ALL-JAPAN: THE CATALOGUE OF EVERYTHING JAPANESE

INTRODUCTION BY OLIVER STATLER

Liza Dalby • Peter Grilli • David Hughes • Christine Guth Kanda
Stephen Longstreet • Jon Spayde • Oliver Statler • Terry Trucco

QUILL

New York 1984

A QUARTO BOOK

Library of Congress Catalog Card Number:
83-63022

ISBN: 0-688-02528-5
ISBN: 0-688-02530-7 (paperback)

ALL-JAPAN
was produced and prepared by
Quarto Marketing Ltd.,
212 Fifth Avenue,
New York, N.Y. 10010

Editor: Bill Logan
Art Director: Richard Boddy
Designer: Liz Trovato
Editorial Assistant: Mary Forsell
Photo Research: Nora Humphrey
Mechanicals: Sue Ewell
Japanese Calligraphy: Nanae Momiyama

Typeset by BPE Graphics, Inc.
Color separations by Hong Kong Scanner Craft Company Ltd.
Printed and bound in Hong Kong by Leefung-Asco Printers Ltd.

First Quill Edition
2 3 4 5 6 7 8 9 10

Cover Design by Liz Trovato

ACKNOWLEDGMENTS

The editors wish to thank
Carol Gluck for her help with the book's outline
and Peter Grilli for his suggestions regarding authors.

Thanks are also due to the principal photographers,
Dana Levy and Tom Haar.

Oliver Statler not only wrote the introduction and part of the text,
but also made many invaluable suggestions regarding the final manuscript.

And thanks to Jon Spayde,
who wrote large parts of the text, and contributed the excellent captions
together with lots of useful advice.

ABOUT THE AUTHORS

LIZA DALBY is an anthropological writer and consultant, with particular expertise in the areas of the geisha and the kimono. She is a graduate of Swarthmore College, having received her M.A. and Ph.D. degrees from Stanford University. Her book, *Geisha,* was selected by *Vanity Fair* magazine as one of the best books of 1983. She was a Fulbright-Hays scholar in 1975–76. She now lives in Chicago with her husband and daughter, where she is researching her forthcoming work, *Kimono: The Grammar of Japanese Dress.*

PETER GRILLI is the Director of Education and Director of the Film Center for the Japan Society in New York City, as well as Adjunct Lecturer in Japanese Film at Fordham University. He earned both his undergraduate and Master's degrees from Harvard University. He is the recipient of a Fulbright Fellowship and a National Defense Foreign Language Fellowship. His principal interests are in the Japanese cultural sphere, and he has both published and in-progress numerous books, articles, and a film. He lived in Japan from the time he was five years old and was raised and educated there for nearly twenty years. He now lives in Grandview, New York, with his wife.

DAVID W. HUGHES is an Ethnomusicologist and Research Fellow at Cambridge University, who currently lives in London. He spent six years working, studying, and researching while living in Japan. He writes, lectures, instructs, and performs Japanese music worldwide. He received both his B.A. and Master's degrees in linguistics from Yale University, was a visiting research student at Tokyo University of the Arts from 1978 to 1980, and is presently a Doctoral candidate in anthropology and musicology at the University of Michigan. He was twice awarded a National Defense Foreign Language Fellowship, and has been a Japanese Ministry of Education Fellow.

CHRISTINE GUTH KANDA is a freelance writer who holds a Ph.D. degree in fine arts from Harvard University. She has written numerous books and articles on Asian arts, as well as lectured on the topic at international conferences and symposia. Her awards include a Mrs. Giles Whiting Fellowship, two Packard Foundation Fellowships, and a Japan Foundation Short Term Professional Fellowship. She was most recently Mellon Assistant Professor of Japanese Art at Princeton University. She resides in Kingston, New Jersey, with her husband and two children.

STEPHEN LONGSTREET, the author of more than fifty books, was born in New York City and educated in Europe. He is a graduate of the New York School of Fine and Applied Arts. He is and has been a frequent contributor to numerous American and European magazines; was the first film critic for *The Saturday Review;* and was an editor for *Time* magazine and the *Los Angeles Daily Review.* He has written for both radio and television networks, as well as acted as screenwriter for MGM, Warner Bros., Columbia, and Paramount Studios. His paintings have been displayed in New York City, Los Angeles, and London galleries. He lives in Los Angeles.

JON SPAYDE, a scholar in Japanese culture and lifestyle, has studied classical and modern Japanese language and culture at Harvard University and the University of Minnesota. He was also a fellow in Comparative Literature at Stanford University. The author of numerous articles about Japanese and American popular culture, his work has appeared in *In These Times* and *Tabloid.* He is currently at work on a Japanese regional cookbook. He lives in Iowa City, Iowa.

OLIVER STATLER is a well-known writer, lecturer, and authority on all aspects of Japanese culture. He currently lives in Honolulu, Hawaii, where he is Visiting Professor of the Asian Studies Program at the University of Hawaii. He received a Guggenheim Fellowship to write about the pilgrimage to the eighty-eight sacred places of Shikoku, and has lived and studied periodically in Japan from 1955 to present. He received his B.A. degree from the University of Chicago and an honorary Doctorate of Humane Letters from the National College of Education in Illinois.

TERRY TRUCCO is an American freelance journalist who has lived in Japan since 1981. Her stories from Japan, and other parts of Asia, on such subjects as art, business, fashion, dance, travel, and sport, have appeared in a variety of publications, including the New York *Times,* the *International Herald Tribune,* the *Christian Science Monitor,* the *Asian Wall Street Journal,* *Advertising Age,* the *Far Eastern Economic Review,* Japan Air Lines' magazine *Winds,* and the *Japan Quarterly.* A native of California, prior to moving to Japan she was an editor at *ARTnews* magazine in New York City.

14

CHILD'S PLAY

15

AFTER HOURS

16

LANGUAGE

CONTENTS

INTRODUCTION

Ever since the first Europeans reached the Japanese islands—in 1543, when some Portuguese traders plying the China coast were blown off course—Westerners have been struggling to understand the Japanese, a people who were persistently contrary in many ways yet disconcertingly similar in others, who could seem barbarous one day and on the next so cultured that their visitors felt like boors.

Those Portuguese traders, being scarcely literate, set down no opinions but, true to the ways of the Western world, the merchants were quickly followed by missionaries—Portuguese Jesuits—and the struggle to convert the Japanese to seeing things our way began. The Jesuits were literate. They were led by Francis Xavier, who found much to praise, concluding that "among the pagan nations . . . the Japanese are the best race yet discovered."

João Rodrigues, one of the Jesuits who followed soon after Xavier, stayed longer, learned more, discovered much to admire, and yet pronounced an indictment that reveals his sense of frustration: "They are so crafty in their hearts that nobody can understand them." He did, however, allow that "they do not use this double dealing to cheat people in business matters, as do the Chinese in their transactions and thieving, for in this respect the Japanese are most exact; but they reserve their treachery for affairs of diplomacy and war in order not to be deceived themselves."

"Nobody can understand them." That is the complaint that has echoed through the centuries since. Another of the eminent Jesuits who came to Japan, Alessandro Valignano, expanded on this theme. "It seems they deliberately try to be unlike other people. . . . It may be said that Japan is a world the reverse of Europe. So great is the difference . . . that it can neither be described nor understood. Now all this would not be surprising if they were like so many barbarians, but what astonishes me is that they behave as very prudent and cultured people."

Some three centuries later, in 1890, the Englishman Basil Hall Chamberlain, published a book titled *Things Japanese.* Chamberlain was a gifted and dedicated student of the language, the people, and the land. *Things Japanese,* which was issued in revised editions well into the twentieth century, was immensely popular and for good reason: It was authoritative and it was interesting. Today its information is dated (and sometimes is valuable as reference because of that) but it is still eminently readable. "We are perpetually being asked questions about Japan," wrote Chamberlain in his introduction. "Here then are the answers . . . a guide-book less to places than to subjects . . . sketches of many things." And so the purpose of *Things Japanese* was very like that of this book.

Chamberlain clearly felt obliged, under the heading "Topsy-turvydom," to list some of the ways in which "Japan is a world the reverse of Europe"—it is a topic that has always engaged foreigners—but he disengaged himself: "It has often been remarked that the Japanese do many things in a way that runs directly counter to European ideas of what is natural and proper. To the Japanese themselves our ways appear equally unaccountable. It was only the other day that a Tokyo lady asked the present writer why foreigners did so many things topsy-turvy, instead of doing them naturally, after the manner of her country-people."

Chamberlain was too knowledgeable to display the kind of frustration that Rodrigues expressed, although he granted that some of those around him felt it. "Logic in the Far East," he wrote, "works by laws differing appreciably from those which the Western mind acknowledges." And he served up a number of examples. For instance, "It is especially in business transactions ...that the European mind and Japanese logic are brought into contact, whence frequently friction and mutual misunderstanding. . . . The peculiarity most often cited is the refusal of Japanese tradesmen to make a reduction on quantity. We Europeans of course argue thus: "I, the buyer, am giving a large order; the seller will in any case make a considerable profit on this single transaction, comparatively quickly and with comparatively slight trouble; therefore he can afford to lower his price. If a dozen goes at the rate of so much, the gross must go at so much less.' . . . But the Japanese dealer views the matter differently. 'If,' says he, 'Messrs. Smith and Co., instead of ordering one bale of silk, order a hundred, that shows that they are badly in want of it, and must be able to pay a good price. Furthermore, if I sell all I have to them, I shall have none left for other customers, which may prove very inconvenient. Their expecting me to reduce my figure is another instance of that unreasonableness on the part of the red-haired foreigner, of which I and my countrymen have already witnessed so many proofs.' "

Difficulties like that have long since been resolved, but others persist, or have arisen since, to bedevil the relations between Japan and the West. Sometimes the cause has been misinformation, or simply lack of information, about how the other operates. Chamberlain, after writing on "History and Mythology," stated that "It is not possible to conclude this sketch of Japanese history with the usual formula, 'Books recommended'—for the reason that there are no general histories of Japan to recommend. . . . A trustworthy history of Japan remains to be written."

That lack was remedied not many years after Chamberlain wrote his complaint; there are today several trustworthy histories of Japan in English. Our knowledge of Japan (and Japan's knowledge of us) has advanced in great leaps since the War in the Pacific, but that knowledge has not always trickled down to those who need it. Witness an American Secretary of Commerce who, smarting from unsuccessful trade negotiations, announced that Japan would have to change its cultural heritage. He might as well have decreed that the Japanese must change their ancestry, their physiognomy, and their language.

This book does not aim to settle weighty problems like the trade imbalance. It is not so immodest. But it offers the expertise of not one but several writers who hope to make things easier and pleasanter for those who are privileged to deal with the Japanese, whether confronting weighty problems or just wishing to enjoy a culture that is endlessly fascinating.

Here then are sketches that focus on the lively arts of living. The Japanese are adept at those, having had several thousand years to fashion a civilization that suits them. It is not perfect— whose is?—but it offers infinite rewards to the outsider who studies it, delves into it, and, most important, accepts it.

OLIVER STATLER
Honolulu, January 1984

技芸

1 • CRAFTS

FOLK CRAFTS

Japan is unique in the world in having legislation that preserves not only tangible art forms such as painting, sculpture, and architecture, but also intangible ones such as the techniques of traditional crafts. It does so by designating craftsmen, both individuals and groups, as *ningen kokuho* (Living National Treasures). During their lifetimes, the *ningen kokuho* receive government stipends, are honored in annual exhibitions, and most important, direct the training of a new generation of craftsmen. When the law was enacted in 1950, thirty-seven people representing thirty-one different crafts were granted the title. Since then, many of the original members of this elite group have died. Thanks to their government's recognition of their exceptional talents, the artistic traditions they represented have not.

The holders of the title *ningen kokuho* have included the makers of textiles, lacquerware, woodwork, stencils, pottery, swords, and even paper. The art of making fine *washi*, the generic name by which the many varieties of Japanese paper is known, has been preserved in the person of Eishiro Abe. His specialty is paper made from the bark of the paper mulberry *(kozo)*; its durability and water resistance have made it the preferred medium for woodblock prints as well as sliding doors and windows *(fusuma* and *shoji)*. Shounsai Shono, a master of intricate bamboo basketwork, is another individual whose unique talents have been recognized by the government. Ayanō

Fujiwara Yu, an individual designated as a Living National Treasure, here models one of his landmark pieces of pottery. In *mingei,* form and function are inseparable.

Contemporary sculptors create people's art at Hokkaidō (the north island). These itinerant artisans produce decorative elements for both shops and homes on this island.

Aided by her daughter (shown), Ayanō Chiba is one of the growing ranks of Japanese women who have been designated Living National Treasures. She has been so honored because of her distinctive and innovative textiles, like this indigo-dyed hemp cloth.

Chiba, a weaver and dyer who spins her own hemp *(asa)* thread, is among the growing ranks of women *ningen kokuho.*

Credit for the enactment of these enlightened laws providing for the support of skilled craftsmen must go at least in part to Yanagi Soetsu (1886–1961). In the early part of the century, when industrialization threatened to wipe out all traces of traditional crafts, Yanagi spearheaded a movement that led to a dramatic reevaluation of Japanese folk traditions. In its wake, Japan's first museum devoted exclusively to folk art was established in Tokyo, and prefectural governments as well as individuals began to assemble collections of fast-disappearing local handicrafts.

The word *mingei* (folk crafts) became a household term because of Yanagi's writings. For Yanagi, *mingei* designated utilitarian objects made for and by the masses—objects ranging from the padded cotton coats worn by firemen (doused with water before approaching a fire) to the intricately carved wooden hooks used to suspend pots over the hearth. Today, however, the word has broader connotations. It may include popular woodblock prints called *Otsu-e,* after the town in Shiga Prefecture where they are believed to have originated, and statuary carved by the itinerant monk-artist Enku.

The beauty of *mingei* is inseparable from their function. Objects that work well are inherently beautiful, declared Yanagi. The fact that they may be unsigned is irrelevant. Yanagi believed that the directness and honesty of *mingei* represented the truest expression of Japan's cultural heritage.

The baskets for flower arranging *(ikebana)* that accompany the warm-weather tea ceremony are becoming increasingly sought as collectibles. Some, known to have been in existence for centuries, have endured because they contain only spare arrangements and are used only part of the year—spring and summer.

TEXTILES

On the fifteenth of the month, rain or shine, they flock to Tōji, a vast temple in southwest Kyoto; on the twenty-fifth, arriving sometimes as early as 6 A.M., they gather on the grounds of the Kitano Tenjin Shrine in the northwest part of the city. "They" are not Japanese, but foreigners hoping to find a bargain at Kyoto's two largest flea markets, one held on the anniversary of Kobo Daishi, Tōji's first abbot, and the other on that of Sugawara no Michizane, the ninth-century prime minister deified as Kitano Tenjin.

As they bend over goods heaped on old newspapers spread out over the sidewalk their objective may not be immediately apparent to the casual observer, but to veterans of these free-for-alls, it is obvious. The hunt is on for old textiles—kimonos made of fine woven silks (but buyer beware, synthetics are slipped in too); cotton robes made in the technique known in the West by the Indonesian term *ikat* but in Japan as *kasuri;* or perhaps a stencil-dyed *futon* cover.

The demand for the indigo-dyed cotton *kasuri*, in which yarn dyed in sections prior to weaving is used to produce a pattern, is especially high today. The market is so great that one young scholar of Japanese art finances his studies in Japan with the profits made from purchases at the flea market sold in turn to dealers in California.

The cotton-filled, quiltlike *futon*, provided with several cotton covers, was traditionally part of a bride's trousseau. Intricate, multicolored designs of cranes and other auspicious symbols of longevity or connubial happiness on the covers were often produced using stencils and rice-paste resist, a technique called

A bright red cotton jacket from the seventeenth century announces that its wearer was a member of a city fire brigade. Sturdy cotton cloth has been used since the fifteenth century for informal garments like the *yukata* (light robe) and *monpe* (trousers worn by Japanese women during the austerity days of World War II).

Paper replicas of clothing make a street-corner display in the northern city of Sendai during the summertime Tanabata Festival. The upper garment is a combination of kimono and *hakama* (pleated trousers)—which in traditional times would have been worn by a member of the samurai class—and are made of silk.

This portion of a *katazome* (stencil-dyed) bed quilt shows the intricate and beautiful effects that the traditional textile artist achieves with this combination of stenciling and paste-resist dyeing. An intricate stencil is cut and laid on the cloth with the aid of punches and fine knives. Then a paste, made of glutinous rice flour and rice bran, is pressed into the stencil in such a way that the paste forms a pattern. The piece is dyed, and the paste-covered portion resists coloring.

katazome. Now hard to come by, *katazome* bedclothes have been upgraded to wall hangings in the homes of foreign collectors.

The Kitano Shrine is not far from the Nishijin district, the center of Japan's centuries-old textile industry. One of the warlord Hideyoshi's first acts after taking over in 1582 was to set up a special quarter for weavers in Kyoto, then the capital. Later, Chinese fleeing from the turmoil in their own country found refuge there and introduced to Japan such weaving secrets as the technique of making gold thread by pasting gold leaf to paper and twisting it around thin strips of silk. Despite the sumptu-

ary laws issued periodically by the Tokugawa government, gold thread was used extensively for garments in the seventeenth century. Today it is still woven into robes worn by Nō actors. The name *karaori* (Chinese weaving), by which these gorgeous, glittering fabrics are known, is a tribute to their origin.

Like *karaori* weaving, cotton is also a relatively recent import to Japan. Although silk was known as early as the Yayoi period (ca. 200 B.C.-A.D. 250), cotton was first cultivated in the fifteenth century. Until that time, various other natural fibers were used by the Japanese for clothing. Most common was *asa*, a hemp-

like fabric much favored for summer garments. The fiber of the *kozo*, paper mulberry, still used for exquisite handmade papers, was the mainstay for clothing worn by commoners. Far rarer was the fabric made from the fiber of the thread banana tree. A specialty of Okinawa, this fabric came to Japan as tribute cloth in the seventeenth century, when that island kingdom lost its independence and became a Japanese domain. The creative designs and technical refinement of all Okinawan textiles delighted the Japanese, and today they continue to excite the admiration of textile collectors and artists all over the world.

CERAMICS

A potter forms the ware called *Bizen-yaki* on a wheel. Bizen, the ancient name for a portion of the modern Okayama Prefecture, has long been a famous center of pottery manufacture. The simple, refined lines of *Bizen-yaki* make it appropriate for the "tea taste," the set of aesthetic standards associated with the tea ceremony. The kilns at Shigaraki, Seto, Tokoname, Echizen, and Tamba are equally famous for superb teaware, ranging in type from the highly sophisticated to the rustic. Some Japanese ceramics are considered artwork on par with sculpture.

Many scholars believe Japan has the oldest ceramic tradition in the world, for based on carbon dating, its origins in Japan have been set as far back as 10,000 B.C. Japan's Neolithic Age is given the name Jomon (cord marked) because of the appearance of the earthenware vessels characteristic of that era. Yayoi pottery, like Jomon, are now considered high art. Over the centuries, clay has been used in Japan in many ways: for the *haniwa* figures of men and animals arranged around the tumuli where the great emperors of the fifth and sixth centuries are buried; for the roof tiles and interior decoration of Buddhist temples in the seventh and eighth centuries; and for an extraordinarily wide range of utensils.

In Japan, unlike the West, fine ceramics are not regarded merely as applied or decorative arts; they are on a par with painting and sculpture. The prices they command at auction—often upward of $25,000 for a single tea bowl—are commensurate with the esteem in which they have long been held by Japanese collectors. The high esthetic standards and the high prices of ceramics in Japan are due in large part to the popularity of the tea ceremony, which since its origins in the late fifteenth century has become something of a national institution. The extraordinary range of shapes and sizes of ceramics reflects the requirements of Japanese cuisine.

Although hundreds of kilns have been abandoned in the past century, many small villages throughout Japan continue to support themselves through the production of ceramics for popular consumption and for the tea ceremony. Mashiko, a village about 120 kilometers northeast of Tokyo, has a century-long tradi-

Left: Three typical pieces exemplify the art of the potters of Mashiko, northeast of Tokyo. *Top to bottom*: A flower vase, a *sake* warmer, and three *sake* cups. The work of Shoji Hamada and his atelier has drawn international attention to Mashiko.

tion of producing simple, sturdy pieces of glazed stoneware for kitchen and table. Mashiko achieved something of an international reputation following the potter Shoji Hamada's selection of it as the site of his kiln.

Large stoneware storage jars with swelling bodies and small mouths are commonly associated with the Shigaraki kilns, located in a valley at the southern end of Shiga Prefecture. Their rough, granular surfaces and natural ash glaze give them a pleasingly rustic apppearance. Shigaraki, together with Seto, Tokoname, Echizen, Tamba, and Bizen, are considered the oldest kilns in Japan. The wares produced there, both old and new, hold a special place in the hearts of those whose passion is the tea ceremony.

Porcelain was first made in Japan in the seventeenth century by Korean immigrants who settled in the Arita district of the island of Kyushu. Lavishly decorated with pictures and designs, Japanese porcelains from the Arita kilns have been avidly collected by Europeans since the seventeenth century. In the West they are generally known as Imari ware, after the port from which they were shipped.

Kyoto, which has always prided itself on being Japan's cultural center, developed its own style of decorated ceramics in the seventeenth century, when the potter Ninsei perfected the art of applying enamels as well as gold and silver to ceramic wares to produce dazzling, dramatic effects. Another Kyoto artist, Ogata Kenzan, produced fine plates and bowls in collaboration with his brother, the painter Ogata Korin. Together, they fused the arts of ceramics, painting, and calligraphy into a harmonious whole.

These bright, boldly patterned dishes are the work of the famous Kyōto designer and ceramicist Ogata Kenzan. Kenzan was closely associated with the eighteenth-century Rimpa school of painters and decorators who revived the design motifs of the Heian Period (794–1185), reinterpreting them with boldness and flair.

Japanese carpenters and cabinetmakers use saws, chisels and planes to work wonders in wood. *Bottom and left:* A small double-edged saw is used for detail work. Japanese saws come in many sizes, from long-handled ripsaws to fine-cutting saws smaller than the one in these pictures. *Top:* A traditional "plane," really a chisel, cuts out decorative motifs, guided by a wooden stick. Japanese tools can be obtained in many specialty shops and Japanese-American hardware stores.

WOODEN CRAFTS

In Japan, trees are objects of reverence; particularly old, large, or unusually shaped trees may be designated as *shimboku* (divine trees), their special status signaled by the suspension of a straw rope around the trunk. This outlook is reflected in the care that goes into the creation of any wooden article in Japan, and especially in the craftsman's sensitivity to the wood's natural qualities—fine grain, color gradations, aroma.

Blessed with an abundance and wide variety of evergreen and broadleaf trees, wood is the medium par excellence of the Japanese craftsman. *Hinoki*, Japanese cypress, which is available throughout the archipelago, is the most widely used. Appreciated for its light weight, fine grain, and distinctive aroma, it is made into shoes *(geta)*, bathtubs, and many household articles.

Although traditional home furnishings are few by comparison with the West, Japanese cabinetry has achieved an international reputation for its simplicity, beauty of design, and craftsmanship. For Westerners, the most readily recognizable form of furniture is the *tansu*, a handsome chest of drawers often embellished with wooden fittings. Of varying sizes and shapes, *tansu* have been used since the seventeenth century in homes, shops, and ships to hold personal belongings, merchandise, and valuables. Most storage in Japanese homes is built in, but *tansu* could be moved easily in case of fire or earthquake, both constant dangers in Japan. (Some especially large and heavy chests are even provided with wheels for greater mobility.)

Unlike smaller objects designed for daily use, *tansu* are often made of costly woods including chestnut, zelkova, and paulownia. Because paulownia grows quickly and its flower is popular and prestigious as a *mon* (family crest), it was customary to plant one upon the birth of a daughter. When both child and tree reached maturity, the lattter was felled and fashioned into a chest for her bridal trousseau.

The sophisticated joinery techniques used in Japanese cabinetry are not suited for all wooden items. Until recently, no home was complete without a bentwood rice bin. To make the bin, a thin piece of wood is shaped into a circular form and tied with cherrywood strips. Although rice bins are sometimes coated with a thin layer of clear or reddish lacquer to protect the surface from moisture, an unfinished one is indispensable in making *sushi.* Similar unfinished wooden containers and trays are used for offerings at Shinto shrines. According to tradition they are used only once, then discarded.

Until about a hundred years ago, the production of wooden household articles was monopolized by groups of itinerant woodworkers called *kijishi.* These craftsmen, who generally left their works unsigned, may have carved the statues of Ebisu and Daikoku-ten, gods of luck and good fortune, often seen in household shrines. Traveling about the countryside with their tools on their backs, the *kijishi* filled commissions in towns and villages throughout Japan. The tradition of the itinerant artisan may have died out in Japan, but interest in the tools of the trade have not. There is a growing market for handmade woodworking tools among Western craftsmen from violin makers to stage set designers.

This *tansu* is a specialized commercial one—the drug cabinet of a traditional apothecary. Each tiny drawer contains a different herbal medicine from the Far Eastern pharmacopia. *Tansu* of all types, including apothecary chests, are popular among foreign antique dealers and collectors.

DOLLS

Webster's dictionary may define a doll as a child's plaything, but in Japan a doll is regarded as a work of art. Dolls are not designed to be cuddled, but to be admired from a distance. Often they take the place of a statue or painting in the entryway (genkan) of a house or in the alcove (tokonoma) of a guest room, their pristine condition preserved by a glass or plastic case. Whether made of porcelain, fabric, wood, papier mâché, or folded paper, most are distinguished by their lavish garments, whose styles are vivid reminders of the aristocratic fashions of bygone days.

The special respect accorded dolls in Japan is rooted in popular religious beliefs and practices. Since ancient times, it has been believed that sins or illness could be exorcised by transferring them from a living person to a substitute, often a figure made in human likeness. Once possessed by the evil spirit the figure was discarded, usually in a river, so it would be carried downstream and eventually out to sea. Flat wooden images with painted faces found in the wells of the eighth-century capital city of Heijo-kyo may have served the same purpose. Until recent times, dolls have also been presented to shrines by concerned mothers in order to ensure the god's protection for their offspring.

Over the centuries, every region in Japan has developed its own distinctive type of doll. The best known are the *kokeshi ningyo* and *nagashibina. Kokeshi ningyo,* especially widespread in the Tohoku region, are tubular wooden dolls with large heads and limbless bodies whose facial features and garments are painted in bright colors. *Nagashibina* are as flat and angular as *kokeshi ningyo* are round

In Japan "paper dolls" are not necessarily child's play, as these elegant dolls made of *washi* (Japanese mulberry bark paper) indicate. Called *renjishi,* they are replicas of the actors who dance the *shishimai* (lion dance) on the Kabuki and Nō stage. Waving and tossing their huge manes of red or white hair, and stepping high to a lively drumbeat, the lion dancers are a spectacular part of Japanese theater. These dolls, despite the sophistication of their costumes, are really not too different from the simplest folk dolls used to exorcise disease.

This antique doll, a baby samurai, is made of lacquer-covered wood. Unlike many Japanese dolls, which are works of art meant for display, this is a genuine toy, intended for the amusement of the samurai children of bygone days.

The Zen patriarch Bodhidarma (Daruma, for short) was so zealous a meditator that his arms and legs finally withered away. Today roly-poly Daruma dolls are lucky charms: You paint in one eye when you begin a project; then add the other if it succeeds.

and smooth. Tottori Prefecture, on Japan's western coast, claims to be the birthplace of these dolls, which are generally made of folded paper and come in couples or groups of ten males and ten females.

Handed down from one generation to the next, many dolls are treasured heirlooms brought out and displayed only on March 3,

the annual Hina Matsuri (Doll Festival). A gala event for all little girls, its focal point is the display of groups of dolls, usually fifteen or more, on tiered shelves covered with red cloth. At the top are the *dairibina*, representing the emperor and empress. Their courtiers are arranged according to rank beneath them. In addition, there are miniature household artic-

les (chests of drawers, toilet cases), musical instruments, and even a palanquin. Offerings of food complete the display. Since no household can be without a collection of dolls for the Hina Matsuri, it should come as no surprise that modern Japan is the largest producer of dolls than any country in the world except the United States.

Of the many Japanese high crafts—the traditions of artisanship whose technical and esthetic demands are the most exacting—three can best typify the evolution of Japanese culture itself. Paper, swordsmithing, and lacquer represent three great "moments" in the long story of Japanese craft and taste.

The making and connoisseurship of fine paper were important in the making of a courtly culture between the seventh and eleventh centuries. Tradition tells us that the Korean monk Donchō, dispatched to the Empress Suiko's court in 610 A.D.—only fifty-odd years after the official introduction of Buddhism—was a particularly well-rounded cleric, being not only an authority on the Confucian classics and a calligrapher, but an artisan who knew how to make scholarly tools: brushes, ink, and Chinese paper.

This most useful of Chinese inventions was in great demand in the pious Nara Period (710–794) when the voluminous Buddhist scriptures were copied and re-copied in the scriptoria of the great monasteries. Chinese paper was essentially the modern product: wood and cloth fibre mixed to give a delicate, fine-grained finish.

In the succeeding Heian period (794–1185), aristocratic Buddhist culture dissolved into a refined secularism that reflected Japanese cultural self-confidence. Literature replaced religion as the chief theatre of the Japanese aristocratic sensibility—and papermaking became a native and a secular art. Heian calligraphy—elegant, spidery and seemingly effortless in comparison with the careful, lucid scribe's hand we see in the Nara sutras—demanded decorative papers in many colors. Fine chinese paper was in demand: Textures and colors were combined in torn-paper designs. Most importantly, the characteristic Japanese paper—*washi*—was invented. *Washi*, a paper made of pure bark fiber (of the mulberry, most often) and unmixed with cloth, has a

HIGH CRAFT

The Japanese touch with fine paper was added to a bit of inventive genius, and the result was the folding fan, one of the few Japanese inventions adopted by the Chinese, instead of the other way around. These fans bear safety and good luck inscriptions.

rough surface, irregular edges, and a truly amazing strength, whether laid thick or thin. *Washi* is the finest of all partners for the Chinese brush and India ink, and, as the merchant classes of the big cities were to find out four hundred years after the end of Heian, it is also perfect for taking the impress of a woodblock. It's doubtful whether the *nishiki-e* (full-color "brocade prints") of the mid-eighteenth century could have been born without a paper that could survive the vigorous rubbing that was necessary to charge it with bright color.

Although Japanese swordmaking goes back to the mixed bronze-iron age of archaic history, and fine blades were made during the peaceful early Heian period, it was the Kamakura era (from 1185 to 1392), the heyday of the aristocratic warrior, that saw the Japanese sword reach a level of perfection never matched elsewhere, not even in the finest forges of Islamic Spain. Even the imperious Chinese recognized the surpassing excellence of the swordsmiths of the east. "Treasure-swords of Japan," says a Sung Dynasty poem, "are got from the East by merchants of Yüeh ...Who wears such a sword can slay the barbarians."

It was higher praise than the Sung poet knew, for swordmaking was, of all crafts, the most intimately involved with the native cult of Shintō. The swordmaker was a priest who obeyed rules of abstinence and sexual continence when bringing an icy blade out of the fiery forge.

The key to the greatness of Japanese blades was the taking of pains and time. A bar of iron was welded lengthwise to two bars of different grades of steel; this triplex was folded upon itself and hammered out again to its original length. The metal was coated with a clay-and-straw-ash mixture, fired, folded again, coated, fired, and so on. The fifteen or twenty doublings and hammerings-out that were usual in the smithing process produced thousands of layers of steel. When, as was sometimes the case, the smith began with three or four *separate* triplexes, welded them and then folded them five times, the sword might contain some four million microscopic steel strata.

Tempering of the edge was no less an art and a science, and swordmaking schools differed primarily on the questions of how long to heat and how long to cool the blades' edges. To call the edge of the Japanese sword razor-sharp is to do it little justice. The finest Japanese sword blades could gently slice through a square of silk dropped out of the air onto their upturned edges.

Another Japanese specialty much appreciated in China was fine lacquerware. Originally an aristocratic delight, lacquer followed the upstart *daimyō* (lords) of the 15th–16th centuries into their luxurious castles, and then began to appear in the homes of wealthy city merchants who were the arbiters of Japan's townsman culture (ca. 1650–1850).

Coating things with the sap of the lac tree was originally a Chinese technique of preservation. It wasn't long, however, before the sensuous properties of fine utensils coated with lacquer came to be appreciated by the discerning eye. There are masterpieces of continental lacquerware in the Shōsōin, Japan's great treasury of Nara era material culture; but native artisans, working over the succeeding thousand years, really made fine lacquer ("japanning") into a Japanese monopoly.

The Japanese lacquer artist is no less patient than his warlike colleague the swordsmith. From twenty to ninety coats of lacquer are applied to wooden cores in the making of fine ware. His brush must be steady and his workshop dust-free.

The truly Japanese touch, however, is the bold and stylish application of gold to the final surface. Gold leaf, gold foil pieces, confetti-like fragments of foil *(hirame)* or fine gold powder *(nashiji)* dance across the surfaces of cosmetic boxes, makeup stands, wooden pillows, serving trays, soup bowls, picnic-lunch boxes, fine chopsticks, testifying to the comfortable budgets and opulent tastes of the 16th- and 17th-century patrons who gave lacquerware its "golden age" in the last great period of traditional culture.

Paper, swords, lacquerware: in all three areas the Japanese are unsurpassed in the world. And, from a modern perspective, it's interesting to note that these three products were Japan's earliest high-technology exports.

A Kyōto connoisseur examines a sword blade mounted on a wooden handle. Fine swords are treasured heirlooms in families of samurai descent.

This lacquerware box with gold inlay depicts gourds on the vine in a lavish style favored by the Japanese merchant class in the eighteenth century. Lacquerware ran the gamut from simple, austere pieces to articles of conspicuous consumption like this.

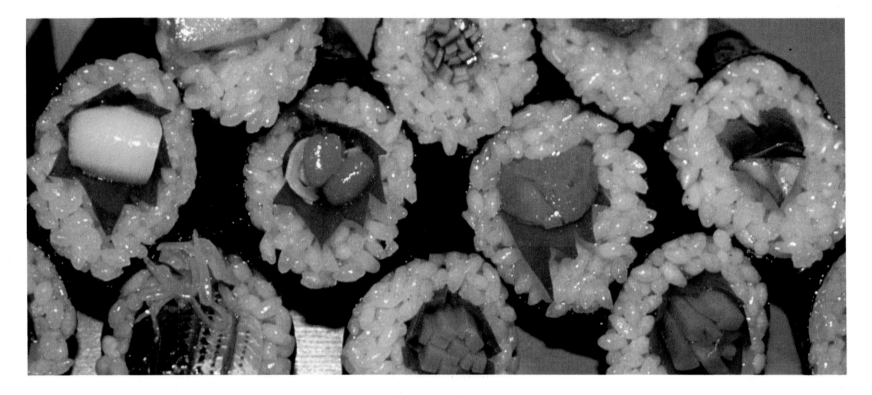

Rolled *sushi (norimaki)*, reproduced in bright vinyl, attracts the passerby to a Tokyo restaurant. Bits of omelet, radish pickle, cucumber, and fish, as well as rice, look like the real thing.

Plastic food serves as a welcome landmark to the hungry tourist traveling in a land where a picture, or better still, a lifelike replica, is worth a thousand words. Although it is not clear where plastic foods originated, the simple fact is that today's tourist could not eat, much less live, without them. Plastic foods make it possible for those unable to speak or read Japanese to distinguish a bathhouse from a restaurant.

Foreigners may be informed, amused, and delighted by these realistic renditions—iced coffee with cream pouring from a pitcher suspended in mid—air or spaghetti with meatballs presented with the artistry of an *ikebana* flower arrangement; the Japanese public takes them for granted. They are regarded as no more than a three-dimensional menu. It should come as no surprise, then, that plastic food is

PLASTIC FOOD

known in Japanese by the generic term *mihon,* meaning simply model or sample.

There are as many varieties of *mihon* as there are foods served in Japan. While *mihon* themselves are uniquely Japanese, the food represented speaks to an international palate. Models of delicate tea sandwiches, curried rice, assorted ice creams, and coffee are displayed in front of "coffee shops" where they are the standard fare. Chinese restaurants may display intricate *mihon,* fried rice made of thousands of individual grains of plastic peppered with helpings of cut vegetables and bits of meat.

Restaurants serving *sukiyaki* present paper-thin slices of plastic meat tinted the same vermilion as Shinto shrines. Invariably, every detail of the original is reproduced with a certain photographic realism. The strange fascination *mihon* instill in passersby stems from this tension between appearance and reality.

Like the life-size plastic statues of Colonel Sanders or the golden arches of McDonalds, *mihon* are a form of advertisement. Models of standard cuisines are readily available in restaurant supply houses throughout the country at prices upwards of $10.00 an item. Uniformity rather than individuality is their hallmark. But in a country where the traveler is constantly assaulted by an overwhelming array of abstract visual images, *mihon* are memorable for their unpretentious directness. They are the *mingei* of modern-day Japan.

Soup, fish cakes, green *soba* noodles, and *tempura* are among the "foods" that grace this display window. High-grade plastic samples like these, unfortunately, are no guarantee of the quality of the real food inside.

In this stand the Tokyo Biken Plastic Food Company displays its wares—"unmeltable vinyl food samples" at "the lowest prices in Japan." Restaurateurs examine Tokyo Biken products here and then place orders; these "sample samples" never leave their display windows.

A more traditional sort of food sample is represented by this *kamban* (shop emblem) advertising a crab restaurant in Kyōto. *Kamban*, which are similar to the tradesmen's symbols used in Europe before literacy was widespread, are remarkable for their wit and elegance of design.

2 • DESIGN

Japanese would say that in the West the house floor is treated as an extension of the road: People tread upon the floor wearing shoes, performing the activities of daily life above, but never on it. The floor in a Japanese house, by contrast, is thought of as an extension of the bed—indeed, the same character is used for both. Everyday activities take place at floor level. The function of the room—eating, sleeping, working—can be changed easily by the placement of a screen, the opening or closing of sliding doors, or the spreading out or removal of bedding. A ''bedroom'' is merely a room that happens to have bedding laid out at that moment.

Japanese were the originators of the prefabricated house. Traditional buildings are designed

ARCHITECTURE

on a grid floor plan by sketching in the number and layout of the *tatami*, the straw mats used as floor covering. From this is determined the placement of the foundation, the walls, the roof—even the garden. By the seventeenth century, building elements had been modularized and cuts of wood standardized, with the result that construction proceeded rapidly from sketch to finished building.

A remarkable continuity that transcends scale and purpose has pervaded Japanese ar-

Sturdily built storehouses *(kura)* are a familiar sight throughout northern Japan. *Kura* like this one at Nuruyu in Aomori Prefecture are reminders that traditional architecture could be massive and permanent.

chitecture. It is true that Buddhist temples imported from medieval China via Korea had a profound impact on Japanese building styles, yet their influence reinforced rather than altered preexisting Japanese preferences for clarity in architecture. Later canons of simplicity, deriving from Zen in particular, have decisively affected residential architecture from imperial villas to farmhouses.

A traditional Japanese residence reveals its architectural components crisply. Supporting and nonsupporting members are visible and unfurbished. Except for the roof, the structure is completely exposed to the eye. Post and beam construction gives a great deal of flexibility in the arrangement of internal walls. Many of the ''walls'' are in fact sliding panels of heavy paper in wooden frames *(fusuma)*, which allow for partitioning the interior of the house, or opening it to the garden. The resulting structural elegance no doubt was the logical consequence of an architecture aiming to enclose human space in the simplest way with the least means possible, but it happens also to project a simplicity that appeals greatly to post-Victorian Western taste.

The main goal of Japanese architecture is openness: A raised floor and walls removable for air circulation; the use of porous materials like wood, clay, and paper to counter humidity; and low overhanging eaves to keep the interior cool—these characteristics are found in traditional houses, in temples, and in shrines. The wooden structure of a Shinto shrine is thought to resemble the longhouses of tropical Polynesia, an architectural argument which in turn is used to support the ''Southern theory'' of the origin of the early inhabitants of the Japanese archipelago. No one doubts that the climatic factors of heat and humidity have had much greater influence on Japanese architecture than have considerations of cold.

The one exception to the architectural ideal of openness is the storehouse, or *kura*. It was the deficiencies of the traditional Japanese house as a functional object that made the beautiful *kura* necessary. The Japanese really have more use for storage space than do Westerners, since the former put away their bedding each day and since they tend to display only a few of the family's possessions at a time. But the traditional house has little storage space, beyond a few closets and space under the kitchen floor. Further, the wooden house is very flammable, and a whole town made of such houses can burn to cinders in a night. *Kura* provided storage space and protection from fire. Though ancient *kura* were made of latticed wood and farmers' *kura* may still have thatched roofs, the more common urban *kura* was made with thick earthen walls covered with plaster, two small high windows for ventilation, and a heavy tiled roof. The single door, as well as the windows, were covered over with plaster when fire threatened. *Kura* proliferated during the Edo period, particularly in depot towns like Kurashiki (meaning "spreading out of *kura*"). Many were beautifully sheathed in dark wood or tiles. When Western architecture came to Japan, vernacular Japanese builders often faked Western houses by using *kura* designs, the closest thing in Japan to Western structures. Today, surviving *kura* are very often converted into either homes or shops.

Top right: This view of a traditional room in the *shoin-zukuri* style illustrates the classic characteristics of Japanese interior design: clean lines, open space, the adroit use of rectangular shapes, and a balance between shadowy privacy and openness to the outdoors. The *fusuma* panel at right can be used to divide the space.

Bottom right: The arch has been called the most basic of architectural forms; in the *torii* ("bird perch") gate, the Japanese have created one of the most graceful and familiar of arch shapes. *Torii* are left unpainted, or like these leading to the Inari Shrine in Kyōto, are painted vermilion, the sacred color of Shintō.

Left: The entryway to the Lefcourte house in Lake Park, Florida, illustrates the Japanese sense of proportion that prevails throughout it. Many of the details were executed by a Japanese carpenter.

Right: Among the Japanese details of the Lefcourte house are *shoji* panels and round windows, which allow soft, diffused light to enter.

Left: This exterior view of the Lefcourte house shows the Japanese-influenced roof lines. Japanese traditional style has been a major influence upon American domestic architecture in the postwar period.

LIGHTING

When one thinks of paper shades in the West, one remembers the heavy brown roller shades drawn down against the baking sun or adding their muddy gloom to the sick room or to the parlors of grandmothers. Perhaps at their best, they relieve the room of its shadows, defeating the intentions of the glass and offering privacy from the white day. What of the shades of lamps? They cast pools of light in a prearranged direction, focusing and expelling it.

How different the situation in Japan, where even before the advent of paper as a medium for walls and lamps, getting light was always at once a matter of holding it off and inviting it in. Sunken hearths and braziers, single candlestands, woven screens created and preserved what the novelist Tanizaki Jun'ichiro has called the "smoky lustre" that best suits the Japanese interior. Only in half light, says Tanizaki, do things Japanese look their best: from lacquer, to dark soups, to the costumes of the traditional theater, to people's skin.

The arrival of paper for *fusuma shoji,* and for lamps—a flat white paper so strong you can't tear it with your hands—brought a cooler elegance to the same idea. Tanizaki, in his wonderfully nuanced essay *In Praise of Shadows*, describes the effect of paper *shoji* in a temple: "The light from the pale white paper, powerless to dispel the heavy darkness of the alcove, is instead repelled by the darkness, creating a world of confusion where dark and light are indistinguishable. Have not you yourselves sensed a difference in the light that suffuses such a room, a rare tranquillity not found in ordinary light?"

The paper lamp, too, whether hanging or standing, creates the same mysterious half

A traditional street lantern in Kyōto glows with a characteristic kind of Japanese light: "sheltered" light without glare that casts the softest of shadows. Such lanterns can be seen at their best at festival-time, when they line the streets or are massed on large parade floats.

light. And today's lamp design, even with the impediment of electric light, tries for the same effect. To see the contrast between exposed and sheltered light, one needs only to walk through Tokyo or Kyoto at night, during a festival. On the Ginza or other nighttown streets, the neon throws off the shadows in a chromatic blaze. In the temples, on the other hand, lit with an array of paper lamps, each light invites its own shadow to accompany it, making the night strangely more companionable for those who enter it.

This modern lamp manages to combine a playfully high-tech look with traditional light-wood-and-paper construction. The Japanese lantern, in old and new forms, has been adapted and used around the world.

This exhibition of modern Japanese lighting design illustrates how a traditional effect can be achieved with electric light. Playful variations on lantern shapes combine tradition and modernity.

CLOTHING

The basic clothing distinction in Japan is native dress *(wafuku)* versus Western dress *(yōfuku)*. European fashions had been adopted by the imperial court and the leaders of the government during the 1880s, and the Western garb of Tokyo high society had its first great fashion impact at this time. Even as late as the 1930s, however, Japanese men usually wore kimono at home, and most women wore native dress most of the time. At the end of the nineteenth century one could see bowler hats, high-collared shirts, and leather shoes worn with kimono. By about 1910, the clothes of East and West, like oil and water, separated out, each to its own domain.

Today both types of clothing coexist, but the kimono survives primarily in its extremes. At its most informal, a kimono is a cotton *yukata*—literally a bathrobe. Otherwise, when the occasion calls for a kimono, it will most likely be the most formal version: a special silk kimono marked by heraldic crests and worn at weddings, funerals, and other times of high ceremony.

During the Heian period (794–1185), the age of Prince Genji and Lady Murasaki, ladies of the court wore as many as twelve layers of flowing robes over a simple "small-sleeved" undergarment called a *kosode.* The esthetic interest of this mode of dress focused on the way the colors of the robes overlapped and harmonized according to the season and the

Far left: A couple enjoy an evening stroll in *yukata,* cool cotton kimono. Spas and hotels usually provide *yukata* for their customers to wear after the bath and at other leisurely moments.

Left: The most formal kimono a woman will ever wear is her bridal robe, an elegant and costly work of silk and brocade. The less formal kimono worn on social occasions, too, is an expensive luxury today.

This bright red jumpsuit of cotton by Yohji Yamamoto is an example of this designer's characteristic boldness of line and color. The flowing looseness of outline is a Yamamoto trademark.

taste of the wearer. By the fourteenth century, when Japan was ruled by the warrior class, samurai and their women scorned twelve layers of flowing robes as effete. They wore instead only two, or perhaps three, *kosode,* now become standard outerwear. These garments were cinched at hip level by a narrow sash called an *obi.* During the Tokugawa period, Japan's three centuries of peaceful isolation, the woman's *obi* grew in width and elaboration to a point where the *kosode,* or *kimono,* came to seem like a mere backdrop for the display of the sash. One theory associates the rise of the *obi* with the popularity of Kabuki theater. Woman's roles were played by men—called *onnagata*—who tended to cover the defects in their femininity with a very broad *obi.* The fashions of the time, says this theory, copied the *onnagata* style.

If a woman opts to wear a kimono today, she must learn the rules for wearing it. Since this is no longer necessarily common social knowledge, schools of kimono have sprung up to teach the basics. The exact form of a woman's kimono outfit is determined by her age, the season, and the level of formality of the occasion. The choice of colors, designs, and material cannot be made randomly, but is governed by a precise code of social appropriateness. These complicated rules, coupled with the great expense involved, contribute to the feeling of many Japanese women that kimono

This voluminous blouse and skirt combination by Rei Kawakubo for Comme des Garçons reflects Kawakubo's intense interest in bodily freedom and circular movement. The shawllike blouse is made of deep pile, dyed according to the traditional *yuzen* technique and swirled over a figured skirt of light rayon. In her recent work, Kawakubo has explored the resources of traditional Far Eastern monochrome tonality, working with bold blacks and whites and a palette of grays. The turbanlike shape of the t-cloth hat is a Kawakubo signature, as are the strong diagonals that give the ensemble both massiveness and a sense of motion.

are completely impractical for modern life. Yet other women wear the garment precisely *because* of these difficulties. Wearing kimono as an expensive, elegant hobby has caught on among ladies of the high bourgeoisie.

Primarily a garment of the leisured classes, the kimono never was terribly practical. Farmers wore it on special occasions, if at all. Work clothes consisted of a variety of leg-encasing jodhpurlike wraps such as *mompe* or *momohiki,* worn with tacked-up or even tubular sleeved jackets. At present, traditional forms of working clothes have been supplanted by Western trousers and shirts.

Whereas Western socks are ambipedal, shoes are different for the right and left foot. It's just the opposite for Japanese footwear: socks have a right and left, shoes do not. Japan has given the world the *zōri,* worn in the West as a flapping rubber-thonged beach shoe. Marvelously suited to the high humidity of Japanese summers, *zōri* and their informal wooden counterparts, *geta,* also have the virtue of being slipped on and off easily when entering and leaving the house.

In general, Japanese follow European rather than purely American fashion trends in Western dress. Recently, Japanese designers like Kenzo, Yohji Yamamoto, Kansai Yamamoto, Hanae Mori, and Rei Kawakubo have begun to make their own distinctive marks on the world of Paris couture.

Rei Kawakubo has said that she tries to emphasize fluid, free movement of the whole body rather than focus on the shoulder line. Here she combines a characteristically free-form blouse of light cotton with a rayon skirt to create an effect of airiness and fluidity that is also highly dramatic. The cloth is meant to accentuate organic rhythms like breathing and walking, while at the same time revealing the complex beauty of its own texture. Kawakubo is one of the most resourceful of the many contemporary Japanese designers who have explored the notable potential of large, simply colored masses of cloth.

GARDENS

Two important garden types sit side-by-side in this Kyōto temple. To the left a pond and mossy rocks evoke the refined taste of the classical aristocracy, while the raked sand expanse reflects the Zen spirit. Rippled to resemble water, the sand is a sort of metaphysical counterpart to the real water nearby.

In most Japanese gardens flowers are incidental, if not positive distractions. Massed beds of flowers, which we regard as the essence of gardens, are seen only in public parks whose history goes back barely a century. Moss, stones, water, bamboo, and sand are the main elements of Japanese gardens. The flowering tree has its place: the plum, peach, and of course *sakura*, the cherry; and certain gardens are noted for their clipped mounds of azaleas, their hillsides of hydrangeas, their groves of camellias. But the garden is not its flowers; its beauty is independent of the blooming and fading of the seasons. The garden is a stage where the human hand has choreographed the particular design for nature to enact on one small patch of ground.

There are easily three quite different styles of gardens to be found in Japan today. The "hill" style (or pond garden, as it is sometimes called in English) is the most aristocratic, the garden of imperial villas. Here will be a pond to stroll around or cross by bridge; a running stream with stepping stones; landscaped hillocks with pine trees, maples, and *sakura;* a raft of iris that bloom in May. Such a garden is a world unto itself.

The moss temple (Saihōji) in western Kyoto has on its grounds a garden with a pond in the shape of the Chinese graph for heart. It was designed by the Zen priest Muso (1275–1351), who is regarded as the most subtle, artful planner of gardens in Japanese history. His work is deemed a masterful combination of the rigorous discipline of Zen with the soignée aristocratic taste of the Heian court. In his gardens are always found both a Zen medita-

tion stone and a graceful weeping cherry.

The Ryōanji temple precincts in Kyoto contain a large pond garden that was once part of a noble villa. Tourists rush right past it (it has somewhat gone to seed) in their eagerness to get to that temple's famous abstract rock garden. This latter style, the dry landscape, is the second major type of Japanese garden. Originally, arrangements of stones and pebbles were just one element in the overall scheme. Muso designed the first independent stone garden in the form of a pebble waterfall.

Rock and sand gardens were most often built on the grounds of Zen temples. Even a "stream" of smooth blue pebbles suggesting water was too representational in the ultimately abstract form these gardens attained. Ryōanji's dry landscape garden is an oblong strip of land filled with raked white sand and fifteen rough stones. Nature is portrayed in its inner meaning rather than its external appearance.

The third type of garden is the tea garden, a carefully planned arrangement of garden, path, and tea hut. These marvelously understated compositions are what strike foreigners as the most Japanese of all gardens. In tea gardens are found the subdued colors and unadorned shapes that accord so well with modern Western sensibilities. Here are the rough-lashed bamboo fences, the irregular mossy stones, the artful stone lanterns.

Running through the whole history of Japanese garden design are two concepts which, specific as they are to Japan, can be of enormous use in the Western garden. The first, variously called *shakkei* or *ikedori*, is most appropriate for the country garden. The second, the *tsuboniwa*, was created for small-space urban settings.

Shakkei means "borrowed view," but the term *ikedori*, or "capturing alive," better shows the spirit of these gardens. Whether a garden is moss or stone, hill or pond, it may practice *ikedori* by including the surrounding view in its design. The most famous Japanese examples are in Kyoto, where gardens may frame the view of gorgeous, maple-encrusted mountains like Arashiyama, Hieizan, or Higashiyama. The middle ground—where the fence might be in a Western garden—is all-important for *ikedori.* Pines or other trees are the most popular device for framing the view in the middle ground. Gateposts are also popular means to *shakkei*, as is a thick mixed hedge. Brilliant gardeners have even used the sky to achieve a captured view.

The *tsuboniwa,* or courtyard garden, has complicated roots. Spare, Zen-style courtyards and small gardens based on Western principles are popular today in Japan, but the classic *tsuboniwa* is derived from the tea garden. Though it may be less than six feet (1.8 meters) square and sandwiched between four buildings, it suggests leisurely activity, not repose. The tea garden was intended to be passed through on the way to the tea house, not observed from the house, so its design concentrates on pathways plus a few details—stones, trees, a lantern, a ritual water basin—that dispose the guest's mind for entering the house. The modern courtyard garden is seldom meant to be walked through, but it retains the basic elements of the tea garden: a stone path, a single maple, a water basin, for example. In cramped urban quarters, it gives the sense of a retreat to which the weary mind retires.

Western imitations of the *tsuboniwa* sometimes look awful because the builders choose the most specifically Japanese elements—a stone lantern and a water basin. A better idea is to adapt the basic principle of the garden, but use local materials.

The south garden of the Tōfuku-ji Zen temple, designed in 1939, is a flamboyant example of the raked-sand garden. Divided into four islands and five mountain clusters, it suggests a lively seascape.

In the summer of 1978, Kyoto geisha Ichifumi apologized to her patron as she handed him a large spatulate fan imprinted with her name and family crest. In past summers she had given him not one, but ten fans. "The bamboo flowered this year," Ichifumi explained. Her patron then realized that entire groves of bamboo had died all over Japan, and that the material used to make the frames of geishas' traditional summer fans, usually abundant, was now suddenly scarce.

Japan's bamboo *(madake; Phyllostachys bambusoides)* produces flowers once every

GARDENING

120 years. All the culms ("trunks") in a grove flower together, blanket the ground with their seed, and then perish. It takes about ten years for the grove to regenerate.

Bamboo has been part of Japanese culture since Neolithic times. Its multifarious uses invariably inspire lists: bamboo as the frame-

work for buildings, for doors, for windowblinds, for ladders; bamboo for umbrella ribs, fishing rods, rulers, hats, fences, birdcages, and chopsticks; bamboo shoots for food; bamboo leaves for food wrappers. Edison used a piece of Hachiman bamboo from a Kyoto suburb as the material for the filament of his first lightbulb. Bamboo is also planted extensively in gardens as an ornament. The dense yet airy feeling created by a stand of bamboo is a perfect hedge for privacy.

The art of Japanese gardening is the art of the unseen hand. Bamboo is exceptional in that its natural appearance in the garden is indeed natural, rather than the effect of intensive tending. In this latter respect, perhaps the most extreme example of the gardener's art is the *bonsai:* miniature landscapes or a single specimen of a tree that, even though barely a foot in height, displays all the dignity of a venerable oak, pine, or flowering plum. Japanese have cultivated small trees and shrubs in pots since the thirteenth century, but the term *bonsai* (tray planting) dates only from 1818. Furthermore, the highly developed technique of using wire to train trunk and branch is an early twentieth-century development.

Bonsai enjoyed its first truly popular vogue after 1905, the period following Japan's victory in the Russo-Japanese War. At this time, a jubilant nation's interest was reawakened in

Not every Japanese tradition is of ancient date; a case in point is *bonsai* cultivation, which began in the nineteenth century. Still, there has been enough time for enthusiasts of this art of dwarf plants to develop many varieties and styles. This large *bonsai* exhibition in Tokyo includes several types of dwarf pine and maple. The range of *bonsai* as a whole is quite wide, extending to mosses and grasses as well as many varieties of tree.

A related art, *bonkei* (tray scenery) creates entire miniature landscapes in a lacquer tray, using pebbles, fine-textured mosses, plants, and many other things, including tiny replicas of such manmade objects as bridges and gates. Both miniature arts enjoyed wide popularity during the period of intense Japanese cultural nationalism at the turn of the century.

native Japanese things. The leaders of the Meiji state were all avid enthusiasts, and participated in the establishment of the canons of *bonsai* taste and cultivation that form the basis of the art today.

The conventions of this tiny world extend to botanical detail. *Bonsai* are classified as trees or grasses. The tree category is the larger. It is subdivided into pines and oaks; flowering trees (plum, cherry, or even wisteria, which is considered a tree in *bonsai* terms); fruiting trees, such as persimmon, chestnut, and crabapple; and foliage trees, the prime example of which is the Japanese maple. Grass *bonsai* are bamboo, shrubs, and mosses.

Similar intensive cultivation is applied to flowers, especially the chrysanthemum, or *kiku.* Chrysanthemums can be displayed as potted ornamentals, as cut flowers, and indeed, as *bonsai.* They can be trained into elaborate forms, shown in competition by hobbyists, and even eaten as a condiment.

Ruth Benedict characterized Japan as the land of the chrysanthemum and the sword. With morbid fascination, she compared the protocol-conscious Japanese character to a chrysanthemum with ''a tiny invisible wire rack inserted in the living flower.'' Modern Japanese rightly resist Benedict's metaphors, but the chrysanthemum remains second only to the blossoming cherry as Japan's flower.

In a quiet corner of the very elaborate Sambō-in garden in Kyōto, this classic tea garden embodies the cheerful serenity of the tea taste. All the basic elements of the tea garden can be found here: a bamboo fence that suggests refined rusticity, a stone lantern, the mossy rocks that seem to breathe the spirit of antiquity, and a stone pathway leading to the tea hut itself. The use of bamboo here is especially notable, far from being an intrusion upon the artful naturalness of the garden, bamboo is very much at home. The hand of man has arranged it in rectangular forms but has not transformed it completely into architecture. Like the stone lantern with its simple contours, the bamboo fence is a human artifact that seems reluctant to let go of its kinship with the works of nature.

GRAPHICS

Japan is a paradise of design for the connoisseur, and a graphically saturated environment for the ordinary person. Emblem, symbol, and sign connect the culture's past to its future: they stand at both the core and the fringe of the riot of language in modern Japan.

Emperor Gotoba, for instance, particularly loved the chrysanthemum. He ordered a symmetrical design of sixteen petals radiating from a central disk and surrounded by two concentric circles to be embroidered on clothing, lacquered into tableware, carved into vehicles, and engraved on swords. This was early in the twelfth century. The chrysanthemum crest thenceforth was associated with the imperial family.

For us, family heraldry has to do with marks of honor from the age of chivalry. We disdain a coat of arms used by the newly arrived, or produced by computer. In Japan, however, crests (mon) were originally decorative, and only later were used as a way to distinguish family from family, friend from foe, on the murky battlefields of the fifteenth and sixteenth centuries. By order of the shogun in 1642, crests were registered and hence legally associated with particular noble and samurai families.

Families of Kabuki actors and traditional musicians are the people who take their crests seriously in Japan today. For most Japanese, a crest becomes important only in its presence or absence at the appropriate spot on a kimono. If you are a wedding guest, for example, your kimono ought to be crested, but it doesn't matter a stitch whose crest it is.

The seal, or hanko, is a similarly stylized graphic element in Japanese life, but one that

This is the imprint of a seal—and no ordinary one. Dated in accordance with 57 A.D., it was granted by the Chinese emperor Kuang Wu of Han to a North Kyūshū chieftain, Kan no Wa no Na, and presumably indicates that this Japanese strongman had entered into a tribute relationship with the continental empire. Discovered in the late eighteenth century, the seal has fascinated antiquarians.

This engraved part of the Kuang Wu seal was probably illegible to the rough-hewn members of Kan no Wa no Na's "court." There is nothing to suggest that literacy in the Chinese language was widespread in Japan before the sixth century A.D. One can well imagine the awe with which the ancient Japanese must have examined this powerful, beautiful example of graphic art, charged with political and cultural authority.

has more immediate everyday use. The ideographs of a person's last name are carved into an approximately symmetrical shape at the end of a stick of wood, stone, or plastic, generally somewhere between the diameter of a pencil and a banana. The seal is pressed into a patty of cinnabar "dragon meat" and its imprint affixed to the document at hand. A person's hanko, rather than the signature, is what literally seals a deal in Japan. Contentless, in a way, and easily forged, the red marks are nonetheless the epitome of truth and probity.

The artistic quality of the advertising posters on the subways is so striking as to tempt susceptible foreigners to follow trains to

Tattooing in Japan is not a matter of one or two pictures on an upper arm; it is an "all-body" art. Among the most passionate tattoo-fanciers are Japan's gangsters, who hide the designs under their sportcoats.

the end of the line late at night, eager to acquire the old ones as they are stripped off for discard by the weary conductor. Europeans and Americans are bemused when English and French words are incorporated into posters purely for effect. A student's shopping bag carries the logo "Don't Pelorian": How does this relate to the picture of the tabby cat in a sailor suit?

The distinguished French critic Roland Barthes called Japan "the empire of signs," and although he didn't have shop signs particularly in mind, his epithet holds there as well. Traditional shop signs depicting crafts or products are an art form in their own right. Often done in folk style, the exuberant imagination displayed on these wooden plaques is one of the great joys of collectors of "things Japanese." From a longer perspective, the arresting sign lives on in neon. The medium has both substance and function, and there are those who think of Tokyo's Ginza as the world's most avant garde gallery of applied neon art.

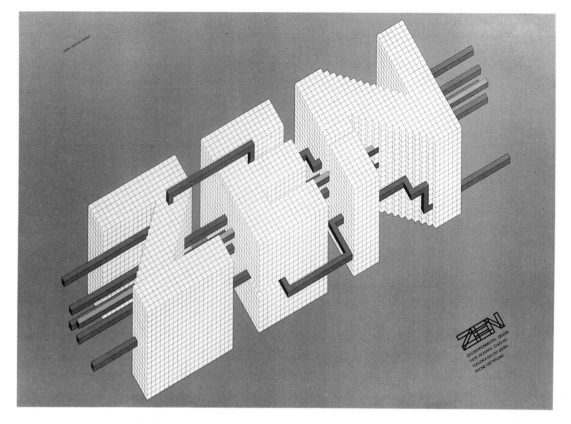

Above: One designer works for another. Takenobu Igarashi's Tokyo studio is known for bold, bright graphic design that makes cheerful use of high-tech ideas like grids, graphs, and exaggerated perspective. Appropriately enough, this poster advertises Zen Environmental Design Corp. of Fukuoka, longtime colleagues and clients of Igarashi.

Left: Neon brilliantly employed turns the major streets of large Japanese cities into graphic wonderlands by night. On the left-hand side, the name of Gekkeikan (Laurel Crown) *sake* appears in handsome Chinese characters. On the right the simple, bold shapes of the *katakana* syllabary—favored by ad designers—lend their authority to a trade name.

Right: A notice for an antinuclear rally in Mie Prefecture is attached to a poster for a worldwide conference on the same issue. The drawing on the poster was made by a Hiroshima survivor. Survivors' drawings, recently published in both Japan and the United States, evoke the horrors of nuclear warfare even more powerfully than photographs.

HIGH-TECH

Just two stops north of Tokyo Station on the loop of the Yamanote train line lies Akihabara, "autumn leaf field," the most famous market for cut-rate, state-of-the-art electronic gadgetry in Japan—and possibly the world. Storefronts take up half the width of the sidewalk with their displays of stereos, televisions, calculators, tape recorders, and computers plus peripherals. Loudspeakers up and down the street demonstrate the virtues of music systems and amplify the voices of barkers advertising deals. Although some bargaining is acceptable—indeed, expected—it doesn't help much to haggle, because storekeepers know what their competitors are charging and nobody can dip much below the already thin markup. Profit is cut to the bone here.

Transistor technology first prodded the Japanese into the high-tech race, where they now speed along in overdrive. In the 1950s Japanese industry plunged into the high-volume production of transistors—cheap, portable replacements for the cumbersome vacuum tube. The Japanese economic prosperity of the 1960s was borne largely on the success of transistor manufacture. Now the silicon chip makes the transistor obsolete, and Japanese industry has retooled itself to rush into the vanguard of computer technology.

The abacus came to Japan early in the sixteenth century. It has been an extremely useful tool for mathematical calculation for five hundred years, but it is now outdated—despite people who will tell the story of some shopkeeper who was able, with his abacus, to beat a computer's speed in adding up a list of numbers. The age of the calculator is here, and if it's hard to imagine a modern-day American

not owning one, it is even harder in the case of a Japanese. Still, just as Americans prefer an analogue watch, the Japanese sometimes buy a calculator that comes with an abacus.

If the calculator is a modern person's electronic workhorse, the video arcade is the electronic rodeo. The mechanical *pa-chink, pa-chink* of pinball machines has been outclassed by the symphony of sound effects available with Asteroids, Centipede, and of course Pac-Man and his relatives. Japanese video game culture has penetrated the consciousness of

American children to the extent that the names Donkey Kong and PacMan are now used for presweetened breakfast cereals, and Nintendo is a household word. Japanese manufacturers are also in the forefront of production of the animated video games that make Space Invaders look old-fashioned.

The most important developing field of high tech at present is robotics, and here too the Japanese seem to be showing the rest of the world where the future lies. Humanoid robots in the R2D2 mold are being developed as toys,

but more serious work is being devoted to the nonanthropomorphic industrial robot. Japanese heavy industry routinely uses robots for material handling and assembly-line work. The robotification of Japanese industry is not perceived as a threat by workers, and its implementation will undoubtedly proceed more smoothly than it will in Europe and America. High-tech work and high-tech play are increasingly coming to have a Japanese stamp the world over. We may even find computers selling computers in Akihabara.

Above: "Cosmo Two" will not only bring you your dinner, he will address you with sixteen separate phrases of correct, polite Japanese. This "Unmanned Conveyer" can be customized to carry many different things; as far as anyone knows, however, he cannot slice *sushi* or mix daiquiris.

Right: Every two years the Honda motorcycle and automobile corporation sponsors a "Honda Idea Contest," inviting employees to submit imaginative inventions and contrivances of all sorts. The 1983 competition saw the debut of this robot rickshawman, complete with Meiji-period clothes and high-tech legs.

Left: The Japanese have pushed the science of robotics far beyond spot-welding and automobile assembly. This mechanical arm, developed at Waseda University, does five-finger exercises on both piano and organ; according to its developers, it can play "as beautifully as any human."

In Japan, the first thing a novice salesclerk must learn is how to wrap a package. Each major department store and traditional specialty shop will have its own beautifully designed wrapping paper for the parcels customers carry away. Every item must have crisp edges and neat ribbons that lie flat, tribute to the consummate skill of the salesclerk. No matter how carefully one tries to preserve all the creases, once opened, it is impossible to rewrap one of these bundles as tidily.

If you are ever given Japanese rice crackers or sweets as a gift, you will first unwrap the store's gift paper, then open the box, then untie one of several cellophane-wrapped pack-

PACKAGING

ets containing one kind of cracker, and finally remove the clear wrapper encasing the single tidbit of your choice. Candies are often wrapped in a translucent papery sheet of *agar*, which is itself edible. Undoubtedly one reason for keeping crisp foods under heavy wrap is the pervasive dampness, but in Japan exquisite packaging goes far beyond just the utilitarian considerations.

Blocks of salted mackerel *sushi* are traditionally wrapped in the tan- and brown-spotted paperlike integument from young bamboos; *fukuro sushi* is wrapped in a thin omelet so that it appears to be contained in a golden bag. Fruit such as apples, peaches, or loquats may be individually wrapped in white paper while still on the bough to protect their delicate skins. The trees growing in the imperial gardens in Kyoto have their trunks wrapped with straw in the wintertime. Tea bowls are wrapped in silk before being nestled into their wooden boxes. The wrapping of things, be it fruit, trees or tea bowls, seems to express respect for the physical objects themselves. There is some-

Decorative boxes of various types and sizes illustrate one aspect of the Japanese genius for enclosing space. From lacquer lunchboxes to wrapping paper, Japanese skill in the art of packaging evokes admiration and adds up to one of the nation's most characteristic and important minor arts.

thing almost magical about a wrapped object.

Amulets come in a variety of forms, but by far the most common is a wrapped brocade packet. Its protective capabilities are literally enfolded within it, and opening the amulet would cause its effectiveness to be dissipated. Modern Japanese may not give a thought to the primitive religious force behind the notion of wrappings, yet they may feel an attraction for the power of its packaging.

Japan's all-purpose wrapper is the *furoshiki*, a square of material that can be small as a child's handkerchief or large as a tablecloth. Originally a *furoshiki* was a cotton cloth to take to the public bath. Like a hobo's bandanna, it was used to bundle up all the bathing accessories one carried along. Folded flat and tucked into pocket or bag, a *furoshiki* is the perfect piece of instant luggage. The most elegant "carrying cloths" are made of heavy silk crepe de Chine. Most women use rayon versions that are practically indistinguishable to the eye, if not the touch. The heavy-duty lugging of larger objects calls for sober cotton cloths. The larger the cloth, the more likely it is to be patterned in the white winged scrolls called "Chinese grass" on a forest green background.

The etiquette of packaging is most evident in gifts. A fresh piece of white paper is held in place over the face of the box by thin paper cords, red from the right, white from the left. An emblematic lozenge shape may be printed upon, or in formal cases affixed to, the upper right-hand side. The giver's and receiver's names are written on the front in an elegant hand. For those of unsteady brush, it is possible to request the store's calligrapher.

In the past, it was possible to tell the contents of a gift package at a glance. This was because specific ways of wrapping were prescribed for specific objects. Gifts were never given as "surprises" in any case, and packaging has always been as important as the object packaged.

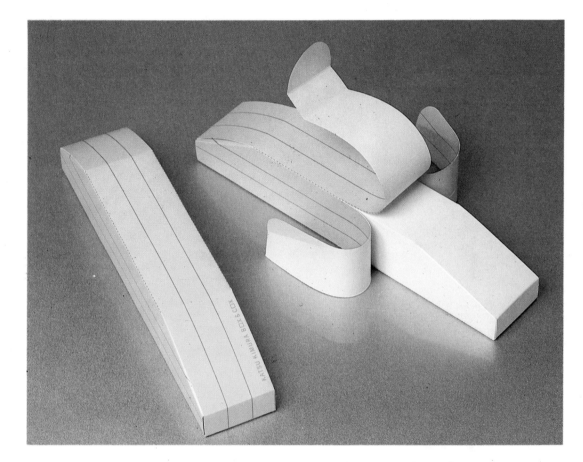

Designer Katsu Kimura creates packages that hold nothing but humor—boxes that mimic the things they ought to contain. The banana box here "peels" open to reveal another box. A square "egg" box opens along a crack to reveal a little square yolk box inside. A parody cigarette pack contains little oblong boxes in the form of filter-tips. Perhaps his most playful creation is a swiss cheese box that is full of holes and looks as if it doesn't want to contain anything at all. Kimura works in fabric and steel as well as paper.

A bright label invites consumers to open this package and enjoy persimmon cakes. Some of the most attractively packaged items on sale in Japan are such local products as cakes, candies, bran pickles, and crackers, bought in their localities as souvenirs or gifts for friends back home. Their wrappings feature regional designs, bits of local literature or other lore, and the usual painstaking multiple layers. Sold at train stations and souvenir shops, they make unique mementos.

美術

3 · VISUAL ARTS

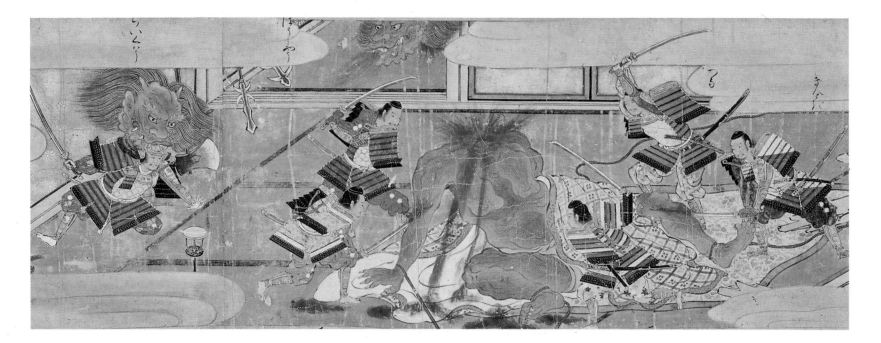

The picture frame, that quadrilateral prison for the image, almost a piece of furniture in the West, was unknown and would not have been appreciated in the traditional Far East. To the Chinese, Japanese, Korean, or Vietnamese artist, a two-dimensional work of art was almost always meant to be easily handled: rolled, unrolled, moved across the room (in the case of screens), slid to one side (doors) or flipped through (albums). The closeness of the hand to the image that we see in the brushwork of the Far East is paralleled by the closeness of the viewer or collector's hand to the object. Scrolls in particular imply loving touch and handling.

There are only two possible kinds of scrolls: "rolls" that unroll horizontally and vertical scrolls or "hangings" (kakemono). The lateral scroll was the original Far Eastern book, and among the many books in scroll form in Nara Japan, the Buddhist sutras were the holiest. The copying and illumination of sutras resulted in masterpieces of precise calligraphy, and in the case of the Kako Genzai Ingakyō (Sutra of Past and Present Cause and Effect), a series of

SCROLLS

vigorous illuminations of the Jataka stories (tales of the Buddha's previous incarnations) in the provincial variant of the high style of the T'ang China.

The Heian period progressively secularized the illuminated scroll, first by illustrating sutras not with antique Indians but with stylish modern court ladies and their gentlemen, and then by developing an exquisite style for illustrating the true "sutras" of this worldly age—the literary tales. A masterpiece inspired by a masterpiece, the Genji Monogatari Emaki (Tale of Genji Scroll) alternates sections of Murasaki's text with illustrations of those passages. It is a rare thing—a work of narrative art that is almost abstract. Sharp or shallow diagonals cut across the unrolling of the scroll, showing us rooms in villas or palaces, where the aristo-

crats of the Genji world sit or stand in quiet repose, their faces almost indistinguishable, their motion frozen but their relationships to one another clear. It is the ideal work of illustration: the enigmatic faces and figures demand to be filled, animated with the reader's own understanding of the text.

In the succeeding era of wars and alarums, however, the handscroll would develop into something quite the opposite of the Genji scroll: a genre of swift, vivid, hyperkinetic pictorial narration, full of incident, precise observation, and a democracy of subject matter that is truly amazing. Everyone in Late Heian and Kamakura Japan, it seems, gets a part in an emaki. Temples had their historical emaki, illustrating renowned miracles. The cataclysmic warfare of the era made for some of the most arresting images of fighting and fiery destruction in all world art. Frightened courtiers, screaming commoners, and masses of cavalry rampage across these scrolls.

Even the netherworld had its chroniclers: the Jigoku Zōshi (Hell Scroll) joined such bril-

Left: The *Ōeyama Emaki* (Mt. Ōe Scroll) is a consciously archaistic picture scroll from the seventeenth century. The painter Kanō Takanobu, whose school was known for its treatment of Chinese themes, here recalls the glories of the thirteenth-century *Yamatoe* (Japanese-style) narrative scrolls in a vigorous scene of demon-quelling. Minamoto no Yorimitsu and four followers decapitate the ogre of Mt. Ōe, whose two heads fly off to help create a nicely balanced three-part composition.

Below: The most famous of all Japanese painters in the Chinese style, the monk Sesshū, worked in both the brusque "broken ink" *(haboku)* style and, as shown here, in a more contemplative vein. The *Sansui Chōkan* (Long Landscape Scroll), from which this detail comes, is a lyrical, rythmical exploration of hills, valleys, and clouds, with here and there some evidence of the presence of man. This fishing hamlet suggests the thousands that dot the Japanese coast, even though all the details are Chinese.

liant grotesqueries as the *Yamai Sōshi* (Scroll of Diseases) and the *Gaki Zōshi* (Scroll of Hungry Ghosts) in providing Japanese artists (notably Hokusai) with unforgettable images of deformity, depravity, and sheer terror.

If the *emaki* represent the turbulent era at the end of the old court culture, the landscape scroll (often but not always a hanging scroll) evokes the politically violent but esthetically more settled era of the early Ashikaga shoguns (1393–1500), a paradoxical period. This period was the birth era of many things we think of as "typically Japanese" in garden architecture, tea drinking, and esthetic theory; it was, none-theless, a time when native Japanese art as such was in disfavor, and every cultivated man modeled himself after a Sung Dynasty Chinese gentleman. The era produced the one Japanese master of the monochrome ink landscape that

the Chinese admit into their own pantheon: Sesshū, who was in fact only one member of a brilliant line of masters in this Chinese genre. The Japanese difference, if there is one, in even relatively early landscapes, is a tendency to-ward the decorative—a shying away from the metaphysical and physical depths of mature Chinese landscape toward a desire to delight the eye. Arrangements in space become some-what arbitrary, brushwork itself becomes a visual pleasure and the viewer can sense the hand and eye of the artist a little more strongly than the presence of spirit. It is too much to call it a resurgence of the Shintō delight in the visible—but it is a signature-characteristic of Japanese art, and it will find its culmination in the sense-pleasing arts of decoration and print-making that dominate the sixteenth, seven-teenth, and eighteenth centuries.

Out of the feudal warfare of the fifteenth and sixteenth centuries emerged a new kind of aristocrat: the powerful local lord or *daimyō*, semi-independent and ensconced in a castle that was no longer a mere temporary or utilitarian fort, but a sumptuous permanent residence, fortified for his safety and decorated to his taste.

His taste, like his ambitions, had grandeur. Oda Nobunaga, the first of the great triumvirate whose ambition, rivalry, treachery, and realpolitik would lead to a unified Japan in the seventeenth century, gave over the decoration of his castle at Azuchi on Lake Biwa to Kanō Eitoku, the most brilliant of a long line of artists. The Kanō school had arisen in the Ashikaga period as a school of monochrome ink painting; Kanō Masanobu, its founder, was a disciple of Shūbun, who had taught the great Sesshū as well. Masanobu's son Motonobu, in a canny act of syncretism, began to introduce into the reflective, sober monochrome style elements of the bright color and overall decorative verve that characterized Yamato-e ("Japanese painting")—the style whose classic starting-point is the Tale of Genji Scroll.

Kanō Eitoku may have been Motonobu's pupil; in any case he is the man who brought this clever style into power and made it the official art of the later feudal period.

Azuchi Eitoku had, as it were, a new canvas to work with. Far from simply decorating the occasional alcove with a hanging scroll, as he might have done for the Zen-fanciers of the Kamakura period, here he had vast spaces to deal with: sliding doors covered with gold leaf from Japan's generous mines; six-section screens with Korean paper hinges, also gilt and ready to receive ambitious images; gloomy indoor spaces that could be set quietly afire with the glow of candles next to gold, red, azurite blue, jadelike green.

And so, although folding screens (*byōbū*, "protection from the wind") had been known

SCREENS

since continental culture first came to Japan, it was at the hands of the great castle decorators of the Kanō tradition—and the even greater masters of the Rimpa style—that they reached their peak of decorative opulence, compositional boldness, and expressive power. Eitoku worked feverishly, painting, so it is said, with a large brush of bundled straw. We can sense the energy of the painter and the age in Eitoku's famous Hawk and Pine Screen, in the collection of the Tokyo University of Arts. The Chinese motif is handled in a thoroughly Japanese

manner: space is flattened to the picture-plane, great rough masses of gilt cloud maneuver about the tree trunk in a semi-abstract pattern. The brilliant green clumps of foliage are executed with the boldness of an oil sketch. Yet trunk and rocks are finely detailed. The result is a fascinating paradox of both precision and abandon, arresting when seen from far away, and increasingly refined and subtle as the viewer approaches it.

These extremes of fine detail and overall compositional boldness persisted in the work of Tawaraya Sōtatsu and the disciple who carried on his work a generation later, Ogata Kōrin. The Sotatsu-Kōrin (Rimpa) school took the Kanō combination of decoration and classical brushwork several steps further, bringing out brilliantly the logic inherent in the evolu-

tion of Japanese design. The Hawk and Pine Screen approaches abstraction very well. The Rimpa masters could find precedents in earlier Japanese art—such as Yamato-e—for becoming more abstract yet. Sōtatsu's Tale of Genji Screen reinterprets the simple, colorful spatial organization of the antique Genji Scroll in the expanded terms of the folding screen: a river curves in and out like a great swathe of silk; foliage dances across the surface in clumps whose placement seems elegantly arbitrary, possessing, like the dark bits of hat or hair in Yamato-e, its own special logic and rhythm separate from the story being told. On flower and foliage screens in another style, the Rimpa masters combined an attention to detail that one usually sees in miniature-painting with simple green tints of great freshness and a compositional boldness that—as always in the art of these great decorators—can be ''read'' and enjoyed across a wide room.

The sixteenth century was a cosmopolitan age in Japan, and Japanese barons liked to surround themselves not only with firearms, astrolabes and iron armor, but with ''foreign''-subject screens and even oil paintings. The Namban (Southern Barbarian) screens of the era are priceless documents of the thriving communities of Portuguese and Spanish missionaries, soldiers, and merchants that existed in southern Japan.

The decorative vigor of the Kanō style at its height is exemplified in the *Matsu Ni Kusabana Zu* (Pine, Grass, and Flower Panels) at the Chishakuin, Kyōto. The strong, sinuous diagonal that the tree trunk makes is a characteristic Kanō resource; it may recur in other compositions as a road or a river.

Exotic Europeans make music in the *Yōjin Sōgaku Zu Byōbu* (Foreign Lute-Music Screen), from the sixteenth century. Evidence of the popularity of foreign motifs among Japan's military rulers in this period, the screen also shows how carefully native artists studied the oil paintings imported into the country during the so-called ''Christian Century.''

PRINTS

Certain screens painted in Kyōto in the early seventeenth century showed wide panoramas of streetlife, festival scenes, and views of popular entertainments like the nascent *kabuki*. Viewers are forcibly reminded of the narrative scrolls of four hundred years before when they see these colorful, energetic, ordinary Japanese (attractive women predominating). *Ukiyo-e* (Floating World) painting, and the explosion of printmaking that developed from it, represent the culmination of the two great native tendencies of Japanese fine art: the narrative and the decorative . . . this time in a democratic milieu.

Not that the early *ukiyo-e* prints were exactly images for the masses; rather, they were illustrations for the sensual and sophisticated young urbanite. It is difficult to overrate the importance of the ''courtesan critique'' in an evaluation of early Edo Period culture. This combination ''buyer's guide'' and sex manual not only suppied the novelist Ihara Saikaku with the model for his pioneering ribald novels but also was the genre to which Hishikawa Moronobu contributed his beautiful woodcut illustrations—illustrations both sedate and salacious. Moronobu did individual prints and album leaves as well, his famous ''singing line'' tracing the graceful clothed and unclothed limbs of the beauties of the evening and their lovers. For a hundred and fifty years the *ukiyo-e* print was to maintain an almost exclusive connection with the licensed quarters, those perpetual carnivals which were the only places in Japan where townsmen, samurai, artists, poets, didactic novelists, exquisites of the flesh, fanciers of things European, and lovely women met on a footing of rough equality.

The theater was the other shrine of the Floating World, and the line of printmakers surnamed Torii (especially Kiyonobu, Kiyomasu, and Kiyomitsu) designed bold actor prints that convey the true Edoite's delight in his muscular style of Kabuki. The Torii also designed courtesan prints and erotica, often indulging the Japanese penchant for the celebration of beautiful cloth patterns. The lines of limbs, so clear and distinct in Moronobu, become entangled with peony motifs, the *oshibori* checkerboard pattern, and the garments' ripples and edges.

Meanwhile the tradition of *ukiyo* painting, on screens and silk, continued brilliantly, with such masters of cloth texture, alluring posture, and seductive sweetness as Kaigetsudō Andō.

One can well imagine the frustration that the printmakers must have felt as they toyed with thin hand-applied color or the rose-and-green duochrome printing that developed after 1740.

Color—deep and bright—came with Suzuki Harunobu in the 1760s. Designing prints for a coterie of young moneyed *samurai*, Harunobu had a bottomless budget and a perfect eye. The *nishiki-e* (brocade-picture) print he invented changed Japanese prints forever—and made them more expensive.

Harunobu's delicate, girlish beauties were a new departure in *ukiyo-e*; not only did his demimondaines lack the robust sensuality of Moronobu women, but he also depicted ''nice'' girls of the middle class while engaged in their gentle diversions.

Downtown Edo (Tokyo) seems busy and serene at the same time in this print by the landscape master Andō Hiroshige, *Nihonbashi in the Rain*. Like his contemporary Katsushika Hokusai, Hiroshige often used Western ''vanishing point'' perspective to add drama and atmosphere to his compositions. This westernism may help account for the powerful effect Hiroshige exerted on European artists like Van Gogh, who copied this print in oils.

The *onnagata* (female impersonator) actor Ogasawara Tsuneyo, by the enigmatic genius Tōshūsai Sharaku, the most famous of all theatrical printmakers.

A young girl plays battledore and shuttlecock in this eighteenth-century print by Torii Kiyomitsu, a major figure in a long artistic dynasty.

Two of Harunobu Suzuki's willowy young women pound cloth with fulling mallets in a scene that restages a classical situation in a modern milieu.

Torii Kiyonaga advanced the Japanese print in two important directions: his beauties lost the attenuated, T'ang-Chinese quality of Harunobu women; they grew stately, tall, adult—anticipating the mature, perfect ladies of Utamaro. And he prophesied the last great age of *ukiyo-e* by giving an unprecedented emphasis to landscape backgrounds.

In one ten-month period beginning in 1794, the mysterious Tōshūsai Sharaku produced some of the most vigorous actor portraits of the entire tradition. By lengthening faces and giving eyes and jaws more tension than had been usual in *ukiyo-e* (or, for that matter, in Far Eastern art in general), Sharaku produced portraits that some have described as "psychological studies," although they can probably be better understood as an effort to create a stronger, more forceful image of the actor's art.

Sharaku executed many of his finest portrait prints in closeup, as did his contemporary Kitagawa Utamaro. But Utamaro's faces convey nothing of the individuality of the actor prints. His beauties retain the cool anonymity that had been traditional since the Genji Scroll, but the fullness of their faces, the fleshed but not fleshy curves of neck and shoulder, convey a presence of the physical that is in no way dependent on the mere illusion of bodily volume. The lines are themselves sensuous, the bodies full but as light as air, indicative of a certain Asian idealization.

In many ways Utamaro took the traditional eroticism of the print as far as it could go. The final burst of creativity in this two-hundred-year tradition came with the landscapes of Katsushika Hokusai and Andō Hiroshige, the former as famous for his bold composition and sense of movement as the latter is for his tranquillity and perfection of atmosphere. Hokusai was a restless, passionate genius who would have been at home in Renaissance Italy. His prints and sketchbooks constitute a joyful, ceaseless pursuit and celebration of the complete visual reality of his homeland. Hiroshige, a more lyrical spirit, appealed to Europeans who saw Japan as a land of poetry and serenity. One of the major ironies of east-west cultural history is the fact that this fine printmaker, coming at the end of a tradition, working in a sense away from it and against it, and so different in mood and tone from the tradition at its peak, should, for many foreigners, have typified the art of the Floating World.

PHOTOGRAPHY

In the eighteenth century, the one serious popular rival of the *ukiyo-e* print was the *Nagasaki-e,* the "Nagasaki picture," showing the exotic scene on the streets and in the harbor of Japan's only foreign-trade port. The *Nagasaki-e* were the popular versions of many visual researches being undertaken by Japanese interested in Europe.

Japan's community of "Dutch scholars" *(rangakusha)* were the first to experiment in a more scholarly way with such devices as the *camera obscura* and the daguerreotype. When Ueno Hikoma, one of Japan's first two full-time photographers, hung out his shingle in 1862, it is certain that he was aware of his intellectual and artistic lineage; he has left us a four-photo panorama of Nagasaki that obeys the stylistic rules of the *Nagasaki-e* perfectly.

Such backward-looking homages were rare in the early days of Japanese photography, however. A nation was in the process of transformation, and lenses were busy recording the activities and faces of young radicals, the façades of new European-style buildings, such great public works as the agricultural reclamation of Hokkaidō, and—for the foreign dollar—hand-tinted exotico-erotica (*Home Bathing, Girls In Bed Room,* and others).

By the turn of the century, a militarily successful and self-confident Japan began to produce a distinctive modern culture. Along with the novels of Sōseki and the accomplished plein-air oil paintings of Asai Chū and Kuroda Seiki came the development of art photography in the painterly mode now called "pictorialism." World War I greatly increased Japanese prosperity, with a resultant rise in amateur photography and increased access to foreign photographic examples. This combination made the 1920s the great age of pictorialism in Japan. The fuzzy, moody gum-bichromate prints of this era sometimes recall the school of Stieglitz—but just as often reproduce the somber, somewhat cool images that abound in Japanese oil portraiture of the period.

The 1930s brought a brief renaissance to the Japanese modern arts, even as war approached. Photographers experimented with hard, bright images of the rapidly industrializing urban Japanese world. German influences encouraged both expressionism (odd angles, visual fragmentation, etc.) and "new objectivity." And modern Japan began its continuing love affair with surrealism.

An unknown foreign photographer took this view of a familiar Japanese symbol, the *torii* (bird perch) gate leading to a Shintō shrine. Both western and Japanese photographers produced such typical exotica for non-Japanese consumption during the late nineteenth century.

A vigorous school of documentary photography provided perhaps the strongest Japanese photos of the 1930s. The masterful Kimura Ihei, in particular, captured in portraits the nervous intensity of the intelligentsia as well as the very different nervousness and vigor of the urban proletariat.

Kimura fell in line with Japanese consumerism and militarism in a way that was sadly typical of his countrymen, finally producing photos devoted to selling both soap and aggression. A survivor, he returned to documentation in the 1950s. Meanwhile, postwar photography leapt ahead.

Ueda Shōji, a prominent prewar experimentalist, returned to making his gently surreal satirical figure studies in bright light against white backgrounds. His almost hallucinatory clarity has influenced contemporary Japanese advertising photography.

At the other end of the stylistic spectrum are Domon Ken and Tōmatsu Shōmei, two giants of postwar photography. Domon's hallmark is texture, and there is little in modern photography as moving as a comparison between his closeups of the ancient wood-grain of Buddhist sculpture and his studies of the ravaged skin of Hiroshima survivors. Tōmatsu is a powerful influence in several directions, a master of both texture and motion. His closeups of muddy ponds and his blurred images of violent action oddly resemble one another and share a brooding darkness that younger photographers like Moriyama Daidō have deepened a great deal.

Moriyama, through multiple exposure and overexposure, seems to corrode his images until they rest uneasily at the very edge of artistic abstraction.

Narahara Ikkō's images are clearer, sometimes, as in his New Mexico series, brightening to a visionary intensity. Like many modern Japanese artists, he is fascinated by the drama of ritual. He portrays Zen meditation as a sort

of occult grand opera. Hosoe Eikō is another dramatist, with a penchant for Genet-like subjects: flowers, rough boys, death.

With young photographers like Akiyama Ryōji, Jūmonji Bishin and Tamura Shigeru, something new and welcome comes into Japanese photography: humor. Jūmonji deftly satirizes both the modern Japanese mentality and the wildly popular Japanese amateur photo in his series of portraits of ordinary citizens—salary men, dads, moms, bikers, and bodybuilders—every last subject's head cut off by the top of the frame. It's a long way from Ueno Hikoma's full-length portraits of frowning samurai stalwarts to these images of people reduced to merely their clothes alone—longer, surely, at least technically, than a mere one hundred years of calendar time.

Five *sumo* wrestlers pose for the camera some time around 1875. While the photographer is unknown, it may be the Baron von Stillfried (see box at right); he is known to have been one of the few photographers of Japan to have employed the albumen print process, by which this photo was made.

SCULPTURE

The earliest Japanese sculpture fell within the Neolithic style. The female figurines of the Jōmon ("cord-pattern") pottery culture, with their massive, ungainly hips, are perfect images of the Earth Mother, charged with the solemn religiosity of this era.

Japanese sculpture didn't enter its next phase until the third century A.D., when the *haniwa* appear. *Haniwa*, four-foot clay figures, were used to form a picketlike fence, lined up closely around the perimeters of the tumuli in which pre-Buddhist chieftains were interred. From solemn religiosity to a secular panorama, the *haniwa* portrayed everything that the ruler enjoyed on earth: armed and armored warriors, caparisoned horses, court ladies with parted hair, musicians, dancers flushed with wine. The first monuments of a distinctly Japanese civilization, the *haniwa*, in their vigor, variety, and naive good humor, laid a groundwork for that joyful final document of traditional Japanese culture, the *Manga* or sketchbook of Katsushika Hokusai.

It was Buddhism, however, that sponsored Japan's greatest sculpture. In the sixth century immigrant Chinese and Korean artists brought their skills to the brand-new temples of the Yamato region. Their work perpetuated the Chinese Northern Wei style: elongated, ethereal, nobly hieratic images of the historical Buddha and the chief Bodhisattvas.

The late seventh century, a time of great distinction in Japanese poetry, was also a high point in sculpture. Without abandoning a heartfelt spirituality, the makers of Buddhas began to give their images a human fullness and softness that gently escaped the linearity of the Northern Wei style. Works like the exqui-

site Miroku (Buddha of the Future) in the Chūgūji nunnery were a prelude to the triumph of the full, ripe T'ang Dynasty style, the style that dominated the Japanese eighth century.

This style, enshrined in the wealthy religious establishments of Nara, Japan's regional version of the T'ang capital, reflected a cosmopolitan civilization at its most vigorous and optimistic. Under Indian influence the human body swelled and filled out; drapery receded and thinned in order to emphasize flesh; portrait sculpture was born. In the statue of the blind monk Ganjin, both human and ideal at once, an astute viewer can see the origin of a genre that came into its glory as Japan declared its cultural independence.

The importation of esoteric Buddhism in the ninth century provided a new departure for Japanese sculpture. The mystery and secrecy of the new cults called up a new and paradoxical sort of image: no longer an idealized body, but a corpulent, more or less grossly physical body with hypnotic eyes that gleam and glare from beneath hooded lids.

If these esoteric images seemed to insist upon a radical split between soul and body, those of the latter Heian period redressed the balance. The refined, secular-minded court of the Heian capital (Kyōto) identified their own gracious palaces and villas with the Buddhist Western Paradise, so it was only natural that their Buddha images should resemble the ele-

This statue of Kannon, bodhisattva of mercy, dates from the early Heian Period (ninth century A.D.), but its ripe, idealized physicality and harmony of line recall the style of the Nara Period (712–794 A.D.). While the Nara sculptor might have chosen dry lacquer or bronze, this image is made of wood; this most abundant and beloved of native materials came to dominate later Japanese sculpture. The entire statue is carved from a single block (ichiboku-bori technique).

gant, vaguely feminine young men (like Prince Genji) who represented their *beau ideal.*

Late Heian and early Kamakura period sculpture evolved beyond Chinese prototypes. The Nara period was the great age of continental techniques like bronze and dry-lacquer work. From about A.D. 900 on, however, Japanese sculptors did all of their finest work in the great national material, wood. The *ichiboku* (one-trunk) technique of the early Heian esoteric Buddhas gave way to a sophisticated peg-and-hole assembly method that allowed for complex asymmetry and detail that went beyond mere surface ornament.

Kamakura sculpture was at its finest at the bottom of the iconographic hierarchy; vigorous, violent images of the Deva kings (wrathful guardians of the Buddhist law) and monk portraits brought living flesh and bone to birth from the intimate contact of chisel and living wood. In this way, as in so many of their arts, foreign stimulus pushed the Japanese toward an ever more fruitful relationship with their own resources—such resources as beautiful wood, psychological realism, and a faultless feel for the "merely" (and triumphantly) human. It is this feel that wins out in the history of Japanese sculpture, in the fine portraits of Kamakura period warlords and their equally courageous counterparts, the men of the spirit, who, in their wrinkly, bony humanity, are as noble as the great Buddhas.

Medieval Japanese religious thinkers and artists developed ingenious ways of combining Shintō, the native cult, with the imported Buddhist faith. Here the sculptor Koshun (fl. 1311–1369) depicts the Shintō war god Hachiman as a Buddhist priest, with more than a hint of the humane realism characteristic of portrait sculpture in this period. The assembled-wood *(yosegi)* technique allows graceful naturalism in robe drapery and the positioning of arms and hands.

Beautiful writing is the queen of the arts in the Far East. No other single art renders, as calligraphy does, the full range of expressive possibilities that Chinese-style culture allows. From the most careful, filial emulation of masters and ancient copybooks to the wildest self-expression, from styles that recall two-thousand-year-old dynasties to up-to-date, elegant brushwork, the calligrapher's art embraces the full richness of the world's oldest continuous civilization.

Chinese characters began with the incised oracle bones and tortoise shells of the Shang Dynasty (1500–1100 B.C.), and the bronze inscriptions of the Chou (1100–221 B.C.). But style-conscious calligraphy is a product of the succeeding ages of national consolidation and empire-building. In the Ch'in Dynasty (221–206 B.C.), a strong bureaucracy standardized a number of regional script variants into what we now call the *tensho*, or "seal style," a style that preserves a strong sense of the early pictographic function of Chinese characters. *Tensho* characters have a combination of naivete and dignity that has appealed to Sinophiles throughout Japanese history.

The Han Dynasty (206 B.C.–8 A.D.), China's Roman Empire, was as fruitful in calligraphic styles as it was in philosophy and political organization. The by-now-archaic seal style began to be written in a cursive form as well, the so-called grass style *(sōsho)*, which allowed the brush great freedom and gave the characters a soft, sinuous feeling. At the same time, the newly organized bureaucratic Confucian state developed a clear, businesslike, and very handsome hand, logically enough called *reisho*, or the "scribe style." From Han-period *reisho* emerged both the modern square or block script *(kaisho)*, the form in which most of us have seen Chinese characters, and the "running hand" *(gyōsho)*, a semicursive version of the block script that allows the hand and heart of the calligrapher a certain freedom while

maintaining the integrity of the characters.

By the time the great Sui-T'ang civilization was knocking on Japan's door in the sixth and seventh centuries, the *kaisho, gyōsho,* and *sōsho* styles had established themselves as the major creative modes, while the seal and scribe hands were still practiced for decorative effect; the latter two styles also spawned a wondrous and bizarre variety of *zattaisho* (miscellaneous styles), in which characters were fashioned from pictures of snakes, tortoises, human figures, clouds, birds, flowers, or tadpoles. The enthusiastic Sinophiles of the Nara period imported and practiced all the styles, with an emphasis on the formal, fully "continental" *kaisho.* The illuminated Buddhist sutras of this period, copied on gorgeous Chinese paper, are *kaisho* masterpieces admired as much by the Chinese as by the Japanese.

In the succeeding Heian period, however, Japanese calligraphy followed Japanese culture generally into a period of self-cultivation. The *sōsho,* highly cultivated in the T'ang, became the foundation for a hand fully as elegant and "native" as the masterpieces of Japanese poetry and fiction, which it was used to transcribe. The Japanese *kana* syllabary itself evolved from *sōsho* cursive versions of characters used for their sound value to write Japanese. The result was an art of elegant abbreviation and sinuousity that ignored Chinese rules of calligraphic spacing. In place of discrete characters occupying essentially square spaces and marching down the page in good order, Heian *sōsho* and *kana* calligraphy made liberal use of elongation, character-to-character connection, and contrasts in size and stroke thickness. While orthodox Chinese

practice called for the maintenance of a good, rich, black India ink tone in every stroke, the Japanese let the ink darken, lighten, grow rich and thin at different points on the page, making for a special graphic rhythm.

The Heian elegance turned to a very idiosyncratic vigor in the succeeding Kamakura period; then as the feudal period progressed, the Heian-based *wayō*, or "Japanese mode," of calligraphy lost much of its creative vigor. As Japan renewed her contacts with the continent, however, the *karayō*, or "Chinese mode" was revived and strengthened. The schools of Zen Buddhism wrote a new chapter in calligraphic history with their powerful, personalized brushwork, executed with speed and strength. In this arresting work, the brush was often allowed to go dry as it rubbed the paper. The result is a classically Japanese sort of art: we are aware of ink and paper, and we are aware of the hand that put the two together.

The scholars of the Edo period strengthened their knowledge of Chinese calligraphy, producing good *kaisho* and *tensho*, while their *reisho* lagged behind. The exciting artistic climate of the period also revived the *wayō* style. In the beautiful work of Hon'ami Kōetsu, the sword-appraiser turned designer, painter, potter, and reviver of the decorative tradition of Sōtatsu, one can see a modernized, highly alert Heian sensibility at work. His spidery, sinuous calligraphy is changeable and cannily spaced out over the leaf or flower motifs of his decorative paper; it is the last great statement of traditional Japanese calligraphic sensibility—a sensibility that was able to both appropriate and extend the heritage of the Chinese brush.

At the start of the new year Japanese schoolchildren participate in a huge calligraphy contest. Calligraphic education is an important part of the national school curriculum. Before the war, students practiced writing nationalistic slogans and starchy moral maxims; in this 1968 competition, several children were working on the phrase "Meiji Restoration Centennial."

DUTCH STUDIES

Far from being a simple, panicky response to Commodore Perry, Japanese awareness of the West has a long history. The Christian Century (ca. 1549–1634), coinciding with a period of terrific social upheaval in Japan, was a high-water mark in the popularity of Iberian Christianity and European material culture. There were churches or cathedrals in every one of Japan's provinces, and vast armies of musketeers battled as though they were somewhere in the Papal States.

The stringent anti-Christian and anti-foreign laws passed in the first decades of the seventeenth century, however, imposed a sort of amnesia, and when a tiny band of gifted—and iconoclastic—intellectuals revived European studies after 1720, everything had to be relearned, this time through the medium of the Dutch language instead of Spanish and Portuguese. These Dutch scholars *(rangakusha)* of the feudal and shogunal domains are the honorable ancestors of the many diligent and courageous teachers who helped Japan mold a modern world view in the nineteenth century.

The geographical focus of Dutch studies was, logically, Nagasaki, where a tiny trading contingent of Dutchmen—strictly confined to the artificial island of Dejima—was allowed to handle the importation of a small number of European goods, and the export of fine Japanese copper and other products. After the shogun Yoshimune relaxed strictures against the importation of foreign books in 1720, a series of colorful scholars visited Nagasaki to obtain Dutch works on anatomy, astronomy, geography, history, and art techniques. Translations and digests of these "barbarian books" followed.

The best Dutch scholars, who liked to toast the Gregorian New Year with red wine, shared a hardy iconoclasm, an independence of mind, and a footloose determination to follow their noses instead of the footprints of tradition. The great botanist, mineralogist, satirist, playwright, ceramicist, and theorist of perspective Hiraga Gennai, who was a *rōnin*, or masterless samurai, rejoiced in a pamphlet with the Rabelaisian title *Hōhiron* (A Fart Treatise): "Permanently bereft of material possessions, I am also spared the futility of servitude to a lord. . . . I go around the places I like and avoid the places that displease me, and I have at least the advantage of possessing myself in freedom for the remainder of my years." Gennai was the first Dutch scholar to make the connection between the new intellectual perspectives from Europe and the study of pictorial perspective in Japanese art.

The prominence of art study in *rangaku* makes perfect sense from both sides of the intellectual equation. The Dutch were heirs of a magnificent tradition of realistic depiction. The Japanese intellectual world, even beyond the confines of Dutch studies, was experimenting with a new empirical doctrine, "the investigation of things," which put a premium on patient attention to the real world instead of the category-shuffling of earlier official Confucianism. The reproduction of objects as the eye sees them thrilled advanced thinkers, whether they were artists, scientists, or philosophers.

Indeed, *rangaku* art study had some complex and surprising results. Hiraga Gennai's most famous disciple was one Satake Shozan, whose northern domain became a *rangaku* center. Shozan, guided by some Dutch engrav-

ings, painted a series of landscapes that reproduced one of the cliches of eighteenth-century European art: a partially seen tree limb and trunk, placed in the extreme foreground, to frame the composition and increase the illusion of depth. Some really consequential artists, among them the print designer Hiroshige, were intrigued by these and other extreme examples of European perspective. Hiroshige, in a number of prints, put a portion of an object into extreme close-up, and contrasted it with an exaggeratedly distant background scene.

When Japanese art became all the rage in France after 1860, the most influential artist was Hiroshige; much admired were his dynamic perspective contrasts between partially seen foreground objects and faraway backgrounds. Toulouse-Lautrec, among others, tried this neat trick. Thus did Europe rediscover itself through the elaborate aid of some minor Dutch engravers, some eager Japanese minds, one truly great artist, and the accidents of time.

Above: Ships of the United States, Britain, and Russia ride at anchor in Yokohama Bay. ''Yokohama prints'' of the 1860s and 1870s, with their views of the exotic foreign settlement, were influenced by earlier ''Nagasaki prints,'' made with the help of Japanese scholars of European studies.

Right: In this *Nanban Byōbu* (Southern Barbarian screen) Portuguese priests and monks adore an image of Christ while Japanese attendants and samurai go about their own business. The cosmopolitan atmosphere of sixteenth-century Nagasaki was altered when all foreigners other than the Dutch and Chinese were banished from the city in the early 1600s. Nevertheless, Nagasaki reemerged as a center of ''barbarian learning.''

文芸

4 • LITERATURE
AND FILM

POETRY

"The poetry of Japan," wrote a medieval theorist, "looks simple but is really difficult." Simple words for a complex truth. If we look just a little way beyond what traditional poems seem to be—delicate and somewhat artless lyrics in one or two simple forms—we can glimpse a poetic universe so different from our own as to challenge it on every point.

Half of the story of Japanese verse is a story of miniaturization. Hauntingly rhythmical "long songs" *(chōka)* are the masterpieces of the eighth-century *Manyōshū* collection. These elegies, praise poems, and almost Homeric war songs give way to the thirty-one-syllable *tanka* (short song) as Japan becomes a settled society dominated by a sophisticated court. The *tanka* is elegantly adapted to the needs of witty, philosophically amorous courtiers. Easy to improvise "off the cuff" (or off the brocade sleeve), and hence the perfect amateur poem, the *tanka* also has enough length to sustain meditation and reward careful artistry. With this form, aristocrats could pursue one of the perennial Japanese poetic goals: to be both effortless and profound at once, to combine the casual cock of the head and the deep boom of the temple bell.

This combination of qualities persisted and was intensified when the Japanese poem shrank to the compass of the seventeen-syllable *hokku* (later *haiku*). But neither *tanka* nor *hokku* practice make much sense unless we understand the other major tendency in Japanese poetic history: As the poem itself, the module of expression, shrank, it came to be part of increasingly sophisticated larger wholes—anthologies, exchanges, and sequences. These larger aggregates themselves

attained brilliant artistry and complex unities, weaving extraordinary poetic tapestries.

As early as the *Manyōshū*, the *tanka* had been a medium of exchange. An amorous verse aimed at one's lover would call forth a responding *tanka* from him or her; since the original verse was often a complaint, the response tended to be a lively act of self-justification, usually turning the accuser's metaphors against him:

You are like those scarves, those white beach waves—I can't go near you, you're cold, my love, yet I long for you.
Just the reverse—it's you who have no time to come near me, as if I were those scarves, those white beach waves.
(Translated by Hiroaki Satō, in From the Country of Eight Islands.)

Tanka were collected and many were made under imperial auspices. In the twelfth and thirteenth centuries anthology making reached its artistic zenith, as compilers crafted long texts out of poems by many pens. Two things aided them in their work: the restricted vocabulary of the poems, assuring that there would be many, many instances of cherry blossoms, autumn moonlight, and plover cries; and the pinpoint specificity within time of most *tanka*. In nonamorous verse, it is almost always clear not only that it is autumn but, for example, the first part of late autumn. Anthologists could trace the Japanese year, subtly moving from the early blossoms to the late. (In fact, the Western anthologist R.H. Blyth made a brilliant, if eccentric, compilation along just these lines during the 1930s.) Or the entire course of a love affair could be followed, from the first sight of a pretty sleeve to the final heartbreak

and recriminations. And, perhaps most important for later developments, the Japanese were fond of verse capping: seventeen syllables by one hand, the remaining fourteen by another.

All these practices flowed together into Japan's most original and profound contribution to world poetry: the *renga*, or linked verse. *Renga* is essentially perpetual-motion verse capping. To the fourteen syllables that cap a *tanka*, one adds another verse of seventeen, in effect starting another *tanka*. Only this new verse continues the thought of the fourteen-syllable verse and (more important) departs from the meaning of the original seventeen-syllable verse, shifting the seasonal identification, the speaker, the mood, or some other significant element. When you read *renga*, you not only feel meaning being added and deepened, you also see it being subtracted, slipping into oblivion, as the old links slough off and away. You become attentive and wary as every link shines and shifts under your eyes. Buddhist critics likened the composing of *renga* to a correct understanding of the impermanence of the world.

There came to be both elegant and comic *renga*. The great Bashō was the master of the latter, bringing to his sharp vision of humble life a great dignity and a deep wit. He was a particular master of the *hokku*, the opening verse, which, by the rules of the game, had to be felicitous in tone, specific as to place, and brilliant enough to spark the mind of the next writer. We recognize all these qualities in what was later called the *haiku*. The *haiku* had a splendid career as a tiny independent lyric, but for Bashō it was always (his word) a "seed" for the great, noble growth called *renga*.

The poet Yamanoe no Okura is one of the most distinctive voices in the great eighth-century anthology, *Man'yōshū*. An ardent Sinophile, Okura wrote moving poems on social and ethical concerns. Using these themes was an exception to the rules of classical poetry, which emphasized individual sensibility as it grew more sophisticated.

Right: The priest Sōgi (in black robe) and poetry-loving friends compose linked verse *(renga)* near the grave of Fujiwara no Teika, by the light of the full moon. Sōgi, perhaps the greatest of all *renga* masters, perfected a style heavily influenced by late classical *tanka* (31-syllable) poetry, of which Teika was the acknowledged arbiter. By convention, the moon suggests the state of Buddhist enlightenment and marks the season (late summer).

STORY

While the brevity of the poems and the kinetic ways in which they fit together make reading Japanese poetry an experience of ceaseless change, perhaps the longest-running tradition in Japanese prose fiction is what a psychologist would call the repetition-compulsion. The most attractive, genial, and self-possessed obsessive in all literature is Hikaru Genji, the focus of the world's first fiction of psychological nuance, *Genji Monogatari* (The Tale of Genji, ca. A.D. 1000) by the court lady Murasaki Shikibu. *Genji* is the greatest product of the Heian court, a group of men and women who were exquisites but not decadents, and Genji himself expresses the romantic side of their ideal. Beautiful, in love with life, yet placid as a mirror, Genji drifts

from affair to affair in a way that we would call "amoral" if its absolute cheerfulness and composure did not tell us that such judgments miss the point. Genji's perfection and emptiness are the pretexts for the unfolding of a brilliant panorama of social, psychological, and esthetic texture. Hikaru means "to shine," and Genji is the light that the reader holds to illumine his now-faraway world.

The very name Genji is a prophecy of darker times in Japanese history and literature, for it is also the surname of the clan that plunged Japan into civil war after the mid-twelfth century. In a bloody time, chanted prose sagas arose recounting the Genji conquest of the Taira, their chief rival. The greatest of these,

BEST TEN PRE-MODERN STORIES
■

KOJIKI The Japanese Myths.

TAKETORI MONOGATARI (Tale of the Bamboo Cutter). A classic folktale.

OCHIKUBO MONOGATARI (Tale of the Lady Ochikubo). A predecessor of *Genji*.

GENJI MONOGATARI (Tale of Genji). The peak of Japanese literature.

KONJAKU MONOGATARI (Tales of Times Now Past). Medieval Buddhist stories.

HEIKE MONOGATARI (Tale of the Heike). The greatest war cycle.

KŌSHOKU ICHIDAI OTOKO (The Man Who Spent a Life in Love). The debut of townsman literature, and of the great Ihara Saikaku.

TŌKAIDŌCHŪ HIZAKURIGE (Along the Tōkaidō on Shank's Mare) by Jippensha Ikku. A great comic picaresque novel.

UGETSU MONOGATARI (Tales of the Rainy Moon) by Ueda Akinari. Buddhist-influenced tales by one of Japan's greatest stylists.

UKIYOBURO (Bathhouse of the Floating World) by Shikitei Samba. Bathhouse tales by a great humorist.

This twelfth-century manuscript of *The Tale of Genji* is one of the treasures kept in the Hōryū-ji Temple in Nara. Many of the masterworks of Japanese secular classical literature were copied, annotated, and preserved by Buddhist monk-scholars in the medieval period. *Genji*, Japan's greatest work of prose, also served as a guide to courtly elegance and high taste for generations of readers.

BEST FIFTEEN MODERN NOVELS

∎

FUTON (The Quilt) by Tayama Katai. The first Meiji naturalist novel: a teacher's infatuation with his pretty student.

SANSHIRŌ by Natsume Sōseki. One of Sōseki's most typical young lovers.

HAKAI (The Broken Commandment) by Shimazaki Tōson. An early novel of social concern.

SANSHŌ DAYU (Sansho the Bailiff) by Mori Ōgai. A story by Japan's first truly cosmopolitan writer.

TAKEKURABE (Growing Up) by Higuchi Ichiyō. A tender story by the premier literary woman of Meiji-era Japan.

SUMIDAGAWA (The Sumida River) by Nagai Kafū. Kafū writes lyrically of the old Tokyo.

STORIES of Akutagawa Ryūnosuke. A modern sensibility confronts the old tales and traditions.

ANYA KŌRŌ (A Dark Night's Passing) by Shiga Naoya. The major novel of the "god of fiction."

JIKAN (Time) by Yokomitsu Riichi. Japan's most prominent modernist.

KANI KŌSEN (The Crab-Cannery Boat) by Kobayashi Takiji. The leading novel of the "proletarian literature" movement.

SASAMEYUKI (The Makioka Sisters) by Tanizaki Jun'ichirō. A stately family chronicle.

MEIJIN (The Master of Go) by Kawabata Yasunari. His most compelling novel.

KAMEN NO KOKUHAYU (Confessions of a Mask) by Mishima Yukio. A great novel of growing up gay.

EROGOTOSHI-TACHI (The Pornographers) by Nozaka Akiyuki. The Saikaku tradition revived in modern Ōsaka.

SUNA NO ONNA (Woman in the Dunes) by Abe Kōbō. A successful existential novel that also became a good film.

---

the *Heike Monogatari,* is another text of repetitive compulsion: the ceaseless and often-renewed lament for vanished Taira glory. This great tale is the matrix of all Japanese war narratives, just as *Genji* lies behind every quiet work that seeks to depict the subtle relations between human emotion and the precise awareness of real time and real space. The same age saw the wide dissemination of Buddhist story collections that brought the riches of Indian, Chinese, and Central Asian traditions into Japanese literature. In succeeding ages, some of the most brilliant of Japanese writers were to mine these jewels.

The Tokugawa Period (1600–1868) was an age of peace and urban plenty, and in literature, a great age of direct and of subtle parody. The prolific poet and novelist Ihara Saikaku turned from spectacular one-man poetry-writing marathons to fiction in 1682, with *Kōshoku Ichidai Otoko* (The Man Who Spent a Life in Lovemaking), the most famous of the era's many works of stylish erotic fiction. Saikaku makes an anti-*Genji* by expanding upon popular contemporary guides to the brothel quarters. The result is a racy, slangy, and elegant catalogue of women, and a city panorama that would have shocked the ladies and gentlemen of Heian.

Modern Japanese fiction struggled free of the lowbrow influence, Saikaku, only to embrace him again as Japan's first great realist. It didn't matter. The modern novel embodies obsessions absolutely different from any that preceded it. The figure who presides over the modern novel like an unhappy angel is Natsume Sōseki (1867–1916). Born under feudalism, and dying during the first great modern war, Sōseki made enduring art out of the struggle of the most intelligent men and women of an ancient race to find values in a world that was changing more rapidly than any Westerner can imagine. Although Sōseki set his face against the pathologically confessional mode of the Japanese "naturalist" or "I-novel," this master of the Japanese *bildungsroman* captured the anguish and isolation of young Japanese intellectuals so vividly that we can understand why confession was the obsession of the age.

Despite the efforts of such distinguished writers as Kawabata Yasunari and Tanizaki Junichirō to restore the estheticism and subtlety of the *Genji* tradition to center stage in the Japanese literary world, the confessional mode has endured. The Japanese novelist has been both the voice and the scapegoat for the forbidden wishes and needs of an energetic but repressed people. The confessional mode is the mechanism whereby he acknowledges these needs, then does public penance. He is an uneasy combination of public fool and honored teacher.

Mishima Yukio, genius and poet of the flesh, the super-cool Ōe Kenzaburō, Abe Kōbō with his densely textured parables, "new journalist" Kaiko Takeshi—whatever their styles, most major writers of the last thirty years have written memorably in the mode of shameful avowal and morbid self-contemplation. It is only slightly middlebrow novelists like Inoue Yasushi or the humorist Inoue Hisashi who bring the relief of a broader focus to what is still a very tense literature, more than nine hundred and eighty years after Hikaru Genji.

One of the most immediately engaging and continually attractive qualities of Japanese traditional literature is the unpretentiousness of the author's voice. Whereas major authors in the Western tradition nearly always have an aura of heroic exaltation about them—whether they are holy men like Homer or prodigies of industry like Dickens and Balzac—the Japanese author is a man among men, tending toward self-effacing disclaimers of genius or even skill, unwilling to stand taller than trees or hills or other humans. Nothing better expresses this spirit than the prominence that very informal genres like the diary and the *zuihitsu* (follow-the-pen) essay have in the tradition.

The literary diary, and Japanese artistic prose itself, begin together in the tenth cen-

DIARIES AND ZUIHITSU

tury with the *Tosa Nikki* (Tosa Diary). This account of part of the passage home (to Kyoto) of a retiring provincial governor from his post on Shikoku was written by the governor himself, Ki no Tsurayuki, a great anthologist and critic. He masquerades as a court lady in the governor's entourage both for the sake of decorum (male diaries were usually kept in Chinese) and in order that the recording voice may be unassuming and free. This device allows for a diverting chronicle of nervous courtiers "on the road," at the mercy of the

elements and the navigational skills of their social inferiors.

The artfulness of the Japanese literary diary was further underscored by the inevitable presence within it of poems written by the diarist, exchanged, or overheard. All classical Japanese literature is poem-rich. The great anthologies often supplied short prose contexts for their selections, and arranged the poems themselves in meaningful sequences. The works of courtly fiction embedded poems and their contexts in elaborate fictional narratives. The literary diary was a sort of sketchbook for fiction, standing midway between the anthologies and the early "novels" in the degree of elaboration it gave to its verses. The classic love affair, with its succession of subtle emotional shifts and its heartfelt poem exchanges, was a natural for the diary form. The *Izumi Shikibu Nikki* (Diary of Izumi Shikibu), for example, follows the romantic fortunes of one of classical Japan's most enigmatic and attractive young women.

Seven centuries later, the hokku master Matsuo Bashō dominated the revived tradition of the travel diary with his incomparable *Oku no Hosomichi* (The Narrow Road to the North), one of the most densely allusive short works in world literature, a rich mix of observation, philosophical reflection, literary self-consciousness, and brilliant poem making. Bashō's work is based upon a real, and long, journey, but is so deftly fictionalized that the seemingly slight entries order themselves in a very complex fashion.

In the *zuihitsu*, the writer either openly or

Critic, anthologist, and the virtual inventor of Japanese artistic prose, Ki no Tsurayuki was one of the most influential men of letters in Japanese history. Tsurayuki not only authored the first literary diary (the *Tosa Nikki*) but also compiled the first of the imperially commissioned poetry anthologies (the *Kokinshū*) and, in its preface, wrote a brilliant and penetrating appraisal of native poetry that stands as the fountainhead of Japanese criticism.

実蕉翁末号

卯槻子笠翁行年八十百二圖

implicitly declares that he intends to jot down anything, just as he pleases and as the moment suggests. He places his own prejudices on view, but denies his own "shaping," "artistic" power by insisting on miscellaneousness. The greatest *zuihitsu* of all is the first: the court lady Sei Shōnagon's *Makura no Sōshi* (Pillow Book). Sei Shōnagon has enchanted generations of readers with her insider's view of the brilliant court that gave us the *Tale of Genji*. This frank lady, in some three hundred little pieces of prose, recounts court gossip, lets us in on her favorite and unfavorite wind instruments, lists the best poetic subjects, evaluates flowering shrubs, good and bad insects, and male behavior in love affairs. She lists "Dirty Things," "Elegant Things," "Enviable People," "Things That Do Not Linger for a Moment." The *Makura no Sōshi* is an index of just how lively a mind could be within the boundaries set by a hypercultivated court.

It took three intervening centuries of military rule and civil war to produce the medieval anti-type of the *Pillow Book*, Yoshida Kenkō's *Tsurezuregusa* (Grasses of Idleness, ca. 1330). Where the *Pillow Book* celebrated the exquisite present in the best of all possible courts, Kenkō is obsessed with the past, with the recovery of ancient forms, old literature and vanished manners. His gentle, stoical estheticism, the creed of a somberly worldly monk, was immensely influential in forming the sensibility we (and the Japanese) now think of as "traditionally Japanese."

The *zuihitsu* flourished in many forms after Kenkō: scholarly ramblings, impressionistic journalism, essayistic literary criticism, were all imbued with the unsystematic, deeply emotional logic of "following the pen." This unclassifiable, fluid form is a monument to the psychological realism of the Japanese, and their almost heroic awareness of the fact that the world and the writer are both fragile leaves floating on the same river of time.

The English anthologist R.H. Blyth suggested that Matsuo Bashō may well have been "the greatest of all the Japanese." Whether or not this is true, it is certain that Japan never produced a greater poet or more profound diarist. A samurai by birth, Bashō gave up all the prerogatives and comforts of his class to become a single-minded devotee of the "way of *haikai*." He channeled his deep knowledge of the Chinese and Japanese classics, seasoned with Zen austerity, into the tiny compass of the *hokku* and the *renga* link. Most important, he trained himself to discover deep, timeless truths in the flux of everyday events and perceptions. His prose masterpiece, *The Narrow Road to the North*, is a profound reading of the events of a long journey in terms of poetry and Buddhist truth.

COMICS

Any trip on any train in Japan will give you a chance to see a cross section of society—students and salary-men predominating—poring over cartoon books: little pocket-sized ones or wide, fat ones printed on cheap pink, blue, or yellow paper. These are *manga. Manga* means, if you want to be literal, "irresponsible pictures."

To the foreigner, that is something of an understatement. An examination of the contents of an ordinary volume, or of the *manga* section of a moderately funky magazine like *Heibon Punch*, can be unnerving. Here we have crudely drawn stories of mah-jong gamblers who tie up and torture women, in the best Japanese "pink-movie" style. Period-costumed heroes who look like a cross between Natalie Wood and Dondi flash their swords, sever limbs, and rescue women who have been... ugh... tied up and tortured.

Then there are the more sophisticated, severely strange *manga* like *Gaki Deka* (Punk, or Devil, Cop). This is a weird little character whose immense square head is topped by a Tokyo Metropolitan Police cap, and who turns into a pig or a block of wood or a voracious hell-mouth, depending on how he feels at the time. The *manga* world encompasses childhood too, of course, and sanitized adventure strips like *Space Battleship Yamato* unfold without tortured ladies. *Hinotori* (The Phoenix) is an imaginative *manga* series that plays with ancient Japanese history and myth, and has inspired a movie.

The connection between *manga* and the movies is deep and direct. Tezuka Osamu, the

Social satire and grotesque fantasy are combined in this panel from Katsushika Hokusai's *Manga*. Near the signboard of an eel restaurant, three lower-class stalwarts do their best to shinny up three mammoth eels. In Edo-period slang, an "eel climb" was a particularly rapid social ascent or business success. Hokusai's aptitude as a social observer was matched by his taste for imaginative oddity; at the same time, he had an engineer's interest in the way machines work.

manga king who modernized Japan's cartoon books in the 1950s, almost single-handedly created Japanese cartoon style by drawing the first very long strips—strips that, movielike, used tens and even hundreds of frames to trace a few powerful gestures. Another strong influence on postwar *manga* were the *kami-shibai* or ''paper-theatre'' men, public story-tellers who used cartoon illustrations. The *kami-shibai* grew up in poor neighborhoods during the Depression, and its first practition-ers were out-of-work *benshi*, narrators who had provided running commentary for Japa-nese silent movies. Displaced by the talkies, these men recreated their art at bargain-basement rates for crowds of attentive kids. Under the twin influences of Tezuka and *kami-shibai*, many of the more serious *manga* art-ists of the postwar period have chosen to call their work *gekiga*, ''dramatic pictures.''

Today, the succession of *manga* panels often resembles the editing of a thriller movie; abrupt closeups and sound effects abound. A recent film *Hokusai Manga*, adapted a stage play and turned it into cinematic *manga*, telling the story of one of Japan's greatest artists with live actors and cartoon technique. The Hokusai film has a delib-erately playful title. *Hokusai Manga* means ''Ho-kusai portrayed in a *manga* style,'' but also refers to that artist's own great collection of sketches and quasi-cartoons of the early nine-teenth century. This multivolume compendium contains a little of everything under the sun. Like Leonardo de Vinci and Walt Whitman, Hokusai ''contained multitudes'': historical characters, monsters, fat people, thin people, people doing magic tricks, people eating noodles, people sleep-ing outdoors, drinking under the blossoms, danc-ing. Castle architecture, matchlocks, ''Dutch'' perspective, the wind in the bamboo, lascivious octopi—if it can be imaged, Hokusai tried it.

Some modern *manga* artists are aware of the noble lineage of their form. Tsuge Yoshi-haru, in particular, traces out the poetic possi-

Foreign residents of Japan cavort in this drawing by Charles Wirgman. Wirgman's *Japan Punch,* begun in 1876, was a British style humor magazine for the Yokohama foreign settlement; despite its parochial focus, it became sensationally popular among the Japanese, and Wirgman is honored as the founder of modern *manga.*

bilities of the modern cartoon, creating surreal dreamscapes and powerful fables. A young man rides a beautifully detailed steam locomo-tive backward into his native village, and makes love with a lady gynecologist while wartime battleships patrol the harbor. In an-other, a sewer lizard ponders life and death, meditating on the curious things that come tumbling down the drain. Tsuge, who rose to prominence in the post-1968 student avant garde, is the best of a small number of artists who can harness the sexual and oneiric energy of *manga* in order to make poetry instead of perverse jokes.

Hyūma Hoshi, consumed with an ambition to become Japan's star baseball pitcher, works out with arm-building equipment. The strip *Hoshi of the Giants* was a big hit in the mid-1960s.

Tsuge Yoshiharu's *gekiga* tale *Neji-shiki* (''Screw Style'') appeared in the experimental cartoon magazine *Garō* in June 1968, at the height of the student movement. According to Tsuge, it is a faithful record of one of his dreams. A boy, bitten by a jellyfish, comes ashore in a mysterious fishing village. Desperately searching for a doctor to sew together the severed artery in his arm, he passes a sinister knife-grinder and confronts an uncomprehending man in·a suit. Near despair, he follows a railroad track toward the next village and is taken aboard a steam locomotive operated by an odd little man in a cat mask. The train ride rocks him back to childhood memories, but his serenity disappears when he realizes that the locomotive has been bearing him backwards to the same village from which he started his quest for a doctor. Suddenly, the streets are full of eye doctors' signs. He asks for help from an ancient woman selling stick-candy in a stall, and the woman reveals that she owns a huge candy factory that is also a gynecology clinic. The boy is suddenly certain that the old woman is his mother, and a mysterious game with the stick-candies ensues. After a lonely walk in which the spirit of terror rises up to threaten him, the boy crosses a rubble-filled courtyard into the presence of a gynecologist. Sitting in her living room while a battleship patrols the harbor, she at first refuses to help; but then, during an encounter with the boy, she fixes his arm with ''the o/x technique''—a ''screw-style'' fastener that stops the blood. Roaring away in a motorboat, he notes ominously, ''When I turned the screw, my arm went numb . . . .''

FILM

It should have surprised nobody that the Japanese once made some of the finest films in the world. A distinguished tradition of narrative painting (unrolling scene by scene on a scroll), an eye for the perfect composition of static elements, a noble history of "action" narrative, a penchant for the erotic, a facility with ensemble arts of all kinds—it's hard to find a traditional Japanese cultural excellence that doesn't carry a seed for cinema.

Something even more pervasive, however, helped Japanese movies to distinction: limit, scarcity. Until recently, there have been few really mammoth movies. Strict limitations on budgets and expressive means, as well as the economic pinchedness of ordinary Japanese life until recently, combined with the ingrained Japanese respect for the real place and the correct name, made some of the most honest images ever seen on the screen. When Frank Capra viewed some very ordinary Japanese films during World War II, he remarked: "We can't beat this kind of thing. We can make films like these maybe once in a decade."

Which is not to say that Japan's filmmakers haven't been chintz merchants, too. The two most characteristic tendencies of the Japanese cinema, the historical costume picture (with swords, usually) and the family drama, have been regularly abused. The former has dripped with gratuitous blood and the latter with gratuitous tears. Yet these two modes also account for most of the classics of the Japanese screen.

The late Yasujirō Ozu, Japan's most distinguished director in the modern mode, said the last word about the Japanese cinema genius on his deathbed. Addressing the president of his studio, he said: "Mr. President, it all comes

In the climactic battle of *Seven Samurai,* the warriors of the title pit their skills against the savagery of horse-riding bandits. Kurosawa's greatest film tells the tale of desperate peasants who hire hungry samurai to help them save their village.

down to the family drama, doesn't it?" And Ozu knew. As the acknowledged master of the genre, he crafted subtle, almost plotless stories of the simplest, strongest actions and emotions of everyday life. A daughter leaves her father to be married. Elderly parents visit their children in Tokyo, and are quietly but completely disappointed with what the young people have become. Unfolding with a slow, insistent, mesmerizing rhythm, Ozu's later works realize the fusion of style and truth that all art struggles for.

The best costume dramas have, in their own way, confirmed Ozu's words. The home drama is the stronghold of psychological realism. Although the costume genre in its everyday

form has been a hyperromanticized and prettified affair, directors like Akira Kurosawa and Kenji Mizoguchi (who, with Ozu, make up the triumvirate of masters best known abroad) have used the gaudy violence of the sword sagas as a point of departure rather than an end in itself. Their psychologically complex costume pictures gave Japanese cinema a world audience in the fifties and early sixties, striking a perfect and unique balance between exotic appeal and intellectual seriousness.

In the late teens and twenties, the Japanese industry was full of people from the politically left-of-center *shingeki* (new theater) movement. An early interest in lower-class characters and their fates crystallized in the "ten-

When an elderly couple from southern Japan visit their children in Tokyo, there is awkwardness and disappointment all around. This luminous work by the late Yasujiro Ozu, *Tokyo Story*, is so deft a blend of comedy and sorrow that it seems to borrow its truth from life itself.

BEST FIFTEEN FILMS

■

SEVEN SAMURAI by Akira Kurosawa.

VENGEANCE IS MINE by Shohei Imamura.

TOKYO STORY by Yasujirō Ozu.

UGETSU by Kenji Mizoguchi.

I WAS BORN, BUT... by Yasujirō Ozu.

A CRAZY PAGE by Teinosuke Kinugasa.

REALM OF THE SENSES by Nagisa Oshima.

WOMAN IN THE DUNES by Hiroshi Teshigahara.

THRONE OF BLOOD by Akira Kurosawa.

BOY by Nagisa Oshima.

THE LOWER DEPTHS by Akira Kurosawa.

LATE SPRING by Yasujirō Ozu.

SISTERS OF THE GION by Kenji Mizoguchi.

YOJIMBO by Akira Kurosawa.

MUJŌ (Transient Life) by Akio Jissōji.

dency film'' of the early thirties. Official disfavor resulted in the fragmentation of the tendency genre into a number of other forms, including screwball comedy with proletarian settings. Most Japanese filmmakers fell in step with their militarist government during the forties; still, the Japanese war movie, with its emphasis on sacrifice instead of hate-the-enemy hysteria, owed a surprising debt to the family drama, and in some cases carried forward the tradition of humanistic realism.

The film of social concern flourished in early postwar Japan, and Kurosawa and Mizoguchi relected the trend. Theirs was a liberal humanism that had no use for political labels. During the sixties, a Japanese New Wave spearheaded by younger directors like Masahiro Shinoda and Nagisa Oshima wrote a new chapter in the history of the political film in Japan by fusing a radical point of view, sophisticated sexuality, and icy irony. They expanded the boundaries of all the genres: the family film, the ''serious'' costume picture, the crime film.

Although many of these directors are still working, along with their elders, the Japanese industry has been rationalized, commercialized, and fused with television to such an extent that the greatest talents have either gone precariously independent or turned into studio men, obligingly making B-grade ''blockbusters'' à la Américaine or ''classic'' remakes starring pop singers.

5 • THE BATH

THE JAPANESE BATH

Few cultures have made as much of bathing as the Japanese. In the most ancient Japanese creation myths, the gods bathed during and immediately after their labor of producing the universe. The Shinto religious tradition has preserved intact the notions of ritual purification that extend far back into Japanese prehistory and has reinforced for all eras of Japanese history the notion that cleanliness is not merely "next to," but rather "part of" godliness. Although the Japanese are not unique in their delight in bathing—one thinks also of the Romans, with the huge bathing emporia they built at Caracalla, at Bath, and elsewhere in the empire; and of the sauna and steam bath traditions of the Scandinavians and the Turks—surely the Japanese are unequaled in the artistry they have lavished on the habits and accoutrements of bathing.

The Japanese bath has been a subject of intense fascination to foreign visitors ever since they first arrived on Japanese shores. Perhaps the first to document Japanese bathing practices were Chinese historians; writing in the dynastic chronicles early in the present millennium, they commented on the Japanese penchant for soaking in hot mineral springs (a habit virtually unheard of on the Asian mainland). European missionaries and traders in the sixteenth and seventeenth centuries were similarly intrigued, remarking on the extraordinary Japanese passions for ritual purity and personal cleanliness. The hot tubs of California and the practice of communal bathing find their origins in Japanese traditions.

For the Japanese, bathing has always been as much a source of pleasure as of practical hygiene. The volcanic archipelago is well endowed with natural geothermal springs, and immersion in the abundant hot water that bubbles up from the earth has soothed tired muscles and eased worn spirits since prehistory. Along with the curative benefits of hot-spring bathing are its social pleasures. Communal bathing for the Japanese, whether in hot springs or in urban bathhouses, has been much like what the town square or local tavern has been to Western societies: a spot where friends could gather to exchange news or gossip. It has provided an atmosphere of relaxation, often even a "democratic" escape from

A beautiful modern bath in the Tawara-ya Inn in Kyōto, complete with garden view, suggests just how pleasurable Japanese bathing can be. The small box on the floor contains soap. Using the bucket that is up-ended on the stool, the bather soaps, washes, and rinses himself thoroughly clean before stepping into the tub to luxuriate in deep water.

the hierarchical distinctions so rigidly observed in other social contexts (after all, how carefully can class distinctions be observed when everyone is nude?).

In modern Japan, where more homeowners and apartment dwellers possess their own baths than ever before, the Japanese still have not forgotten the warm communal benefits of group bathing. An outing with friends to a hot spring resort remains a favorite pastime, and many city dwellers prefer nightly visits to the public bathhouse to a solitary bath at home. And private baths, though small, are usually large enough to permit a relaxing deep soak together by at least two family members, who would abhor the functionalism of a quick, efficient shower.

Unlike steam bathing, where the body is cleansed by its own perspiration in an atmosphere of hot steam and later rinsed by a bracing cold shower, Japanese bathing practices for the most part call for total immersion in a tub of water as hot as the bather can bear. Bathing etiquette and consideration for others who will later soak in the same hot water require that the bather first wash his body thoroughly and carefully rinse away all soap and grime *before* entering the tub. This sequence is followed whether one is bathing at home, at a large public bathhouse, or at a hot spring resort. Thus, the cleansing process takes place outside the tub; the bather should already be sparkling clean when he slowly lowers himslf into the deep tub, and the subsequent long soak, neck-deep in hot water, serves more to cleanse and restore the soul than to wash the body.

The large *hiragana* characters in both of the pictures at the right say *yu:* literally, ''hot water,'' the sign of a public bath. These business curtains *(noren)* also give directions to the separate men's and women's sections of the bathhouse. Mixed bathing lingers only in the remotest country places, while public bathing as such is popular everywhere.

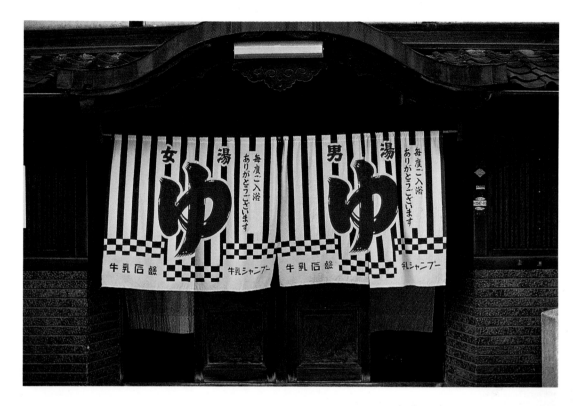

Thanks to the volcanic nature of their islands, the Japanese people are blessed with abundant natural hot water emerging spontaneously from the earth. In many rural areas, expensive fuels can be saved for uses other than heating water for the daily bath. The Japanese have exploited their natural geothermal springs to the fullest, developing around them great resort towns that attract pleasure seekers to the spas and offer all manner of other entertainment as well.

Onsen (hot springs) are found throughout Japan, in mountainous canyons, in caves, in riverbeds, along sandy beaches. If the natural hot water is not too hot, it may be entered and

HOT SPRING BATHS

enjoyed right where it bubbles forth from the earth. Or it may be piped into the grand pools of huge resort hotels. For bathers who like to commune with nature while enjoying the warmth and hygienic benefits of bathing, tubs are often carved out of rocky outdoor grottoes or built in forest thickets, on cliffs overlooking the ocean, or in other scenic spots. Similarly, the large public baths of resort hotels (nowa-

days, usually segregated into men's baths and women's) invariably occupy the finest spot in the hotel and usually command sweeping views from wide glass windows. A recent popular phenomenon has been the development of "jungle baths." These are generally huge greenhouselike structures built on the roofs of high-rise hotels or in hotel gardens, densely filled with many types of tropical plants that flourish in the steamy atmosphere that rises from the hot pools. The hedonistic spirit of the *onsen* visitor demands a wide variety of different baths in which to immerse the body: surrounding the clean pools of natural hot water may be smaller tubs of milk baths, wine

This unusual *onsen* in the spa city of Ibusuki is a "jungle bath," a combination bath and greenhouse in which tropical plants as well as bathers luxuriate in the steamy atmosphere created by hot water. The statue of a European style water sprite is intended to add to the general air of refined hedonism that such fancy bathhouses promote. Hot springs come in many varieties and sizes; the biggest and best-known are vacation spots for notable people. Others have a clearly popular flavor. Wherever they are, however, *onsen* allow a welcome respite from the tensions and formalities of daily life. Just as hot water soothes muscular tension, the jovial, informal, music-filled atmosphere of *onsen* refreshes the spirit.

baths, murky sulphurous baths, hot sand baths, mud baths, even baths of heated coffee beans!

One of the greatest pleasures of many *onsen* resorts is the *rōtenburo,* or "open-air bath." These may be small natural pools or huge man-made outdoor enclosures where the bather can soak comfortably in the ever-flowing hot spring water, even in dead of winter when the pool is surrounded by snowdrifts.

Japanese legend has it that many hot springs were "created," or opened up, by the saintly ninth-century Buddhist sage Kobo Daishi, who in his pilgrimages around the country is said to have frequently struck his staff on a rock, causing an endless stream of hot water to flow forth. Actually, many hot springs were discovered by hunters tracking their prey into the mountains. Wild monkeys were frequently seen to bathe in warm springs, and wounded animals entered the hot mineral waters to heal their injuries. New hot springs are routinely discovered deep in the mountains by hikers or cross-country skiers, and are added to the thousands that have already been developed as resorts and listed in travel guides.

Today a visit to a hot spring may be anything from a simple family outing to an elaborate trip by a club or group of friends, even an entire company of co-workers, who spend a weekend in a large hotel bathing together, eating, drinking, and enjoying the other entertainments provided by the resort. Large hot spring resorts like Noboribetsu in Hokkaido, Atami near Tokyo, or Beppu in Kyushu rival Las Vegas or Atantic City in lavishness and variety of entertainments. Hundreds of other *onsen* towns—Narugo, Minakami, Kusatsu, Hakone, Shimoda, Kinosaki, Tamazukuri, Ibusuki, to name only a few—are smaller versions of the same thing: entire towns devoted to the pleasures of hot spring bathing. The festive atmosphere in each is completed by the throngs of guests strolling in colorful *yukata.*

A solitary bather at the Ibusuki "jungle bath" enjoys a dramatic water-and-rockscape. Many small *onsen* are nothing more than places where volcanically heated water bubbles up among the rocks, to be captured in natural or manmade pools.

Kings of the Ibusuki "jungle," these men lounge and chat by a heated pool. The eighteenth-century humorist Shikitei Samba's book *Ukiyo-buro* is a witty *tour de force* of conversation in a bathhouse, a place where all men are naked and—temporarily—equal.

DOMESTIC BATHS AND PUBLIC BATHS

Wherever Japanese bathe, at home or in urban public bathhouses or in resort hotels, the procedure is the same. One first sheds one's clothing in an antechamber; upon entering the bathroom proper, one washes thoroughly outside the tub. Hot water for washing and rinsing is dipped from a deep tub or pool or run from faucets; the bathroom floor is equipped with a drain to carry away the rinse water and overflow from the tub. Only when the body is completely clean, hair shampooed and soapy water rinsed away, does one step into the scalding water of the tub. No soap is ever introduced into the tub (that would be the greatest offense to other family members or other guests at a hotel), and the tub is not drained after each user. Its hot water may be replenished from time to time, but everyone soaks in the same tubful of water. Only when everyone has finished his bath is the tub emptied.

It should be noted that Japanese bathrooms are exclusively for bathing. The toilet, commonly found in Western "bathrooms," has no place in the immaculate Japanese bathroom. Its function has nothing to do with bathing, so it is totally separate from the bathroom and often located in another part of the house.

It is only in recent decades that individual homes or apartments have been equipped with private baths. Throughout history, the Japanese have bathed communally, and even among modern city dwellers today there is an often-expressed sense of loss of the communal spirit engendered by bathing privately at home. Individuals and families who enjoy the convenience of a bath at home still occasionally go off to the local public bath, where they can enjoy a long hot soak together with friends.

The finest tubs in Japan are still constructed of soft woods—*hinoki* (Japanese cypress; *Chamaecyparis obtusa*) or *maki* (Chinese black pine; *Podocarpus macrophylla*) are considered best suited to the purpose—carefully handcrafted to be leakproof and to swell with wetness and contract with dryness without cracking. A soak in such a tub is an indescribable pleasure, enhanced by the softness of the wood and by the gentle aroma it gives off when wet. But suitable wood has grown scarce in Japan and extremely expensive; no less rare are skilled craftsmen willing to devote the time and effort necessary to building a fine tub. Consequently, such tubs are rapidly becoming the exclusive privilege of the very wealthy. Far more common today are varieties of tubs made of molded plastic, fiberglass, or enameled steel. Functional, easy to clean, and relatively inexpensive, they have made the convenience of a private bath available to virtually every house or apartment. Unfortunately lost along the way to functionalism, however, is the extraordinary sensual pleasure afforded by the old-fashioned wooden tub.

Public bathhouses are located at intervals of several blocks in most Japanese cities. Although they have lost much of the exotic vitality they enjoyed in earlier centuries, when they were great urban gathering places at the center of popular culture, today's public bathhouses remain more than merely functional, hygienic facilities. Friends and neighbors still meet at the bath to exchange local gossip while enjoying a long, hot soak together. The bathhouses are privately owned, but since they provide an invaluable hygienic social service, the costs of construction, fuel, and maintenance are heavily subsidized by public funds.

Urban bathhouses are also divided into a men's section and a women's section. The bather pays his fee upon entering, checks his shoes in a locker, and proceeds to a large antechamber where he undresses, placing his clothing in a basket or locker provided for this purpose. The dressing room opens directly into a large tiled room, heavy with steam and crowded with other bathers. Along the lower section of the walls are faucets for hot and cold water, as well as shower spigots. The walls may be elaborately decorated with large murals depicting famous scenic spots, usually rendered in mosaic. Sunk in the floor in the center of the bathroom is one or more tile pools full of hot water for soaking, each large enough to accommodate thirty people or more. Since all bathers have washed outside the pool and since soap is never carried into it, the communal water usually remains clean until the end of the day. After closing time, the tub is finally drained and scrubbed. The next day it is refilled, and a constant stream of fresh hot water, often flowing from a fountain, replenishes the pool as bathers climb in and out.

Japanese public bathhouses don't waste money on fancy decor or elegant atmosphere. Simple pipes convey wash water to this bather. Sitting on a plastic stool, he fills his plastic basin and washes, shampoos, and shaves. Then he joins neighborhood friends in the big common pool for a relaxing soak that soothes the spirit. Although more and more private flats and apartments have tubs, one can still see flushed and happy people returning from the public bath, dressed in cool cotton *yukata* and carrying their towels over their arms.

茶道

6 • THE TEA
CEREMONY

RITUAL

The tea ceremony, *cha no yu* in Japanese, is "nothing more than boiling water, making tea, and drinking it," declared Sen no Rikyu, its sixteenth-century patron saint. Yet since its inception a century earlier, what were then ordinary, everyday activities have become so ritualized that their mastery requires hours of study and practice. Even Westerners are drawn by the drama. Every aspect of the ceremony is carefully regulated: the way the host enters the room to greet guests, the gestures accompanying the preparation of tea, even the folding of the silk napkin used to wipe the tea scoop and ladle. Yet when orchestrated by a consummate master, the *cha no yu* is an intense, satisfying, spiritual and esthetic experience.

From its beginnings as a form of relaxation and withdrawal, *cha no yu* has become, in a rigidly stratified society, a classless art form for millions of Japanese. In the process of transformation, women too have mastered its intricacies; along with flower arranging *(ikebana)*, it has become one of the social graces required of young ladies of marriageable age.

The tea ceremony cannot be learned from books. Like Zen Buddhism, under whose influence its ritual took shape, it too can be transmitted only from master to disciple. The Urasenke, Omotesenke, and Mushakoji, each under the direction of a grand tea master claiming descent from the legendary Sen no Rikyu, teach the secrets of the art.

The esthetics of *wabi cha* (poverty tea), the most austere, intimate, and influential form of the ceremony, which stresses spiritual fulfillment through the renunciation of material things, were formulated by Rikyu, tea master to the warlord Hideyoshi. Rikyu's pursuit of material simplicity, out of step with the splendor of the times, incurred Hideyoshi's wrath,

and he was forced to commit suicide.

Time has been on Rikyu's side. Sen no Soshitsu, the fifteenth-generation grand master of the Urasenke, the most successful of the three schools, heads a multimillion-dollar international conglomerate. His school not only teaches the principles of the tea ceremony, but through an elaborate franchise system certifies teachers who wish to establish their own branches, and even controls the production of the tea utensils they need.

The heart of *cha no yu* is, of course, the drinking of tea prepared, as a sign of humility, by the host himself. Before the event, the tearoom and adjacent garden are cleaned, a fire is laid in the sunken hearth, water put to boil, and a painting and a flower placed in the *tokonoma*, an alcove designed for this purpose. At the appointed time, the guests enter the garden and, one at a time, rinse their mouths and hands with water from a stone basin. As a token of their humility, the guests enter crouching through a low doorway; originally this practice ensured that no weapons were brought in.

Only the guests partake of the green tea called *matcha* that looks like a brew made from clippings from a freshly mowed lawn and is decidedly bitter. The host focuses on simmering the water in the kettle, using a bamboo scoop to ladle it into the tea bowl, and then whisking the powdered tea into the required frothy consistency. Because only a limited number of tea bowls are used, the guests drink one after another—while one sips, the host must carefully wash the bowl to be used by the next guest. This sharing of bowls contributes to the sense of community among participants which, however momentary, is the essence of *cha no yu*.

Left: In the relaxed curve of the tea master's body and the attentive composure of his face one can see the mood and spirit of the ceremony.

Famous tea kettles and bowls are recognized as works of art by tea-fanciers and laymen alike; no less beautiful are the whisks that blend water and tea.

OBJECTS

Cha no yu involves a union between discriminating individuals and beautiful objects—the tea utensils and the art works in the *tokonoma.*

The tea bowl, *chawan,* is the centerpiece of the ritual. Its appreciation comes only through use; put under glass, it looks dead. *Chawan* may be of many shapes and sizes, of Japanese manufacture, or imported from China or Korea. Chinese *temmoku* wares, with their lustrous brown-black glazes, were highly prized by the fifteenth-century Ashikaga shoguns in whose court *cha no yu* was born. Over the centuries, vessels owned by the shoguns were classified as *daimeibutsu* (great objects of fame), and could command a king's ransom. The design of the tea bowl used in *wabi cha* was so important to Rikyu that he personally supervised their production by the Kyoto tilemaker Chōjirō and his family. Called *raku,* these low-fire, rough-textured, red or black bowls, each a unique sculptural entity, continue to be the tea bowl par excellence.

Likewise, tea caddies, the two-inch-high jars that hold the powdered tea, have been avidly collected over the centuries. Both ceramic and lacquer ones are used; the former called *chaire,* for thick tea, the latter called *natsume,* for the thin tea taken in summer. The great care lavished on them is reflected in their numerous accessories: an assortment of specially designed ivory lids and, for safekeeping, drawstring bags made from precious fabrics with exquisite design and craftsmanship. These command great admiration among tea aficionados. Tea caddies may also be classified as *meibutsu* and given poetic names like River of Memories (Omoigawa) or Maiden of the

Bridge (Hashihime) in recognition of their appearance or ownership. Their names and pedigrees are inscribed on the box or boxes in which they are preserved.

The insignificant strip of bamboo used as a spoon to transfer the tea from the caddy to the bowl may be the most direct expression of the tea master's personality. Since they are often crafted by their owners, no two are alike. Cracks or wormholes in the bamboo are not considered defects; quite the opposite. Imperfection is desired. As one of the founding fathers of *cha no yu* declared: "I do not like the full moon in a cloudless sky."

The objects in the *tokonoma* must be appropriate to the season and the occasion. To alleviate the heat of a muggy summer day, an ink monochrome landscape painting with a scene of a refreshing waterfall would be appropriate. The host might choose special objects to create a mood for a particular day, such as New Year's, the first day of spring, or a birthday. Appropriate to commemorating and honoring Rikyu, the host might place in the *tokonoma* one of Rikyu's own letters—if he were wealthy enough to own one—and a flower in a hollow bamboo container. Rikyu was the first to use bamboo for this purpose. The tea utensils would also conform to Rikyu's preference for rustic simplicity. The art of *cha no yu* involves a kind of mixing and matching of personal and traditional elements, a combination in which a host's cultivation and discrimination are expressed.

Left: This flower arrangement is appropriate for a winter tea ceremony. The section of bamboo is particularly expressive of "tea taste."

Above right: This seventeenth-century tea bowl depicts the ocean and a crescent moon.

Right: The austere beauty of the ladle adds visual interest to the tea ceremony. Like a conductor's baton, it is a symbol of mastery.

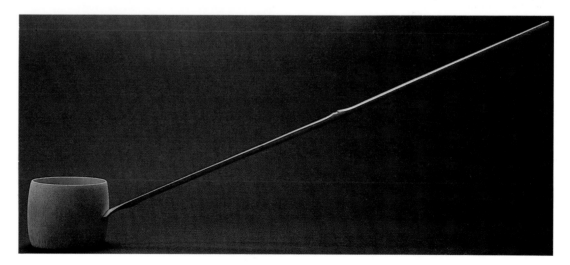

SURROUNDINGS

Whether a special enclosure within a private home or a detached building, the tearoom (chashitsu) invariably incorporates elements of the Japanese farmhouse and of the scholar's study. Unpretentious in appearance, it has roughly finished plaster walls, a bamboo lattice ceiling, and small paper-covered windows. Only a dim light filters through, bathing the occupants in a shadowy warmth. The novelist Junichirō Tanizaki wrote an entire essay "in praise of shadows"; they are keys to understanding the esthetics of traditional Japanese architecture, the tearoom included. Human in scale, the walls of the tearoom are no more than six feet (1.8 meters) high; the standard floor space, four and a half mats, is a mere ten feet (3 meters) square. Constructed of fragile, natural materials, the chashitsu is subject to age and decay, recalling the Buddhist dictum that all things are impermanent.

The garden surrounding the teahouse is a prologue to the experience within. Often the garden is little more than a "dewy path" or rōji, punctuated by stepping stones, lit by a stone lantern, and refreshed by a stone basin into which water flows from a bamboo conduit. The basin may be no more than a well-worn foundation stone; objets trouvés are popular in the tea world. Flowering shrubs are frowned upon as too distracting, although aromatic ones are acceptable. In designing the rōji leading to his Tai-an teahut, Rikyu went so far as to plant a six-foot-high hedge to prevent his guests' eyes and minds from wandering to the spectacular view beyond the garden.

In the summer of 1587, Toyotomi Hideyoshi addressed an invitation to "all earnest practitioners of cha no yu" to attend a ten-day tea ceremony in the pine groves of the Kitano Tenjin Shrine in the northwest part of Kyoto. Participants were told they could erect two-mat huts as enclosures or simply spread mat covers or rice hull bags on the ground. Those in attendance, from warriors to farmers, would have occasion to see Hideyoshi's personal collection of meibutsu, and better still, to drink tea prepared by his hands. But the crowning glory of what came to be known as the Grand Kitano Tea Gathering was Hideyoshi's own portable gold teahut, three mats in size, covered with scarlet felt imported from the West, and edged with red and gold brocade. Like an oversized jewel box, the ceilings, walls, and even the window frames were covered in gold leaf.

Although ostentatious displays of priceless art treasures are not unknown, extravaganzas like Hideyoshi's gold teahut are rare in the history of tea. They are frowned upon by Rikyu's descendants, who rule the tea world with as iron a hand as Hideyoshi did the nation. For them, the humble soan or "grass hut" style teahouse is the setting most appropriate to the ideals of restraint and spiritual tranquillity that animate cha no yu.

The dripping of water from a bamboo pipe into a stone cistern enhances the peace and stillness of a small tea garden. Good water is the basis of good tea, and it is no small part of cha no yu connoisseurship to know the best wells and finest tasting waters. The bamboo fence pictured here is another standard tea-garden element.

This photograph illustrates the visual harmony between tea implements and tea-ceremony surroundings that is an important part of *cha no yu* esthetics. Picking up the warm earth colors of the *tatami* and the wall panels, the implements complement the crisp, angular architectural shapes with their round contours. While the architecture suggests the formality of the tea ceremony, the implements express its intimate, individualistic aspect.

料理

7 · FOOD
AND DRINK

SASHIMI AND SUSHI

The most important element in Japanese cooking is rice, the Alpha and Omega of a good meal. But the best thing, the most exciting and eagerly-awaited thing, is raw fish, or *sashimi*. All the virtues of good Japanese cooking and eating are present in beautifully sliced *sashimi:* freshness (nothing *fishy* is allowed), seasonal savvy (fish, like fruit, must be taken at the right time), an almost occult skill with the knife, and eye-pleasing presentation. If all these requirements are handsomely met, the *sashimi* course at the beginning of the meal may very nearly upstage all the rest.

Sashimi is such an important experience for the serious eater that it is even favored as a prelude to *sushi*—Japan's vinegared-rice treat. And, as more and more Western diners are coming to learn, the most delicious of all *sushi* is topped with raw fish!

It's safe to say that most of the new *sushi* eaters are thinking of that Tokyo-area specialty *nigirisushi* when the dish comes to mind. And that's perfectly reasonable. The *nigiri* (hand-shaped, or perhaps more accurately, riceball) variety provides the peak of *sushi* pleasure. An elongated ball of lightly vinegared rice is smeared with paste of the *wasabi* root—a bright green fusion of horseradish and mustard, tastes the Japanese have nicknamed *namida* (tears). (Put a dab on your tongue to discover the origin of this nickname.) This already delicious snack is then topped with a piece of the most exquisitely fresh, lusciously hued raw fish or shellfish.

Pick up the whole morsel with thumb, index, and middle finger, invert, and dip the fish (never the rice) in a little of the *sushi* shop's special fortified soy sauce (to which sweet

Intended not only to please the palate, sushi and sashimi must provide esthetic edification. Shown here are the traditional accouterments, as well as a tantalizing array of the types.

Left: Sea-bream *sashimi* is one of the most felicitous of Japanese fish dishes. Served with head and eyes intact, it is just the thing for New Year's wedding banquets and other congratulatory occasions.

sake and bonito flakes will have been added). Eat in one bite. Order more—there is a world of beautiful fish arranged before your eyes at the counter, and the cheerful chef will custom-fillet your choice, providing you with two *nigiri* at a time. For dessert, you can't beat the sweet omelet *sushi* washed down with green tea.

It sometimes pleases foreign visitors to Japan to maintain that they prefer ·Kyoto, that ancient seat of culture and learning, to the noisy monster Tokyo. *Nigirizushi* rightly understood, however, can give you a real taste for old Tokyo and its virtues. After all, *sushi* itself probably originated near the edge of Tokyo Bay, where vinegared rice was used as a fish preservative. And the most colorful, if not quite the best, *sushi* shops in Japan are the tiny ones just a stone's throw from the Tokyo Central Fish Market, the biggest wholesale fish market on the planet. Every good *sushi* shop is imbued with a little of the downtown Tokyo spirit: bright lights, good cheer, hearty voices, straightforward enjoyment of the gifts of the sea.

Not that *nigiri,* or even Tokyo, are the whole story of *sushi.* Osaka and Kyoto contribute *oshizushi,* a pressed-together square block of rice topped with a thin slice of marinated or boiled fish. After Tokyo *nigiri,* with its succulent hunk of tuna, mackerel, or shark meat trailing down a good half inch at either end of the rice, *oshizushi* can seem underwhelming. It does look lovely on a lacquered dish, though, testimony to the intense sightliness of Japanese cuisine.

A way around the prohibitive price of *nigiri* is the *maki* route. *Makizushi* (wrapped *sushi*) results when strips of vegetable and/or fish are rolled into the center of a cylinder of vinegared rice, and the whole is wrapped in *nori* (seaweed). Ordinary Japanese, who prefer to eat their *nigiri* at a restaurant or have it delivered by a bike messenger, will often make up a *nori* roll at home, refrigerate it, then slice it into rounds as needed, or gnaw on the roll.

Another home favorite is *chirashizushi* (scattered style), an embarassingly simple and utterly delicious meal in which cold seafood bits are in or on a vinegar-rice bed in a bowl.

Whatever sort of *sushi* takes your fancy, make sure you eat it in the right spirit. Eighteenth-century playgoers in Edo (Tokyo) took it to the Kabuki with them and munched it while they watched their favorite actors. Eat *sushi* eagerly, hungrily, and as copiously as your pocketbook permits. Learn the Japanese names of the fish (see Glossary). Let the stalwart spirit of the true Tokyo native seep into your soul as the *sushi* goes down.

A typical *nigirizushi* plate includes roe *(ikura),* shrimp *(ebi),* fatty tuna *(toro),* eel *(anago),* tuna *(maguro),* a rolled piece *(maki),* and pickled ginger, which clears the palate.

SUSHI GLOSSARY
■

AKAGAI a red-meat clam

ANAGO a type of eel, served already in a sweet sauce; don't dip it in any other sauce

AWABI abalone

EBI shrimp

FUTOMAKI various pickled vegetables and rice, rolled in *nori* seaweed and sliced

HAMACHI young yellowtail

HIRAME flounder

IKA squid

IKURA salmon roe

KAPPAMAKI cucumber and rice, rolled in *nori* seaweed and sliced

MAGURO red meat of the tuna

ODORI live shrimp, delicious and expensive

SHIME-SABA marinated mackerel

TAKO boiled octopus

TAMAGO a sweetened omelet

TEKKAMAKI *maguro* tuna and rice, rolled in *nori* seaweed and sliced

TORO succulent, fatty cut of tuna

UNI sea-urchin roe

NOODLES AND BEAN CURD

Two of the most pleasant culinary gifts of China to Japan are noodles and bean curd, or *tōfu*. Both of these good things are enjoyed in Japanese and Chinese forms in modern Japan.

Noodles as such need no introduction. It's pretty certain that they originated in China and passed to Europe—if not in the saddlebags of Marco Polo, then probably in the caravans that crossed Asia when it was one great Mongol principality. They have been Japanese favorites at least since the seventeenth century.

Like so many Japanese institutions, noodles express the primary cultural division of Japan between the West (Kyoto and Osaka) and the East (what is now Tokyo). Tokyoites claim *soba*, thin, grayish buckwheat noodles, served in soup or "naked" with a dipping sauce, as their specialty; Western Japan boasts of its *udon*, fat, flat white noodles made of wheat, chewy and somewhat reminiscent of German noodles. In warm weather *udon* are often served saucrloss and then dipped; otherwise, they are served in soup and piping hot.

Soup noodles are to be eaten right away; the

Steaming *udon* noodles tempt the passerby to a counter restaurant. *Udon,* a specialty of western Japan, are enjoyed in countless variations throughout the country.

Japanese hate to linger over their traditional "fast food." The only way to do this is to slurp in a good deal of air as you chopstick them into your mouth. The result is a cheerful sound—quite rude to the Western ear, but just the right sound to make if you consider yourself a serious eater.

Dipping sauce is a delicious blend of soy sauce, sweet *sake*, and the fish and seaweed broth called *dashi*—that is to say, it contains the three most important Japanese flavoring agents. The basic soup for hot noodle immersion is based on the same trinity of flavors, but milder and with far more *dashi* and just a hint of soy. Noodle lovers in Japan have always preferred the simplest saucing, much as real Italian epicures love perfectly *al dente* linguine served *al burro*, with nothing but butter, some grated cheese, and a dash of pepper. Still, anything can be added to a bowl of Japanese noodles, from green onion to shrimp *tempura*, and almost all of the hundreds of thousands of noodle shops of every description in Japan offer a generous variety of accompaniments.

Tōfu (bean curd) is probably the best-known Japanese food in America, and that's altogether appropriate, since the Japanese now obtain most of their soybeans from farmers in Iowa, Illinois, and other Midwest states. What Japanese *tōfu* makers do to the beans, however, is a Far Eastern specialty: The beans are boiled and crushed, and the resulting liquid is firmed up with a coagulant. The curds that result are either drained (for a firmer *tōfu*) or left moist (for the delicate-textured curd flavored for inclusion in soups) and chilled with water in square molds.

The result is a milky-white cake with a pleasant, uninsistent flavor (there is a faint, cheesy tang). Fresh *tōfu* from one of Japan's home factories is delicious all by itself or topped with a little soy sauce. But *tōfu* comes into its own when its flavor is augmented, either by frying or by inclusion in a myriad of dishes. No *dashi* stock soup, whether clear or rich with *miso* (bean paste) would be complete without little *tōfu* squares sitting at the bottom of the bowl, absorbing flavor and greeting the tongue with their agreeable texture.

Yudōfu (hot water *tōfu*) is a simple and elegant dish in which heated (but never overcooked) *tōfu* is treated like noodles. A warm dipping sauce of *dashi*, soy sauce, and sweet sake is placed before each diner, along with spicy condiments like green onion, fresh ginger, and grated Japanese radish. The condiments go in the sauce, the *tōfu* squares are dipped in gently, and you enjoy little concentrated cubes of "the taste of Japan."

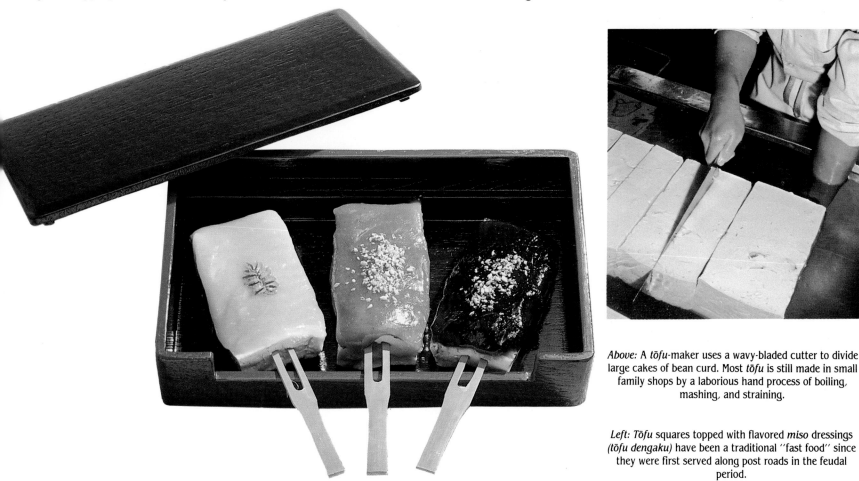

Above: A *tōfu*-maker uses a wavy-bladed cutter to divide large cakes of bean curd. Most *tōfu* is still made in small family shops by a laborious hand process of boiling, mashing, and straining.

Left: *Tōfu* squares topped with flavored *miso* dressings *(tōfu dengaku)* have been a traditional "fast food" since they were first served along post roads in the feudal period.

THE JAPANESE MEAL

One of the major responsibilities of the Japanese chef is to select plates and bowls that show the food to best advantage. The matching of these two elements of fine dining is a creative art in which the haute cuisine cook takes care not to repeat himself; putting, for example, simmered eggplant into the same kind of bowl three times in a row would prove a real lack of imagination on the chef's part. This photo shows a variety of accommodations between food and dish. At the upper left, the simplicity of *sashimi* (raw fish) is underscored by a plain wooden tray, while a rice roll makes a vivid impression set against dark, gleaming lacquer. The covered lacquer dish contains soup.

Japanese restaurant menus in America all too often obscure the architecture of the Japanese meal. We are encouraged to think of *tempura* or *teriyaki* as entrees, accompanied by a raw fish "appetizer" and a "side" of rice. Well, here as in so many cases when we deal with Japan, a shift in perspective reveals a much more interesting truth.

First of all, rice is the heart of the matter. In Japan, a meal without rice is either an informal affair (noodles gulped at lunch) or an absurdity. Rice, a bit of pickle, and tea together constitute a sufficient if spartan repast, and one that satisfies all major cultural requirements for a basic meal.

Beyond rice, then, what is required for a basic sit-down dinner? A soup and three dishes. After a bit of fresh vegetable and soup (the clear *suimono* or the rich, cloudy *misoshiru*) comes the raw fish course. The succulent *sashimi* is scarcely an appetizer! It's the high point of the meal, the flower of the cook's art. Since it's so good, we get it early, and this early point is already the time to judge the meal. If the *wansashi* (soupbowl and *sashimi*) are good, then expect the pleasure to continue. The second of the three will be something grilled, perhaps a whole small fish on skewers or chicken *yakitori*, or maybe a deep-fried dish like *tempura*. Third in this harmonious trio is a steamed or simmered dish: shrimp with spinach and Japanese squash, perhaps. Fish broth and soy sauce simmering sauces are among the most delicious resources of the Japanese cook.

Soup and three dishes finished, the meal ends with rice, pickles, and green tea.

Such a meal is the sort you might have at the home of a friend, or in the standard, medium-priced Japanese restaurant in the USA. Suppose, however, that you decide to patronize a grander establishment, and order the *omakase* (the "leave-it-to-them" dinner). The parade of dishes will resemble the soup

Grilled sweetfish *(ayu)* makes a delicious lunch, served in style at a Kyōto river-fish restaurant. The little fish, a great Japanese favorite, has been skewered with the *unerigushi* technique, so that it looks as if it is swimming upstream. Tea, rice, pickles, *miso* soup, and a raw egg for dipping complete the meal, which has been designed to embody a refined simplicity. The fish itself, for example, is served in a section of bamboo.

plus three, but only in the sense that an angel on the Sistine ceiling resembles the one on a Christmas tree.

Part One: familiar from the more modest meal. A simple appetizer *(zensai)*, soup (the clear variety), and *sashimi*, beautifully garnished. Part Two: a delicate symphony of all the major Japanese culinary methods: a grilled dish, then a steamed one (why not abalone steamed in *sake*?); a simmered dish (radish steamed in broth, soy, and *sake*, for example); then something deep-fried, like the wonderful chicken *kara-age*. To top it off, and freshen the palate, "vinegared things" *(sunomono)* or

"combined things" *(aemono)*, small salads in thin and thick dressing, respectively. Sesame, *miso*, or pureed bean curd provide bases for the thick dressings. Part Three, the curtain-puller, is the familiar rice, pickles, and tea, but augmented with *miso* soup and a final bright bit of fresh fruit, perhaps the famous *mikan* (mandarin oranges) of the Izu Peninsula.

Such a meal can even be had in a large, formal Japanese restaurant in any American or European city where Japanese businesspeople have established themselves. Invite friends, ask for the *o-makase*, and be sure your American Express card is in good repair.

Pristine freshness, visual elegance, seasonal appropriateness, careful coordination with beautiful serving ware—many of the most precious attributes of good Japanese cooking owe their refinement to the tea ceremony of the fourteenth to fifteenth centuries. *Kaiseki-ryōri,* tea-taste cooking, was and remains an important part of this remarkable medieval art in which performer and audience are one. After welcoming his guests to the little three-mat tea cottage where the ceremony is to take place, the tea master serves rice and miso soup, along with three dishes—chicken, mountain vegetables, game, nuts—in tiny portions, resting on exquisite lacquer-ware or pottery utensils.

As his guests quietly enjoy this visual-gustatory treat, the master withdraws to the adjoining room to finish preparing a light clear soup and a course of two fishes. He serves these along with warm *sake.* The tea, as in

CEREMONIAL FOOD

every Japanese meal, comes at the end, and is the "ceremony"; but the full *kaiseki* reminds us that the tea ceremony is as much a ritual *meal* as the preparation of a single exquisite beverage. The tea ceremony is a banquet, on an intimate scale, conducted according to exquisite canons of taste. It is intended to be relaxed, cheerful, with a conviviality that expresses itself as inward warmth instead of outward boisterousness. This secular and social ceremony, compounded of many kinds of connoisseurship—garden, art, pottery, aroma, taste, even water, are all to be evaluated and enjoyed—is nevertheless not an "art event"

but an occasion for sociability, a lift for the spirit. And Japanese food eaten in this spirit is always eaten correctly.

The oldest ceremonial food—ceremonies bringing us back beyond medieval days to Japan's immemorial *shintō* spirit-food—is *mochi.* The product of the ritual pounding of cooked glutinous rice, *mochi* has a magical tradition. An ancient gazetteer records a story about a *mochi* cake that was used as an archery target. When the arrow transfixed it, it turned into a white bird and flew away. *Mochi's* virture is such that it has long been eaten as a restorative after childbirth or travel.

During the joyous New Year holiday, it's the all-purpose offering. The rural tradition is to drop *mochi* bits down the well on January first as an offering to the god of water. On the eleventh, it's offered to farmyard crows. If they snap it up, that's an omen of a good harvest.

Above: These beautifully wrapped *mochi* cakes are part of a New Year's display at a Tokyo *sushi* shop. The making and eating of *mochi* are age-old New Year traditions.

Right: Japanese cuisine reaches its height of refinement in *kaiseki* (tea-ceremony cooking).

Left: Carefully wrapped and tied, *mochi* cakes await purchasers. *Mochi,* a taffylike rice cake, is made from glutinous rice *(mochigome)* that is steamed, never boiled.

In both country and city, the fifteenth of January, "little New Year," is the heart of the celebration and the time when the family itself partakes of *mochi,* on its own and in a hearty meat and vegetable stew called *ozōni* (miscellany). Other New Year foods include rice gruel *(kayu),* red rice (sticky rice with red beans), and sweet *sake.*

The ceremonial food of this most important of all holidays dominates the whole calendar. On Girls' Day (March 3), *mochi* is formed into diamond shapes and these are tinted pink, green, or white. Sweet *sake* sprinkled with peach blossoms is also served. The Boys' Day (May 5) favorite is *mochi* wrapped in bamboo or oak leaves. Moon viewing, an August festival that comes near the rice harvest, is an occasion to offer up red rice and sweet potatoes. During the September harvest, the New Year trio of sweet *sake, mochi,* and red rice

reappears. October is called the "godless month" because this is when the stalwarts of the Shinto pantheon are presumed to abandon their local shrine homes for the annual convention at Izumo. Human beings see them off and welcome them back, usually a month later, with red rice.

Nearly as important as rice and rice products for making a festive atmosphere is seafood. Fat pink sea bream *(tai)* is served on many celebratory occasions, especially at weddings and on the New Year. For maximum felicitousness, *tai* should be served whole; the Japanese term is *o-kashiratsuki,* "tail and head attached." In the days before modern commodity distribution, villages far from the sea had to make do with dried or smoked fish on holidays—or, failing these, seaweed, or failing even that, salt. Some part of the meal had to invoke and evoke the ocean.

Fruits and vegetables can be offerings too, of course. Persimmons, peas, turnips, and oranges find a place on New Year altars. The souls of the dead are welcomed back to our world during the Buddhist All-Souls' festival (Obon) in July, and are offered gifts of fish, eggplant, and cut cucumber. Noodles are provided as "ropes" for tying up the gifts, and horse and cow images cut from eggplant and melon represent the pack animals that will bear the gifts back to the underworld.

Still, rice remains the most profound ceremonial food. When someone dies, a "pillow meal" of a single bowl of pure white boiled rice is placed at the head, with a single chopstick stuck upright in it. It is a solemn thing to see, and has created two meal taboos that most Japanese respect: Never leave your chopsticks in your rice, and always eat more than one single bowl.

Japanese food is famous for its eye appeal. Beyond simply looking lovely, however, Japanese food when correctly served is part of an even more complex design. There is supposed to be a smooth continuity between the decor of the restaurant, the design of the table, the table decorations, the serving and eating dishes, and what is in them. This continuity can be very explicit. Go to dinner in the autumn at an elegant restaurant, and you will be able, first of all, to view brilliant red maple trees from where you sit; on your table, cut chrysanthemums also bespeak the season. In your soup, bits of boiled chrysanthemum continue the theme, and as a garnish for your *sashimi* (raw fish), you might find *momijioroshi*, (red-maple radish), Japanese radish

GARNISHES

ground together with a bit of red pepper.

Japanese garnishes decorate, invoke the season, and generally remind the eater that food originates out in the world. A leaf sprig next to a piece of grilled or simmered fish is a faint but unmistakable reminder that rivers and oceans are near neighbors to groves and forest.

Of course, garnishes taste good too. Noodle dipping sauce would be incomplete without the chopped green onion and grated radish with

which you are provided in little dishes. Even *kinome*, the tiny laurel-like leaves of the *sanshō* plant, among the commonest and most "visual" of Japanese garnishes, are good to eat. *Kinome* is often found in clear soup *(suimono)* as a visual accent. Other *suimono* garnishes include bits of trefoil (a parsleylike vegetable) and *yuzu* (citron) rind. *Kinome* and *yuzu* are traditional garnishes for simmered foods too, and so is fresh ginger.

Sashimi garnishes are, collectively, a vast garden of shapes and tastes. The Japanese eye simply can't resist pairing the simple, colorful pieces of fish with little intricate bits of vegetable. The slices rest upon a bed of lacy white grated radish, or carrot or cucumber filaments. Beside the *sashimi* you might find tiny squares of "rock moss" *(iwatade)*, the ubiquitous *kinome*, parboiled young asparagus tips, edible chrysanthemum petals, a bit of *suizenji nori* (a freshwater alga) or bright red *benitade* sprouts. Even okra, the West African vegetable that enriches gumbo stews in Louisiana, has been adopted by the Japanese as a raw fish accompaniment.

These garnishes are subtle in flavor and aroma. When stronger-flavored grilled foods are on the menu, the Japanese like to garnish them with tangy, acidic things like pickled ginger, pickled shallots, yam slices in vinegar, lemon, pickled radish, or cucumber. *Yakitori* (skewered chicken) and *teriyaki* (grilled meat basted with a soy-based sauce) are often accompanied by green onions or green peppers that have been charcoal-grilled.

Left: Not all Japanese garnishes come from the world of nature. The greenery in this commercially produced *bentō* (lunch box) is thin corrugated plastic. The sesame seeds on the rice, however, are real.

The knifework required to create ornamental garnishes is nothing short of spectacular. The rose in the center has been cut from a tomato, as have the butterflies in the upper right.

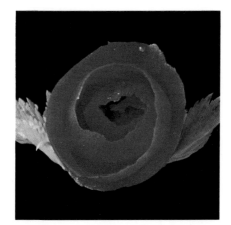

The Koreans believe that a human being can live and thrive on a diet of nothing but white rice and *kimchi* (their hot and spicy pickles made of cabbage, carrot, and seafood). The Japanese have a parallel faith: rice and *tsuke-mono* (their own far milder pickles) make a meal. It was this faith that presided over the birth of the *bentō*, the Japanese portable lunch, a good-sized snack that thousands of people pick up every day on the train or in the station, at highway rest stops, at temples and shrines, even in restaurants.

The feudal lord Oda Nobunaga, the most successful of Japan's brutal sixteenth-century warrior heroes, invented the humble but serviceable *bentō*. It was Nobunaga who first portioned out a carefully limited and spartan lunch to an assemblage of his vassals. It soon

PORTABLE MEALS

became customary to issue a *bentō* (divide the amount) ration to feudal troops. This consisted of a riceball plus pickle, generally the tart and reputedly medicinal pickled Japanese plum *(umeboshi),* wrapped in a convenient leaf.

When a permanent ceasefire came in 1600, it wasn't long before the warlike *bentō* became one of the loveliest ornaments of peace. Bourgeois families on springtime cherry-viewing parties packed *bentō* in handsome little boxes of lacquer or oak. They took them to the puppet theater or the kabuki and nibbled them

between acts, giving the *makunouchi* (between curtains) *bentō* its name. Edo period *bentō* had already become a fairly elaborate "convenience food," augmenting the *nigiri* riceball and *umeboshi* with other interesting pickles and whatever else was reasonably dry, mild in aroma, and unlikely to spoil.

The tidy, convenient *bentō* was a natural lunch for train travelers. In 1885 the first *ekiben* (station *bentō*) were sold on the Ueno-Utsunomiya line in the capital. It was a return to the basic model: A couple of riceballs and pickles, leaf-wrapped as in days of old, but it established a modern tradition. *Ekiben* hawkers quickly became an indispensable part of the atmosphere of travel on Japanese rails. Today one may still order them from trainside sellers in the stations or, on fancier trains,

Sushi is a perennially popular *bentō*-filler. The people of pre-modern Edo (Tokyo) brought *sushi bentō* to the theater to eat between acts, and the little rice sandwiches are still among the most portable and adaptable of delicacies. This shop offers several varieties, including mackerel *sushi* (second from the left) and *sushi* in the *kamigata* (Osaka-Kyōto) style, at right. While *nigirizushi* (fish-slice) makes a rather expensive *bentō*, the simpler seaweed-wrapped varieties are affordable, homey fare, such as the rice balls, dried fish, pickled plums, chicken and egg dishes that make up the vast majority of *bentō* meals.

This elaborate multilayer *bentō* box is used during cherry-blossom season and other special occasions.

A *bentō* stall in a railway station offers lunches at nine different prices. Station *bentō* are not only convenient for travelers, but they also reflect local cuisine.

from young ladies who push carts down the aisles in the manner of stewardesses.

Bentō are also on sale in the rest areas of the nation's transprefectural highways. While some pretense of regionality is maintained at these counters and vending machines, one's basic choice is among three options: Japanese, Western, and Chinese-style *bentō*.

If you put all your *bentō* options together, regional, national, and stylistic, you get some-

thing like 1600 varieties currently available. Needless to say, you need to go to Japan to sample this sort of variety. Still, many larger Japanese restaurants in the West serve a *makunouchi bentō* as a regular menu item, and many will make up *bentō* for you or your group. A *bentō* box, divided into a warren of little compartments, each filled with a small bright item, is an interesting example of Japanese "modular" design as well as a tasty meal.

A *bentō* packed full of *nigirizushi* and, in the lower left corner, rolled *sushi (norimaki)*. The ginger in the upper row helps refresh the palate.

We use the terms "nectar" and "ambrosia" figuratively, but which of us has ever tasted the drink and the food of the deities on Mount Olympus?

Yet we can be as gods—Japanese Shinto deities—when we sip *sake*, Japan's rice wine. The Japanese divinities, all "eight hundred myriads" of them, were a simple, hearty group who make Athena and Apollo seem like Freud's patients in Vienna. These merry gods

SAKE

were fond of *sake* and its riotous consequences, and so were ancient Japanese human beings, who have left us frank, funny poems and songs in praise of it. In their day, *sake* had

a ricier look, thick and milky. What we drink today is beautifully clear, like *mashimizu* (true clear water).

Sake is not wine because it is not produced by the one-step vintner's method, whereby the natural yeasts that cover the grapes in a powdery must are allowed to act upon the fruit sugars to create alcohol and carbon dioxide. *Sake* brewing is a two-step affair like beer making. The grain is steamed to turn its starches into sugar; only then is yeast added. Of course, *sake* will remind nobody of beer. It's a light, smooth beverage that doesn't effervesce, and runs from 15 to 17 percent alcohol. It takes a couple of months to produce and is ready to drink when it's made. It is an accessible, scrupulously honest beverage.

Yet no one should think that *sake* is simple. There is as much taste variety in the *sake* spectrum as there is, say, within the domain of a given wine. The basic divider of *sake* types is the question of sweetness. *Amakuchi* (sweet taste) *sake* occurs more or less naturally, and *karakuchi* (dry) is created artificially. Male connoisseurs complain that sweet *sake*, favored by women and the newly affluent young, is driving the good dry stuff of prewar years off the market. *Karakuchi* does taste more astringent, more "Japanese" in the medieval sense, but it's likely that the *sake* of 1300 years ago was sweet— and you can't get more traditional than then.

Sake is available in many kinds of containers—from single cups dispensed by vending machines to large casks like this one, made of wood and "tapped" like beer kegs. Bars display colorful rows of these casks.

And for sheer variety of varieties, *sake* is hard to beat. There are around three thousand breweries in the country—and only one in Tokyo! *Sake* brewing is a specialty of western Japan and the North. The ancient port of Nada in Hyogo Prefecture and history-rich Fushimi near Kyoto together account for half of the country's production.

Sake of whatever provenance and degree of sweetness can be enjoyed warm or cold, or at room temperature. Hot *sake* served in a narrow pouring bottle *(tokkuri* or *chōshi),* and poured into a tiny cup *(chokko* or *sakazuki)* is perfect to stir the blood in autumn or winter. In the hot months, which are very humid in Japan, sensible people are fond of *reishu* (cool *sake*) in square measuring cups of unfinished wood. Somehow the simple beauty of these cups is the perfect accompaniment to the limpid wine.

Sake happily accompanies any Japanese food, but is especially good with *sashimi* and grilled meat or fish. It's fine alone too, or with the many side snacks *(otsumami)* you can get in a Japanese tavern.

And finally, you can brew *sake* at home. I have an old friend in rural Iowa who, though no Japanophile, is an accomplished *sake* maker. He got his formula from a standard home brewer's recipe book, and he makes a brew that is a little bit milky and quite sweet. We drink it with spareribs and pickled okra.

Above: This *sake* brewery is in the city of Takayama, where traditional crafts, products, and architecture thrive.

Right: Sake, the favorite drink of gods and men, is an important offering. These large wooden tubs of rice wine, bearing many brands, have been consecrated, for divine enjoyment, at a Shintō shrine in Kyōto.

BEER AND WHISKEY

The Japanese manage to maintain both a hearty tradition of social drinking and a very low rate of alcoholism. A belt or two—or more—with the boys is an inevitable adjunct of ordinary life, not only tolerated but expected; a pleasant rite without poetic or passionate associations for most people. The Japanese body, however, does not have enough tolerance for alcohol to allow alcoholism. Above all, the accent is on what surrounds the social glass: the atmosphere of the bar, the mood of the crowd, the style of enjoying the libation. Drink vivifies and connects in Japan.

The liquors the Japanese prefer prove this. They invented *sake*, a truly civilized drink perfect for social intercourse, stuff that doesn't fuddle you. And they have taken to beer, the "liquid bread" of the jollier nations of northern Europe. Actually, it was Americans and not Germans who were instrumental in bringing the hop-and-barley brew to Japan. The Spring Valley Brewery opened in Yokohama in 1870, under the direction of a Yank named Copeland. This was strictly a colonial operation, providing brew for the foreign trading community in that city, and exporting the stuff to such colonial outposts as Shanghai and Saigon. Six years later, an American agricultural expert named Thomas Antisell began cultivating hops on the island of Hokkaido under the auspices of the Meiji government, which was encouraging American-style pioneering on Japan's long-neglected northern island.

Copeland's venture ultimately became Kirin Beer, and a German-trained Japanese brewer named Nakagawa Seibei turned Antisell's foresight into the Sapporo Beer Company in 1877. After a visit from no less august a personage

On a bamboo scaffold, a workman puts finishing touches on a billboard for Suntory blended whiskey. Domestic whiskeys, and a few highly favored foreign brands, are indispensible accompaniments to serious entertaining, especially in the business world. Costly whiskey is also a stylish gift.

than the Meiji emperor himself, in 1881 the Sapporo concern began to make money. Benefiting from this sort of publicity, the brewing industry as a whole expanded throughout the 1880s and 1890s until, on the very eve of the new century, Japan's first public beer hall opened on the Ginza in Tokyo. Competition was so intense that by 1901 most of the little breweries had been forced out of business, leaving the field to the likes of Kirin and Sapporo.

For forty more years, beer grew in favor in

Japan's great cities. It wasn't until after World War II, however—and to be more precise, not until the fifties had run their course—that beer drinking became a truly national pastime. In 1960, five makers produced all of Japan's beer: Kirin, Sapporo, Asahi, Suntory, and Takara. In twenty years, this situation hasn't changed. Beer drinking, however, has expanded explosively. Mammoth department store rooftop beer gardens light up the summer nights. Huge *chokki* (steins) crowd the tables. Ground-floor beer bars run by the breweries themselves carry on year-round. Vending machines dispense beer on street corners and in hotel corridors. Bars of all sorts, from the tiny *nomiya* (drinking places) that are little more than open air stalls to hostess clubs and cabarets keep the golden brew flowing. And it's commonsense hospitality, whether you're eating at home or in a fancy *tempura* place in the best quarter of Osaka, to order a few big two-liter bottles for the center of the table. You never pour for yourself; instead, you keep your neighbor's little glass full, and he reciprocates. That way you maintain conviviality and forget just how much you've drunk.

If beer is the convivial drink, then whiskey is the stylish one. In Nikka and Suntory whiskeys, Japan has two distinguished contributions to international inebriation. But the inevitable prestige whiskey is Johnny Walker. It's a must item in stateside duty-free shops where Japanese tourists congregate, and the highlight of the small Japanese counter bars where whiskey highballs are the drink of choice. Nothing could be a better gift for Japanese friends visiting you than a gift-wrapped fifth of Red or Black Label. For yourself, Japanese whiskeys are a treat. These carefully blended concoctions are smooth and mild and made to go with food. If you've tried them, and *sake*, and one of the fine Japanese lager beers (also made for accompanying food; tastier than American beers but less filling than German brews), you've made your way around the three basic drinks the Japanese favor. Suntory is pushing its vodka, aiming at the youth market, but such American mainstays as the martini and the gin and tonic haven't had time to put down deep social roots in Japan. This is changing, of course. One Japanese desk calendar includes, with each daily entry, a recipe for an exotic Western drink. On National Foundation Day (hallowing the mythical origin of the state in 660 B.C.), one learns how to make a sloe gin fizz.

A brace of Japanese beer labels. From modest beginnings in the late nineteenth century, the beer-brewing industry has grown fast in the postwar years. Mild and flavorful, Japanese beer has also been a success overseas, not only doing well in the export market, but also influencing the composition of other Asian beers.

COFFEE SHOPS

This Tokyo coffee shop can stand for thousands throughout the country: unpretentious, even undistinguished little places that offer a quiet corner for private thoughts in a very public society. The coffee is almost never bad and is sometimes superb.

On the intuition that we would be surprised, a Japanese friend and I decided to count the coffee shops we could find in six city blocks of Shinjuku, Tokyo. This particular part of Shinjuku is thoroughly Manhattanized, a concrete canyon-land. The banks and insurance headquarters and brokerage houses line up shoulder to shoulder, and the predominant colors are slate gray and high-tech mirror black. We counted twenty-seven coffee shops. Of course, we were in a moving car and may have missed a few.

In Ginza or Shibuya or Harajuku, where they're serious about coffee shops, well, they probably have to keep track of them by computer. A surrealistically hectic city of eleven million people—a city that has precious few park benches—needs coffee shops. People who live in apartments the size of squash courts and can hear three neighbors at once need quiet and cheerful places where the price of one cup of java buys you relative peace and solitude for as long as you want—no table-rushing in a Japanese coffee shop.

The convenience and ubiquity of the shops make them seem something like a public utility; and yet each shop or *kissaten* (tea-drinking shop, a term for a larger coffee place) has a vivid personality of its own, the better to snatch you in off the busy and distracting Japanese sidewalks. Snappily suited businesspeople close deals or talk office politics over *mōningu sābisu* (morning service), a light breakfast, in spacious, elegant *kissaten* dotted with ferns and decorated in tasteful shades of avocado or beige. Japan's *yangu* (young) people—college students, first-year salarymen and OLs (office ladies)—gather in cozy pairs under huge photographs of Lester Young or Milt Jackson; the music on the predictably superb house audio system is high-grade bebop.

Book lovers in Kanda-Jimbōchō, Tokyo's vast paradise of bookshops, dash into tiny glassed-in corner cafés to protect themselves and their new books from the rain. They drink tea, Coke, cocoa, ice cream floats, or the perfectly roasted and lovingly brewed Japanese coffee—coffee so rich it tastes a little like chocolate, and so smooth it doesn't need milk. For a bite, there are Japanese sandwiches, dainty things made with sugary white bread and cut into canapé-like triangles, or small portions of curry rice, the student staple, which are filling, tasty, and cheap.

In Harajuku, the boutique heaven where fashion designer Mori Hanae has her headquarters, you're likeliest to find the Georgetown or nouveau-Haight sort of café: Mucha posters of Sarah Bernhardt on the walls, warm wood all over, a connoisseur's selection of coffees. At the top of the list: Blue Mountain, the expensive brew named for the mountain that rises behind Kingston, Jamaica. The music is likely to be *chanson* or Parisian *jazz hot.* There are other places in Harajuku where you can listen to techno-pop and stare at primary colors.

There was a *kissaten* on the ground floor of the building where I worked in Tokyo: a real *kissaten,* wide, bright, and more than a little garish. It was our second office, the place where deals were struck, where gossip flowed, where ambitious employees had breakfast with the boss, and where many of us joked and relaxed after six. The coffee and the beer were all right; the food was dreadful. But it was the space that mattered, a modern magic space, not a Zen garden or a Nō stage, just a place for the ancient aleatory arts of relaxation.

The framed poster and bentwood chairs in this coffee shop mark it as one aimed at well-off urban young people—students, white-collar workers and OLs (office ladies), whose tastes run to things European. Here they can enjoy a wide variety of fancy coffees, prepared with painstaking care and served with individual filters.

音楽

8 • MUSIC

If you ask a native to hum you a typical Japanese traditional melody, you will quite possibly be given a bit of either of two songs about that quintessential Japanese topic, nature: ''Akatombo'' (Red Dragonfly) or ''Hotaru no hikari'' (The Light of the Firefly). The former was written in 1923 by European-trained composer Yamada Kosaku, who chose to be known in the West under the pseudo-Slavic spelling Kosczak Yamada; the first thirteen notes are a direct steal from Schubert. The latter song is none other than ''Auld Lang Syne'' with Japanese lyrics.

The Japanese of today is a musical polyglot. Ancient Chinese music coexists in Japan with punk rock. I once attended a Housewive's Association musical evening in which the same group of ladies took lessons in traditional Japanese folk song for one hour and in ball-

AN EASTERN MELTING POT

room dancing for a second hour—without even a change of clothes. It's all Japanese music, in the sense of ''music performed by and for Japanese.'' Citizens are, of course, aware that a rice-planting song and a Beethoven symphony spring from quite different cultural roots, but the audiences for these two events are not always as separate as we might expect.

Japan has borrowed musical elements—instruments, especially—from the Continent for well over a millennium. Significant Western influence dates only from the 1860s, but the past century has seen successive waves of

musical importation from Europe and the Americas in roughly the following chronological order: military music, classical music, prewar pops, jazz, rock, bluegrass, folk, electronic . . . and the beat goes on. Traditional music has for the most part coexisted peacefully with these invaders, sometimes standing aloof, sometimes mingling with varying degrees of success. The diverse musical life of modern Japan is reflected also in the names of the performers: Tanaka Denzaemon XVII, heir to a famous lineage of Kabuki percussionists; bluegrass picker Josh Otsuka; early Beatles clones the Spiders; veteran jazz saxman Hidehiko ''Sleepy'' Matsumoto; Pro Musica Nipponia, who perform modern compositions for traditional instruments; the Sadistic Mika Band, who manage to merge avant garde rock with the sounds of traditional Japan.

Left: A contemporary ensemble of guitar, piano, voice, and *koto* (the Japanese zither). Experiments with combinations of European and Japanese instruments began in the late nineteenth century and continue in both serious and popular music.

Above: The bassist Naoyuki Miura performs in a New York church. Miura's nonprofit Music From Japan organization promotes the performance of contemporary Japanese concert music in the United States and gives many works their American premieres.

DRUMS, FLUTES, AND STRINGS

The *biwa*, or Japanese lute, is one of the nation's most ancient links to world musical culture. It is first cousin to the very similar Chinese *pi-pa*, which in turn is a version of the Turkish instrument, the *barbat*. The Turks adapted their lute from the antique *barbatos* of Greece. These *biwa* are on display in Fukuoka.

Individual Westerners may have very different views of Japanese music depending on their particular experiences. One person has seen only a performance of Gagaku, the ancient and majestic court music, and reveled in the complex wash of sound drifting from the fifteen-odd peformers. Another loved the solo recital by a wizened old lady whose subtly modulated voice lagged skilfully behind the melody of her thirteen-stringed *koto*. A third could hardly sit still when the near-naked drummers of the Ondekoza, bodies glistening with sweat, made the rafters ring with their ensemble of drums large and small. All these, and more, are traditional Japanese music.

Few Japanese actually like all genres of traditional classical music *(hōgaku)*, any more than a Westerner finds equal enjoyment in Machaut, Vivaldi, Wagner, and Steve Reich. After all, each type of music developed to serve a particular audience in a particular setting. Take the Tokugawa period (1600–1868), for example. The *sankyoku* trio—koto, three-stringed *shamisen*, and vertical bamboo flute *(shakuhachi)*—provided the women of the newly affluent merchant class with a refined music in keeping with their aspirations to culture. In a more honest moment, the merchant would hie himself to the Kabuki theater, where the *shamisen* took on a much more extroverted character in the company of drums and piercing *fue* (horizontal flutes). The *shakuhachi* likewise produced a very different music of long, meditative notes in the hands of wandering ascetics. In the shogun's castle, the condensed, concentrated emotion of the Nō was translated by the drummers into drawn-out vocal wails, each followed by a single drum stroke—an icon of the self-discipline by which the samurai focused his strength. At the emperor's court in Kyoto, the ancient ritual music was continually being revived after periods of lapse due to various disturbances. In the peasants' villages, still other types of music were performed in a continuous tradition.

As society changes, tastes and needs change too. Playing the koto, for example, was until recently a necessary skill for a prospective upper-middle-class bride; now she is more likely to study piano. All in all, though, *hōgaku* is doing quite well, considering that educational policy had for so long consigned it to oblivion. Its success is due in no small part to the infamous *iemoto* system of artistic transmission. To learn Nō singing, for example, you join one of the five lineages or ''schools'' of Nō and study by rote a style approved by the school's head *(iemoto).* You do not offer your own interpretations; you simply imitate. Progress is marked by a series of much-coveted certificates, culminating in the awarding of a professional name. The prestige of earning a name has been a strong incentive contributing to the survival of many arts. However, the system is frequently criticized for stifling creativity (and funneling wealth to the *iemoto),* and for placing certificate chasing ahead of love of music.

Certain musical features, common to many of the diverse genres of Japanese music, distinguish it sharply from Western music. First of all, Japanese music is nonharmonic. Instead of melodies supported by chords, we find heterophony, a sort of loose unison with each instrument performing its own version of a basic melody. The interest we find in harmony, the traditional Japanese finds in melodic ornamentation—the subtle grace notes and vibratos that make it difficult to notate the melodies accurately. Scales are mostly pentatonic, seeming from a Western viewpoint to have gaps in them. Free rhythm is common. There is also a great interest in tone color or timbre, extending even to the use of ''extramusical'' sounds such as the *shakuhachi* player's sharp expulsion of breath, the *koto* player's lengthwise scraping of the strings, and other sounds incidental to the tones produced.

Features such as these have made it difficult for East and West to meet musically. Most young Japanese have developed a taste for harmony, but in vain do they search their guitars for the chords to accompany a traditional *shakuhachi* melody. One solution is to write new pieces for Japanese instruments, retaining certain elements of traditional style— say, the pentatonic scale—but adding Western elements such as chordal harmonies and triple rhythms. Miyagi Michio (1894–1956) created many such mixtures, and met with great popular success. Some critics claim that a piece such as his famous ''Haru no Umi'' (for *koto* and *shakuhachi*) is neither fish nor fowl; but a composer who attempts to write new *hōgaku* as if it were still 1850 will be dismissed as summarily as the European who tries to write a Beethoven's Tenth.

Drummers give it all they've got for a shrine festival. The *matsuri-bayashi* (festival music) of popular Shintō is one of the most accessible of Japanese musical styles: The combination of drum, flute, and bell, played in syncopation, is irresistibly exciting.

The mendicant monk playing his *shakuhachi* is a familiar figure in Japanese literature and legend. The instrument, a type of end-blown flute, produces a breathy, reedy tone that is full of a loneliness and mystery that evoke medieval Japan.

EAST-WEST INFLUENCE

An American visitor once had the temerity to ask a Japanese player of the viola da gamba why he had not chosen instead a "more Japanese" instrument such as the *shamisen.* The musician pointed out that the gamba and *shamisen* were of equal antiquity in Japan, both having been imported during the mid-sixteenth century!

Of course, the anti-European isolationism that soon followed eliminated practically all traces of the music imported from the West during Japan's Christian century. But the century following Perry's forced reopening of Japan in 1853 has had a more thoroughgoing influence on musical life. The wholehearted acceptance of all things Western extended to music: To compete militarily and economically with the "barbarians," it would surely be necessary to adopt their music as well. By 1881 the emperor's court orchestra could play several national anthems—on Western instruments. Ever since, the court musicians have been masters of both native and European instruments.

According to the government's music education policy, all vocal and instrumental training in the schools was Western style; only since World War II has authentic native music attained a tentative, subordinate position. As a result, most Japanese were weaned on Western melodies (the lullaby may well have been Brahms). And although not all this music was of great quality, by the 1920s an aspiring violinist could have heard Heifetz, Zimbalist, Kreisler, and Elman; would have studied with a European teacher; and could have listened to records and radio broadcasts of the great performances.

The Japanese have obviously developed a taste for Western music. Yamaha sells over 200,000 pianos a year—90 percent of them in Japan. There are nine professional symphony orchestras and six major music colleges in Tokyo alone, and Japanese have recently been flooding music schools and orchestras abroad as well. Beethoven's Ninth Symphony, a year-end ritual, is heard nearly 100 times each December in performances by professional and amateur groups across the country. The Tokyo String Quartet's Bartók recordings are generally considered definitive.

Even with all this, one still hears the charge that Japanese artists are mere technicians aping a "foreign" music, products of Suzuki-style violinist factories. (Most Suzuki method pupils are in fact Westerners.) To one critic, Tokyo String Quartet typifies the "East Asian" approach: Their attention to detail and sound production (they play on matched Amati instruments) does not redeem their interpretations from occasional "emotional immaturity." Certainly it is true that Japanese pedagogy does not encourage creativity or originality of interpretation; the *iemoto* mentality is still potent. But both Westerners and Japanese are often reluctant to accept a priori that Japanese culture *could* produce sensitive Western-style musicians. Perhaps we need a rigorously con-

JAPANESE RECORDINGS
■
CLASSICAL DISCOGRAPHY
■

"The Hiroshima Masses." Chorus, *koto* orchestra, and soloists of Elizabeth University. Lyrichord 7180.

"Japan: Semi-classical and Folk Music." EMI/Odeon C064-17967.

"Japan: Traditional Vocal and Instrumental Music," featuring *shakuhachi, biwa, koto,* and *shamisen;* soloists of the Ensemble Nipponia. Nonesuch Explorer H-72072.

"Japanese *Shamisen;* Chamber Music with *Koto* and *Shakuhachi.*" Lyrichord 7209.

"The Metropolis Wind Quintet, Art of Woodwind Quintet." PolyGram Special Imports K25C 134.

"Hiroko Nakamura Plays Piano Favorites." CBS/Sony 30AC 66-7.

"Nippon: Impressions From the West," featuring compositions of Ohki, Fukai, Kiyose, and Yamada; by Shigenolou Yanaoka and the Yomiuri Symphony Orchestra. Takanori Kobayashi, piano. Varase Sarabande VX80161.

Aki Takahashi, "Piano Space 1." Toshiba/EMI 60153.

Toru Takemitsu, "Quatrain; A Flock Descends into the Pentagonal Garden." Deutsche Grammophon, DG2531210. "Quatrain II; Waterways; Waves." RCA ARL1-3483.

Tokyo String Quartet, "Complete Quartets of Bartok." Deutsche Grammophon 3-DG2740235

Yoshio Unno with the CBS Symphony Orchestra, conducted by Tadashi Mori. CBS/Sony 22AC 184.

Left: Japanese pianist Aki Takahashi rehearses. She represents the contemporary generation of internationally recognized Japanese players.

The Tokyo String Quartet has achieved an international reputation with its Bartok recordings for Deutsche Grammophon and its concert appearances.

ducted series of blind listening tests to elicit unbiased reactions from such critics.

Composition, of course, is another matter. Unlike a performer interpreting the product of another culture, the confident composer creates from within his or her own culture. Even when writing for Western instruments, the better Japanese composers draw on elements, musical and otherwise, of their traditional culture. Two such composers are Takemitsu Tōru and Miki Minoru, both born in 1930.

Takemitsu has experimented with almost every modern composition technique and has written for both Japanese and European instruments. But constant throughout his work, as M. Kanazawa has pointed out, is a preoccupation with "timbre and texture—and with silence." Even before his personal "discovery" of Japanese traditional music around 1961, these three elements were present in his compositions. So was his very Japanese concern with the sounds and rhythms of language and nature, as heard in "Vocalism A•I" (1956) and "Mizu no Kyoku" (1960)—the latter consisting entirely of recorded water sounds.

When Takemitsu uses Japanese instruments, as in the world-famous "November Steps" for *biwa, shakuhachi,* and orchestra (1967), he seldom demands any significant extension of traditional technique. Miki has been much more adventurous in that respect (although less so in others), working closely with performers to develop new kinds of virtuousity. Yet Miki too has a very Japanese sense of timbre and texture, and his Stravinsky-like rhythmic sense actually derives, he says, from the dance music of his native Tokushima.

Miki's English-language opera, *An Actors's Revenge,* a tale set in the world of Kabuki, opened in London in 1979. One reviewer, praising Miki's way with text setting, pronounced him the successor to Benjamin Britten in this regard—very high praise indeed. But the question is, had Miki mastered British techniques? Or was Britten's own approach to text setting actually quite Japanese? And does it matter?

Jazz and Japan shouldn't mix. After all, the essence of jazz lies in improvisation—a concept largely absent from both traditional Japanese music and Japanese society as a whole. Japan may adapt, but it does not improvise. Still, considering the popularity of impromptu poetry, jazz may not be so foreign after all.

Regardless, jazz has found a happy home in Japan. Indeed, except for a brief period during World War II when contacts with foreign musicians were curtailed, jazz in Japan has kept pace with developments in the United States. Swing, bebop, cool jazz, hard bop, fusion have all flourished in their turn. And in the last decade, Japanese musicians have gained increasing recognition and respect from their foreign colleagues.

In the prewar period, as in the West, jazz found its home in urban dance halls. Surveys in the 1930s showed that one adult in five enjoyed jazz—exceeding the figure for many genres of traditional music. Then as now, the audience was primarily young and urban. Foreign bands occasionally visited, and several

JAZZ

Filipino musicians stayed behind to become mainstays on the Japanese scene.

World War II nearly eliminated "the enemy's music," but the market provided by the Occupation forces soon brought home-grown jazz to a new peak. Following overseas trends, postwar jazz became more and more a music for listening rather than dancing. The dance hall gave way in the 1950s to the jazz *kissa* (tearoom-coffeehouse), where live bands played for audiences of students and young adults.

Another major development in the 1950s was the true internationalization of Japanese jazz. Foreign acts flooded into Japan, and Tokyo became a standard stop on the world jazz circuit. Visiting performers such as pianist Oscar Peterson, much taken with the enthusi-

asm of their Eastern counterparts, offered encouragement and advice.

The next big step was taken when, in 1956, pianist Toshiko Akiyoshi won a scholarship to Boston's Berklee School of Music—*the* school for jazz. Her full acceptance as a working musician, composer, and arranger in the United States and Europe showed the way to others back home. With economic prosperity, a slow trickle of emigrants during the 1960s turned to a steady flow in the 1970s.

There is no question that Japan can produce artists of world-class caliber; indeed, several have already worked as sidemen for such major figures as Sonny Rollins, Art Blakey, Chico Hamilton, and Charles Mingus. Success in the West of course spells fame back home for the elite few: Akiyoshi (b. 1929), who now cofronts (with husband Lew Tabackin) an internationally renowned "big band"; "Nabesada" (Watanabe Sadao, b. 1932), sax-tooting son of a *biwa* teacher, whose recent albums regularly sell over 100,000 copies; trumpeter Hino Terumasa (b. 1942), whose fusion sound has pro-

Left: In his first film under the direction of Akira Kurosawa, Toshirō Mifune played the troubled, terminally ill gangster "hero" of *Drunken Angel* (1948). Kurosawa used jazz to evoke the atmosphere of nightclubs and beer halls in the chaotic years following Japan's surrender.

Right: Pianist Toshiko Akiyoshi is the most prominent of the Japanese jazz expatriates. Her work as a soloist and with the Akiyoshi-Tabackin Big Band has placed her securely in the front rank of world jazz. Akiyoshi's success helped clear the way for other first-rate Japanese players.

pelled him to television fame as a purveyor of Nikka whiskey.

Others who have worked regularly abroad include guitarists Masuo Yoshiaki, Kawasaki Ryō and Watanabe Kazumi; Suzuki Isao (bass, vibes); Omori Akira (alto sax); and Tana Akira (drums). But many fine artists rarely or never leave their native soil—among them "Sleepy" Matsumoto and pianist Maeda Norio.

It is still an open question whether Japan can contribute anything specifically Japanese to world jazz. The flirtation with Indian elements in the 1960s has had limited long-term effect. At the 1982 Berlin Jazzfest, which spotlighted several Japanese artists, Sakata Akira's band featured traditional Japanese percussion, but the sound system rendered it inaudible. (East Asian woodblocks have of course long since become standard in jazz percussion.) Pianist Aki Takase is reputed to have a funky *koto* style, and American John Neptune is introducing the *shakuhachi* to a wider public as a jazz instrument. Some of Akiyoshi's pieces seem to show a certain Japanese sensibility.

As with other forms of "Western" music, it is difficult to be objective when evaluating the Japanese jazz artist. The generally held opinion seems to be that the music offered in Tokyo's jazz spots is still somewhat stilted. The word "still" is important, for it assumes that progress is being made. Why not listen for yourself?

JAPANESE RECORDINGS
■
JAZZ DISCOGRAPHY
■

TOSHIKO AKIYOSHI/LEW TABACKIN BIG BAND, "Long Yellow Road." RCA JPL1-1350.

TERUMASA HINA, "Double Rainbow." Columbia 37420.

TOSHIYUKI HONDO & BURNING WAVES, "Spanish Waves." PolyGram Special Imports K28P-6051.

EIJI KATAMURA, "Swing Eiji." Concord CJ 152.

RYO KAWASAKI, "Trinkets and Things." Timeless SJP 123.

TAKEHISA KOSUGI, "Kosugi." Bellows 003.

KIKUCHI MASABUMI, "Matrix." Catalyst 7916.

MIKIO "MICKEY" MASUDO, "Corazon." PolyGram Special Imports SKS 8004.

SADAO WATANABE, "Fill Up the Night." Elektra/Musician 60297.

YOSUKE YAMASHITA, "Breathtake." West 54 Records 8009.

MASUO YOSHIAKI, "The Song Is You and Me." PolyGram Special Imports K28P-6043.

医術

9 • MEDICINE

At a Japanese public bath, one invariably sees at least one older person decorated along his or her spine with two parallel rows of round scars, about the size of peas. They are moxibustion scars, the marks left after tiny wads of dried *mogusa* leaves have been burned on the person's skin in accordance with principles of traditional medicine.

The three most important components of non-Western medicine as it is practiced in Japan today are moxa cautery, acupuncture, and the herbal pharmacopia called Chinese medicine *(kampōyaku)*. Moxa and acupuncture are based on the same system of understanding particular points and connections throughout the body. These points are stimulated—by heat in the case of moxa, needles in the case of acupuncture—to promote the body's own regenerative powers. A licensed practitioner of one can usually perform the other as well. Moxa is considered a milder treatment, and many households keep a packet of the crumbly pale-gray substance to administer to family members. Acupuncture is always left to the expert.

Both techniques are believed effective for the relief of chronic aches and pains, especially of the legs and back. Old people suffering from rheumatism often set up a regular regimen that includes massage (shiatsu), moxa, and acupuncture. The general rule is that if there is tenderness or inflammation that would make the pressure of massage painful, the number of moxa points should be increased while the burning time for each is shortened. Conversely, if massage feels good and the body is relaxed, fewer moxa points of greater heat should be applied. It is recommended that any of these techniques be performed at least thirty minutes after meals, and preferably after bowel evacuation.

Moxa cautery and acupuncture were introduced to the West in the eighteenth century by the Dutch doctor Rhyne and the German

TRADITIONAL AND FOLK REMEDIES

Kampfer, who had observed Japanese physicians inflicting these odd treatments on their patients. In the late nineteenth century Japanese turned away from their needles and *mogusa* to adopt Western medical knowledge and techniques. Now there is something of a resurgence of the old ways, sparked in no small part by the interest of Western scientists in the physiological principles behind the effectiveness of these treatments.

The philosophy of traditional medicine is based on the notion that humans live in and are thus susceptible to the influences of the natural environment. If they cannot adapt to its fluctuations, their bodies will become sick. External factors such as wind, temperature, and humidity, and internal factors like fatigue or emotional stress, lie at the root of illness. The internal organs are thought to be connected to certain places on the skin—hence the notion that by stimulating those spots with needle or heat, the state of the organ will be affected. The goal is to restore a person's proper balance of yin and yang in congruence with the environment. This may be accomplished externally with moxa or acupuncture, or internally with herbal medicines.

The subtle combinations of vegetable substances used in traditional Chinese herbal medicine are not yet understood by modern pharmacology. There are specialty shops that carry only *kampōyaku,* but one can also find some of the more popular combinations prepackaged and sold in a special section of any drugstore. Ota Isan is an antacid powder concocted by Mr. Ota many years ago from a variety of ingredients culled from East and West. It is considered to be far superior to Alka-Seltzer by most Japanese, so when, for a time in the 1970s, the U.S. Food and Drug Administration banned the importation of Ota Isan while it tried to ascertain what its ingredients actually affected, anxious Japanese residents of the United States importuned visiting relatives to smuggle the tins of clove-scented powder into the country with them.

There are few areas of Japan now where people seriously believe that children's diseases and tantrums are caused by a *mushi,* a "bug." In the past, however, a plethora of folk

A small Japanese drugstore proclaims (on the little statue in the foreground): "Satō for Medicines!" Such shops carry traditional medicines as well.

remedies was available to cure children of such bugs. One was to give a child some bit of food received from a household in which lived three generations of healthy couples. Another was to feed (or threaten to feed) the brat broiled tree frog. Quite plausibly the idea behind the latter cure was that the frog would "catch" the bug causing the bad behavior.

Moxa cautery is a traditional remedy for naughtiness that is not infrequently practiced on children even today. Moxa is used by adults for a number of ailments, and in small, less intense doses, is thought to temper childish obstreperousness. Unpleasant, although said to be quite effective, is the cure for bedwetting: burning a pinch of moxa on the tender triangle of flesh between the lower thumb and the rest of the hand.

The Japanese equivalent of the hot toddy, drunk to ward off an impending cold, is a cup of hot *sake* fortified with a spoonful of sugar and a beaten egg. A warm, overall feeling of well-being is said to ensue. Children are given a hot nectar produced from boiled tangerine peels and sugar. Every Japanese family has a collection of favorite home remedies like this, concocted mostly from ingredients likely to be found right in the kitchen.

The dreaded hangover is a disease that strikes Japanese males in particular. Although dark and quiet are the optimum conditions for reducing the ache of a big head, recovery can be speeded by drinking a tincture of boiled cloves.

Egg white mixed with a tad of soy sauce is believed to be an effective poultice for burns, and rashes will be soothed by being rubbed with slices of cucumber. Chewing roasted tangerine seeds is said to relieve a sore throat, while chewing a handful of raw brown rice will get rid of intestinal parasites. A headache may be helped by application of equal parts of sesame oil and juice of fresh ginger root, while the recipe for fever medicine, with minor

changes, could double as dipping sauce for *tempura:* take one tbsp grated daikon radish, two tbsp soy sauce, and one tsp grated ginger; brew together in one liter of water; strain; drink.

Bamboo—charred, powdered, and mixed with water—will settle a queasy stomach if it doesn't unsettle it, and diarrhea can be staunched by drinking peony-root tea. Charring also brings out the benefits of pine needles and eggplants, which may then be applied to an aching tooth. Perhaps the most generally used item in the kitchen pharmacopia is the plumply wrinkled, salty-sour pickled plum, or *umeboshi.* Anyone not feeling well for whatever reason in Japan can nurture his system with a bowl of rice gruel accompanied by a couple of *umeboshi.* Japanese mountain climbers carry a packet of the moist, acidic red plums to prevent dehydration. Popping pickled plums may have the same physiological effect

as swallowing salt tablets is said to have.

To keep one's health robust, one's body immune from the miasma of germs ever ready to invade, Japanese have available numerous elixers and concoctions from both traditional Eastern and "scientific" Western sources. Modern Japanese are quite as conscientious as Americans about their *bitamin* quotient. Vitamin C in particular enjoys a great vogue in Japan. The liquid synthetic vitamin Orinamin-C is sold in one-gulp bottles at every cigar stand in the country. Ginseng, garlic, and various molds that can be incubated at home on top of the television set are cultivated by people serious about maintaining their disease resistance. Germs may also be kept at bay by wearing a gauze mask over the nose and mouth. Ostensibly a way of preventing the spread of germs by a carrier, in fact, psychologically, the effect for most Japanese who wear the masks is prophylactic.

Above: All of the dishes in this meal are made from bamboo, in one form or another. Bamboo has a variety of uses in folk medicine, including settling queasy stomachs.

Right: Bamboo, the most versatile of all East Asian plants, can be transformed into scaffolds, brushes, chopsticks, food, medicine, and more.

Two professions have always been open to the blind in Japan. One is the musician—a blind *koto* player has an undeniable edge over his sighted confreres; and the other is the masseur, or *anma.* One lives by his ears, the other by his fingers. A professionally trained *anma,* who today must be certified by the board of health in the prefecture where he practices, is similar to a chiropractor. His hands are his instruments, and the technique of "finger pressure"—*shiatsu*—is the most important skill in his repertoire.

The origins of *shiatsu* lie in the practical philosophy of judo: a thorough knowledge of

MASSAGE

the body, its weak points, the flow of energy, the strength to be found in one's "center," and the importance of flexible joints. This traditional wisdom of the body was allied with Western holistic health theories to produce the art of *shiatsu* as it is practiced in Japan today.

The basic technique is the "rectification" of a person's vertebrae through controlled pres-

sure applied along the spine. Although Japanese love to massage each others' stiff shoulders, actual *shiatsu* is usually left to a professional, for the amount of pressure to be applied must be carefully gauged to the body type, general health, and age of the person receiving treatment.

The practitioner begins by kneeling over his supine patient and stroking down the spine with his palms. Then, placing his right hand on top of his left, he presses for three or four seconds at each handspan from neckbone to tailbone. By this process he may ascertain the state of the spine—if it is curved, if there are

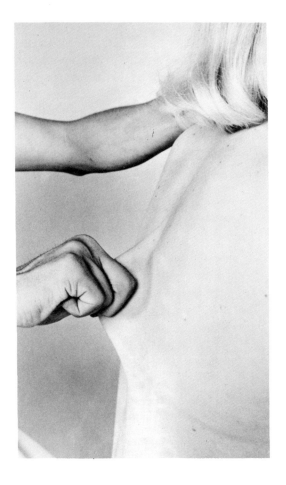

The *shiatsu* therapist relieves back tension by pulling the muscles. The technique also aids circulation.

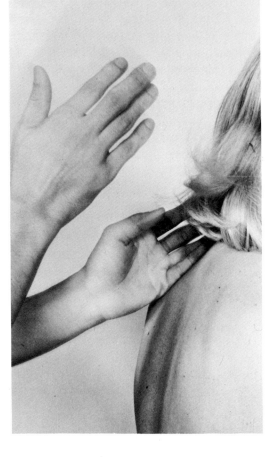

"Karate chops" with relaxed hands can help to ease muscle fatigue all along the back and the hips.

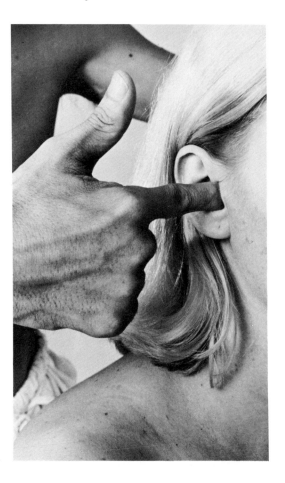

An odd-looking but effective way to relieve mental fatigue and nervous tension is "vibrating the ears."

lumps. With his wrists and thumbs, he pays particular attention to any irregular spots. Neurological disorders are thought to be caused by malalignment of the spine, and *shiatsu* is held to be effective in their cure.

The technique is called "finger pressure," but in fact the weight of the massseur's entire body is being conducted through the fingers, zeroing in on stiffness. The *shiatsu* master's experienced fingers tell him just how much pressure to apply, and at what rhythm.

Manipulation of the joints is also important in *shiatsu*. Stretching and rotating works out the body's kinks and is considered to promote general good health and physiological well-being. It is very important that the patient be relaxed, however, for a sudden tightening of the muscles could be disastrous—especially when the neck is being rotated.

Japanese think of *shiatsu* for relief of conditions like high blood pressure, insomnia, rheumatism, and gastrointestinal disorders, as well as the common headache, stiff neck, and fatigue. In general, *shiatsu* is practiced on chronic conditions and is not recommended for persons in a weakened state, with fever, with all-over aches, with a tumor, or with an inflamed appendix.

Toe rotation and flexing the toe joints is a milder form of *shiatsu* that has many devotees all over Japan. Although there are specialists in this too, it is easy (and safe) for a person to work on his or her own feet. The result is felt immediately when one sits lotus fashion, grasps the big toe with thumb and forefinger, and rotates it firmly thirty times clockwise. It is as if a rubber band holding the shoulders taut were suddenly let go.

Shiatsu techniques are practiced in the West through chiropracty, which it has heavily influenced, and also by specialists trained in Japan. *Shiatsu* workshops are advertised on college campuses, in the counterculture newspapers, and increasingly, in most larger cities.

Sliding two fingers along the patient's back, the therapist makes a diagnosis. Like acupuncture, *shiatsu* associates areas of the spinal column with internal organs and "reads" disorders via spinal irregularities.

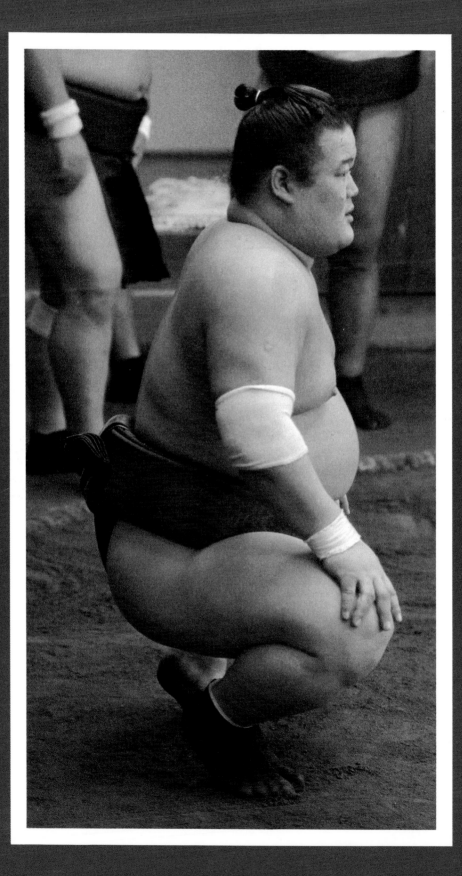

体育

10 · SPORTS

SUMO

Above, wrestlers grapple under the watchful eye of the referee in his sixteenth-century garb. At right, a competitor anticipates a bout in a practice ring. *Sumo* matches, most lasting less than a minute, require intense concentration.

They call it the sport of major proportions, and the pun is intended. Few sports are as strong on pageantry, history, and tradition as is Japan's national sport, Sumo. But Sumo is also a thrilling spectacle, alive with drama and excitement. The wrestlers are of major proportions, indeed, massive men who usually stand at 6 feet (1.8 meters) or less but rarely weigh in under 300 lbs (136 Kg). To watch a Sumo tournament, or *basho*, as the six yearly fifteen-day fighting events are called, is to delve to the

core of Japanese culture and history. To many Japanese, these well-conditioned behemoths are the last of the samurai.

Sumo looks like no other sport in Japan or, for that matter, the world. Unlike boxing or professional wrestling, the ring or *dohyō*, where the wrestlers grapple, is round. Fights, which rarely last more than a minute, are over when one of these hefty grapplers succeeds in knocking down his opponent or removing him from the ring. While the action is swift, per-

fectly tailored for an era of instant replays, the preliminary warmups seem to go on and on.

Clad only in bright-colored silk *mawashi*, as the Sumo belt is called, the wrestlers bow, touch the ground, clap their hands and throw salt into the air, all in a graceful cadence. They also glare and glower at each other, trying to seize upon the best tactic for winning. It is this blaze of ritual, rich in tradition and symbolism, that underscores Sumo's uniqueness. It also serves as a tantalizing buildup to the matches.

Nearly every aspect of Sumo is at least three centuries old. Modern-day Sumo traces its origins to the Edo period (1603–1868), about the same time as Kabuki began—the mid-1600s. But references to the sport are found in Japan's two oldest histories, the Kojiki and Nihonshoki. Indeed, legend has it that a Sumo match decided which group of gods was to rule the nation (the victor was supposedly a distant ancestor of today's imperial family). With such significant roots, Sumo not surprisingly is associated with the ancient Japanese religion, Shinto. Early Sumo was usually performed at a local Shinto shrine in conjunction with rice planting and crop harvesting, a ceremony to please the gods. Even today, many shrines still have their own *dohyō*. Tokyo's enormous Yasukuni Shrine, for example is the site of a special tournament in honor of the war dead each spring.

The depth of ritual is staggering. Every movement has some special significance. The hand clapping prior to a fight is done to attract the attention of the gods. Foot stamping is designed to drive away demons. Salt is hurled into the air to purify both wrestlers and ring.

Like ballet dancers, Sumo wrestlers start their training at an early age. Tokyo's Ryogoku district, site of the wrestling stadium, is also home of some thirty-five *heya*, or stables, where the sport's 700-odd wrestlers eat, sleep, and grapple. Boys can enter a stable when they have completed junior high school, but it is a demanding existence for the young. In return for room, food, and training, but no pay, they must care for the stable, prepare the *chanko nabe* (the hearty stew wrestlers wash down with vast quantities of beer and rice), and act as manservants to the senior wrestlers.

As a wrestler progresses through various levels in this highly stratified sport, his lot improves. Life becomes attractive when he reaches the Jūryō level, the lower end of Sumo's top division. In addition to a salary, he

Wrestlers stand in a circle during the ceremony that opens the day's round of *sumo* bouts. A full tournament comprises fifteen days of matches and is called a *basho*; the *sumo* calendar is made up of six yearly *basho*.

is allowed to wear bright-colored *mawashi* instead of the ugly canvas belt used by the lowest levels, his long hair is styled in a *chonmage*, a lacquered topknot shaped like a ginko leaf, and his fights are often seen on television.

An even sweeter promotion is to the Makunouchi division, which means "inside the curtain." The salary is higher, though still less than that of a professional baseball player, and the wrestler is eligible for promotion to Sumo's top ranks—Komusubi, Sekiwake, Ōzeki, and the most treasured of all, Yokozuna, which means grand champion. At this writing, only fifty-eight men in modern Sumo history have achieved it. It is the pinnacle, and in addition to high pay and popularity, *yokuzuna* usually become masters of their own stables upon retirement. Lesser-ranked men often open restaurants when they hang up their *mawashi.*

Though the sport is intrinsically Japanese, a handful of foreigners have been drawn into it, notably an enormous wrestler named Takamiyama. Born in Hawaii in 1944, the former Jesse Kuhaulua even won a tournament back in 1972 (he received a congratulatory telegram from then-president Nixon).

As with so many things Japanese, Sumo is a tough world for the foreigner. The wrestlers even speak their own style of Japanese. But the Japanese, who take enormous pride in their national sport, like it this way.

Pro ball under the lights in Tokyo. The Japanese follow high school and college baseball avidly as well.

BASEBALL

America's official national sport ranks as Japan's unofficial national sport. Baseball enjoys a nationwide following. It's the sport everyone seems to enjoy—from the schoolgirls, who weep when their teams lose, to the emperor, whose dignified presence at a game in 1959 lent this upstart sport regal approval.

Twice a year, 49 teams of teens vie for the national high school championship crown, and their heroic efforts are followed as closely as America's World Series. Television programs are preempted for live coverage. Japan's two professional leagues, the Central and the Pacific, enjoy equally fervid attention.

The nation's television stations plot the year's broadcast schedules around baseball season, and viewers can see at least one baseball game nearly every night. Those who miss out can catch up with nightly baseball wrapups, filmed inning-by-inning highlights from almost every team. For the true devotee, five major sports dailies report on every imaginable

facet of the game, from player performances against specific pitchers to a speculative glossary of team hand signals.

To the casual observer, baseball seems pretty much the same on both sides of the Pacific. The umpire calls "Purei Bōru!" at the start of a contest. The game consists of nine fielders, nine batters, nine innings, four bases, four balls, three strikes, and three outs. Some teams sport the same names, such as Tokyo's Yomiuri Giants and the San Francisco Giants; these two even share identical colors—orange and black.

But just as the English-language word "baseball" sounds little like its Japanese counterpart *yakyu*, the stylistic and psychic differences are wide. Baseball in Japan is ultimately a Japanese sport, right down to its emphasis on the group over the individual. Baseball was introduced to Japan in 1873 by Horace Wilson, an American professor at Tokyo University, and though the countries' rules are virtually

the same, professional American players imported for their power hitting and, one suspects, their colorful personalities frequently find it hard to succeed in Japan. Baseball is an ideal example of how the Japanese have borrowed liberally from the West, yet managed to keep their own culture.

At the heart of this difference is *bushidō*, the thirteenth-century samurai code of behavior. Filtered for baseball, it stresses loyalty, duty, honor, obedience, and the importance of being a "team player"; as the well-worn Japanese saying goes, "The nail that sticks up gets hammered down." Japanese baseball players never quibble over contracts, do not demand huge salaries, try not to draw attention to themselves, and stick to the established form and procedure; individualistic pitching or batting stances are frowned upon, no matter how these may enhance the end result. Players, all mindful of their status as team members, routinely meet during the off season, report for

A pitcher for the Hiroshima Carps stares down a batter in a televised game. Japanese baseball stresses "fighting spirit," discipline, and team-consciousness over personal heroics and flamboyant style, to the consternation of some U.S. players on Japanese teams.

"voluntary training" weeks in advance, and forego time with family to be with the team.

Under baseball's samurai code, training is strict. You don't see many pot-bellied pitchers, following a daily training regimen lasting from 7:30 A.M. to 11 P.M. and including five-mile runs; calisthenics; batting, catching, base running and defense practices; an intrasquad game; drills for players with problems; a daily review and voluntary after-hours shadow pitching and batting routines.

Japanese baseball is serious business. They've taken the fun out, lamented Reggie Smith, the former San Francisco Giant who played with the Yomiuri Giants in 1983. "It's strictly business, more like 'work,'" he told The Japan Times, a Tokyo paper. According to Smith, one problem with this keen emphasis on what the Japanese call "fighting spirit" is that players overextend themselves, and injuries occur. It's not unusual for a weary pitcher to hurl more than nine innings since, under the code, he must show the fans he has the desire and spirit to win, even if he no longer has an arm. In his excellent book The Chrysanthemum and the Bat, Robert Whiting describes a manager's typical comment after the team lost seven in a row: "I apologize to the fans for this disgrace. I just hope we will get better. I don't know what has come over my pitching staff. They have lost their fighting spirit."

Baseball's samurai code also requires those in charge to take full responsibility for each player's performance, no matter how little control they have over the situation. When the Yomiuri Giants suddenly lost their ten-game lead over the Hiroshima Carps in the 1983 season, both the team manager and the head coach promised to resign if the team failed to finish in first place.

To show fighting spirit, Japanese players labor constantly to make their plays look hard, display their efforts; it's the opposite of American players who try to make everything look graceful and easy. Players are also expected to be a shining example for the youth of the nation. When Shigeo Nagashima, the former Yomiuri Giant who was once Japan's most popular star, was asked what he would do if a power failure occurred when he was talking with his girlfriend, he replied: "I would not take advantage of the darkness. I would never grab her hand, because I'm a gentleman. I would wait quietly until the lights came back on."

Reggie Smith cites the Japanese ability to bunt and "execute fundamentals" as two national qualities. "Mechanics are repeatedly stressed," he says. Anyone watching an evening's baseball highlights can look forward to some thrilling plays—a diving catch, a fearless slide, a running leap to blunt a home run. What you don't get is an American sense of individuality or spontaneity in style, ideas, even appearance. Indeed, there's no long hair, facial hair or gold neckchains. What is overwhelming is uniformity on every level, including philosophy, drive and mental attitude. The players are products of similar backgrounds, schooling and training. They can play some terrific baseball. But always, it is first and foremost Japanese baseball.

MARTIAL ARTS

In the West, the martial arts have gained popularity as effective tools of defense. America's FBI and Secret Service agents routinely study *aikidō*, a method of disarming, throwing, or evading attackers. Big-city dwellers assiduously review *jūdō*'s broad vocabulary of hip throws and leg sweeps. Styles of *karate*—Japanese, Chinese, and Korean—proliferate in the West.

But in Japan, where the martial arts have been cultivated since primitive times, philosophical rather than physical reasons are usually behind mastery of *aikidō*, *karatedō*, *kyūdō*, and more than sixteen other skills, including *sumo*. Far more than mere fighting skills, the martial arts seek to unite body, mind, and spirit. Those who integrate the martial arts into their lives stoutly maintain they undergo lasting—and positive—changes in ideas and attitude. In an article in *The East* magazine, Russian-born *kyūdō* student Grisha Dotzenko wrote: "*Kyūdō* (the martial arts' distinct method of archery) is not a body builder. You do learn to control your body, muscles and bones, but your exterior does not change. You do, however, learn to respect and understand your limitations and potentials. And your achievements are acknowledged by a ranking system, which serves as a measuring device for your progress."

The martial arts are essentially about discipline, but they also seek to make an individual's instincts work to their fullest to protect him. For the master, this process allows him to deal effectively and in the most natural way possible with any pressures from the world around him. At the center of the fighting arts is the Japanese concept of *suki*, which means

Above: The practitioner of *kendō* wears a mask to protect his face from the blows of bamboo swords.

Right: Waseda University *karate* students assume a fighting stance during a practice session.

an unguarded point, an opening, or an opportunity to attack. People with a lot of *suki* can be vulnerable to accidents and often, by their demeanor or bearing, even invite attack. The martial arts seek to purge all *suki* from body and soul—and when needed, to allow one to take advantage of an opponent's personal supply. It's no surprise the martial arts were practiced and perfected by the samurai; for the professional warrior, these techniques could mean the difference between life and death.

As with most strains of philosophy, study of the martial arts can last a lifetime. Achieving sufficient strength and technique to protect oneself is the first step, but the master also reaches *haragei*, which translates as "belly art"—a centralization of the spirit in the lower abdomen. It is this that facilitates effortless control and tranquillity. With mind and soul in harmony, the artist can call upon his formidable inner strength, a lasting commodity that has little to do with muscular skill.

Though the spiritual goals of martial artists are much the same, actual techniques vary

MARTIAL ARTS STYLES / BY BONNIE YOUNG

■

It must be kept in mind that while these are the major styles of Japanese weaponless martial arts today, there are differences in each style from school to school and master to master. If one is seriously contemplating studying a martial art, careful consideration should be given to the initial choice of a school. It is important to observe classes firsthand, and to look at a few schools and watch the instructors to find the one best suited to one's needs.

■

AIKIDŌ means "the way to meet the spirit." It is a practice based on the concept of natural rhythm: flowing and yielding. It emphasizes being so in tune with your opponent as to sense his intentions and use his own force to defeat him. The physical techniques emphasize throwing and grappling.

GO-JU RYŪ or Hard-Soft Style karate, was founded by Chojun Miyaki. Go-ju integrates soft, circular-motion Chinese techniques with the harder Okinawan style, combining fast and slow movements, tension and relaxation. Emphasis is on body conditioning and breath control. It is a strong fighting style.

ISSHIN-RYŪ karate is derived from many of the basic styles of Okinawan karate, and was founded by Tatsuo Shimabuku after World War II. Isshin-Ryū is popular in the United States.

JŪDŌ is a synthesis of armed and unarmed Jūjitsu fighting techniques. It emphasizes throwing and grappling, and is popular as a sport.

KYOKUSHINKAI, meaning "ultimate truth," karate was founded by Mas Oyama. Kyokushinkai combines several systems of karate using full-power fighting techniques; competition employs full contact with emphasis on "one punch, one kick" to determine victory. Tameshiwari (breaking of objects) is practiced to test strength and skill.

SEIDŌ karate, meaning "sincere way," was founded by Tadashi Nakamura in 1968 when he broke away from Mas Oyama and the Kyokushinkai organization. Seidō karate utilizes hard and soft techniques, with *kata*, (complex formal exercises), *kumite* (free fighting), deep breathing, and zen meditation practice all being integral aspects of the training.

SHITO-RYŪ karate was developed in 1928 by Kenwa Mabuni. Shito-Ryū derives from Shotokan but follows more closely the traditional Okinawan style of strong, simple movements. This traditional combat approach has limited the growth of Shito-Ryū outside of Japan.

SHOTOKAN karate started when Gichin Funakoshi, an Okinawan school teacher brought the martial art of karate to Japan for the first time. Shotokan emphasizes close-range fighting, low stances, and powerful techniques. Funakoshi introduced more flexible stances and kicks to the Okinawan style. Shotokan is a power style well suited to competition. In 1957 the Shotokan school founded the Japan Karate Association to promote karate through competition. The emphasis on the sporting aspects of karate led to a rift in the Shotokan organization. In 1956, a separate school called Shotokai broke from Shotokan to preserve the true *budō* nature of karate. Shotokai karate employs more flexible techniques with strong emphasis on each movement of *kata*. Competition is not promoted. Shotokan Karate International (SKI) was founded by Hirokasu Kanazawa. SKI parted with the Shotokan organization as the parent organization placed greater emphasis on karate as a sport. SKI permits competition, but the emphasis is on the traditional practice of karate as a martial art.

WADO-RYŪ, or "way of peace," was founded by Hironori Otsuka in 1939. Wado karate uses many snapping techniques which depend upon speed for their power. *Kata* training is emphasized, as well as *kumite*.

dramatically. *Kendo* (the way of the sword), *karatedō* (the way of the empty hand) and *jūdō* (the gentle way) all differ in skill, training, and athletic content. Other strains include *kyūdō* (archery), *jodō* (stick fighting), *jūkendo* (bayonet fighting), and *aikidō*. Within each type of fighting, numerous schools exist, each with a more or less distinct training philosophy. There are, for example, hundreds of separate styles of karate taught in Japan. Still, some styles—especially of karate—are very eclectic, including elements of many of the fighting arts in their programs.

The list of martial arts is still growing, with new strains added from time to time. Among recent additions is *shintaido*, which means "new body way." A technique that uses dance to bring mind and body together, it was begun in the early 1970s by Hiroyuki Oaki, a former *karatedō* instructor.

Despite deep roots in Japan's history, the martial arts withered briefly during the Meiji period (1868–1912), when modern day Western weapons were introduced to Japan. Today Tokyo is home to more international martial arts headquarters than any city, though these twentieth-century martial arts are flourishing predominantly as sports. Yet for many Japanese, the arts are also a cherished link with the nation's samurai past. Yasuhiro Yamashita, one of Japan's most skilled *jūdō* champions, is far from rare when he explains that he approaches each tournament in the spirit of the samurai: "I always take a bath, and I try to keep my surroundings neat so I won't be ashamed even if I die during the competition," he has said. He plays martial songs to stir his soul. The spiritual side is prominent, too. "The pressure before tournaments is so strong I like to ask for the help of *kami* (the gods)," he concludes.

A female *judōka* (*judō* practitioner) throws her male opponent, who demonstrates the correct way to take a fall. A martial art that has become an international sport, *judō* is practiced by both sexes and all ages.

11 • RELIGION

FESTIVALS

Yanagida Kunio (1875–1962), the near-legendary founder of Japanese folklore studies, described *matsuri* (festivals) as the gateway to Japanese culture. Striking for their frequency and variety, *matsuri* are held in Shinto shrines, large or small. Through them, many indigenous traditions are kept alive in this age of robotics.

Whether they celebrate the founding of a community or a historic happening, the focus of the *matsuri* is prayers or offerings of thanks to the *kami*. *Kami* is an all-embracing and indefinable word that designates anything possessed of an otherworldly, numinous aura—a deified government official, an ancestor, even the forces of nature. According to Japanese mythology, there are eight million *kami:* Japan is almost as densely populated by divine beings as by mortals.

Not surprising in a country where rice was traditionally the measure of life, *matsuri* are most common in the spring rice planting season and following the harvest in the fall. To ensure the *kami's* favor at these crucial times, rice, *sake,* and other delicacies are offered to them. At the Ise Shrines, dedicated to Amaterasu Omikami, the ancestress of the imperial family, and Toyouke no Mikoto, the foremost rice god, paddies are set apart for the cultivation of rice exclusively for their delectation.

But the *matsuri* does not involve only such solemn rituals; it is also a joyous celebration of life expressed in dancing, singing, dramatic performances, horse racing, and Sumo wrestling matches. Racing may be the sport of kings in the West; in Japan, it is the sport of

the gods: their will determines the winner. A race between two horses down a long straight track before the Kamigamo Shrine in Kyoto is the highlight of its annual *matsuri.* Although today Sumo is more often held in sports arenas than on shrine compounds, its Shinto origins are in evidence: The referees are shrine priests who instantly stop the match at the slightest nosebleed because blood, a form of pollution, is taboo in or around shrines.

Many *matsuri* include a procession around the whole area considered to be under the *kami's* protection. During this event, the *kami* (one or more), embodied in a sacred emblem such as a mirror, is borne in a special palanquin or *mikoshi* by parishioners. Local youths, stripped to loincloths, may, in a kind of rite of passage, be selected to carry it. Often the procession is held under cover of darkness down a steep mountainside, and there is the thrill of danger and bravery inherent in rites of passage the world over.

Most spectacular of all *matsuri* are those celebrated during the summer. Originally such *natsu matsuri* were intended to prevent epidemics, posing a threat to both man and crop, caused by the proliferation of insects during Japan's long rainy season. The ceremonies are often held at night, and the participants, carrying huge pine torches, wind about the city streets or rice paddies calling on the *kami* for protection. The torches do not simply light the way; their fire is believed to have the power to destroy evil and to purify.

Originating over a thousand years ago, the Gion Matsuri is the most famous of the sum-

mer festivals. Held between the seventeenth and twenty-fourth of July at Kyoto's Yasaka Shrine, it reaches a climax in a pageant of floats, some up to twenty-four meters high and weighing as much as twelve tons. Decorated with dolls, statues, spears, and other symbols of the *kami,* with lighted paper lanterns, and in one instance, with a seventeenth-century French tapestry, these floats on great wooden wheels are drawn through the streets of Kyoto, dazzling all who see them. Rooted in ancient beliefs and practices whose significance is long forgotten, such *matsuri* continue to foster a sense of community and continuity with Japan's long and rich religious heritage.

Left: These views of massive illuminated floats all come from the Nebuta Matsuri in the city of Hirosaki. Japanese festivals range from local shrine observances to ancient national rites like New Year's Day and Obon (the Buddhist All Souls' Day).

Right: When the city of Kyōto was delivered from a plague centuries ago, the Gion festival was born as an expression of gratitude. The towering portable shrine floats that make their way through the streets are accompanied by music and fan-waving.

RITUALS

Thirty-two days after the birth of a boy and thirty-three after the birth of a girl, the newborn is carried to the local shrine to be introduced to the *kami.* Called the *hatsu miya mairi,* this visit signals the child's recognition as a shrine parishioner or *ujiko*—and so the child becomes a member of society. No matter where he lives, he always remains a parishioner of the shrine where he made his *hatsu miya mairi.* It is but the first of a long parade of rituals marking the mortal cycle.

Subsequent visits to the shrine may not occur until the ages of three, five, and seven *(shichi go san).* Worship of the *kami* does not involve attendance at weekly services, much less any form of religious education. November 15 is the day set apart for the children's *shichi go san,* a gala event. Girls decked in brightly patterned *kimono* and boys in the traditional *hakama,* a kind of split skirt, are taken to the shrine to seek the gods' protection for the coming years. Standing before the entrance to the sanctuary (which only priests may enter) the children dutifully ring a giant bell, clap their hands to make the gods aware of their presence, and intone a brief prayer before returning home to festivities.

Until modern times, shrines were also the sites of elaborate individual coming-of-age rites, held between thirteen and eighteen for a boy, and at first menstruation for a girl. On this occasion, boys were given the clothes of manhood *(gempuku)* and girls an underskirt *(koshimaki).* But Japan has entered an era of mass production and secularization: today the coming of age is signaled by a civil ceremony held every January fifteenth for all who will become twenty in the calendar year. They are legally recognized as adults and can marry with or without parental consent.

Wearing cotton summer kimono, young women light incense sticks among family graves during the *obon* (All-Souls') festival in mid-July.

More often than not, marriage takes place with parental consent, following a lengthy matchmaking process so hedged in by rules and traditions that it has become a ritual in its own right. This so-called *omiai* seeks to match future partners on the basis of social standing, education, interests, age, and compatible horoscope readings. Love is irrelevant. Women born under the sign of fire in the year of the horse, according to the Chinese sexagenary cycle, are marked for life: Thought to be fiery tempered, they often remain spinsters.

If matters involving birth, coming of age, and marriage are entrusted to the *kami*, those of the world beyond are the responsibility of Buddhist deities. A Japanese asked his religious affiliation is tongue-tied: the exclusiveness of Western religions has never been a part of the Japanese mentality. Shinto, Buddhism, Taoism, and Confucianism have mingled to such a degree that it is impossible to draw lines between them. Funerals, however, are invariably held in Buddhist temples. Through Buddhist influence also, cremation has been practiced in Japan since the sixth century.

Stone pillars, circling Buddhist temples, incised with the names of the donors signal their association. For a price, one can install a marker at the temple of one's choice. The environs of certain temples, such as Kongobuji on Mount Koya, founded by Kobo Daishi (774–835), one of Japan's great holy men, are in great demand. According to tradition, Kobo Daishi himself has sat for over a thousand years deep in a trance within a grotto on Mount Koya, awaiting the coming of Miroku (the Buddha of the Future). When Miroku descends to earth, Kobo Daishi and all those around him will be among the fortunate few to hear the Buddha preach and so will attain salvation.

A solemn three-year-old and his five-year-old sister pose on the steps of a shrine for their official *shichi go san* festival portrait.

In the past twenty years, *zazen* (seated meditation) has become familiar to many Westerners through the writings of Daisetsu Suzuki and the Zen centers of California and New England. Many university and college campuses now offer weekly *zazen* sessions for students. In Japan, the value of meditation has been recognized since the introduction of Buddhism in the sixth century.

Meditation exemplifies Buddhism's original emphasis on individual salvation, an emphasis not shared by the indigenous Shinto tradition, in which community welfare comes first and foremost. Sakyamuni, the father of Buddhism, gained salvation by meditating on the Four Noble Truths: all life is sorrowful, sorrow comes from craving, sorrow ceases when one gives up craving, and this end can be achieved by mental and physical discipline. Members of Japan's multitudinous Buddhist sects, both monks and laypeople, continue this practice to achieve the same goal, or perhaps simply to realize peace of mind and respite from the worries of the workplace.

For Zen adepts, *zazen* in its purest form is just sitting, giving up all thoughts without becoming trapped in a conscious process of no thinking. The blows of the *keisaku*, a stick used to bring the drowsy practitioner to attention, may be the only interruption during the long meditation session. *Zazen* is as much a physical as a mental discipline. According to legend, Bodhidharma, the founder of the Zen sect, meditated for nine years facing the wall of a cave until his legs rotted off. (This provided the source of inspiration for the pot-bellied legless Daruma dolls seen throughout Japan.) Sometimes the adept is instructed to ponder over a *koan*, a kind of riddle for which there is no intellectual solution, only an intuitive one that may come after prolonged meditation. This is undoubtedly what the eccentric Zen monk-painter Sengai had in mind when he inscribed a painting of a bullfrog as follows:

"Zazen to shite hito ka hotoke ni naru narawa....."
If a man becomes a Buddha just by practicing *zazen*....."
(Then could the bullfrog who always sits in meditation have gained enlightenment already?)

Meditation can be practiced anywhere, and not necessarily while seated. The monks of Shokokuji, a vast Zen temple in Kyoto, are instructed to meditate on a given topic while sweeping the great gravel walkways of the temple compound. The thirteenth-century monk Myoe Shonin meditated in the crook of a pine tree atop Mount Takao, a place then much appreciated by reclusive monks. Certain monks meditate on the same mountain, while standing under an icy waterfall.

Meditation and seclusion often go hand in hand. Many of Japan's great holy men are said to have acquired supernatural powers by leading a life of asceticism and meditation in remote mountain recesses. Sacred mountains such as Yoshino, Kimpu, and Omine—sacred because the *kami* are believed to reside there—have long been regarded as especially propitious sites for such practices. The traditional veneration of individuals who have withstood the rigors of such a life still follows members of the Shugendo movement. Although not as influential as it once was, this blend of Buddhism, Shinto, Taoism, and shamanism still has many adherents in rural Japan. Called *yamabushi* (priests who lie down in the mountains), they make pilgrimages, singly or in groups, to the ancient holy spots, there to meditate and perform secret rituals from which women are barred. (In fact, until recently women were prohibited from climbing many of Japan's holy mountains for fear of pollution.) The rigorous life of the *yamabushi* is believed to cleanse both mind and body and so to enable him to achieve spiritual illumination.

But such practices are not for eveyone; they are simply too demanding. Far more popular, especially among women, is the chanting of the name of the Buddha Amida, the master of the Western Paradise where all hope to be reborn after death. Faith in Amida, symbolized by the invocation of the phrase *Namu Amida-butsu* is all that is required to achieve this goal. The vast gulf that separates the practice of calling Amida's name from the more strenuous ones described above is summarized by the terms *jiriki* and *tariki*, "self power" and "other power." Though radically different, these two approaches toward salvation have coexisted in Japan for over a thousand years.

Above: Under the eyes of a superior with a *keisaku*—a stick to surprise the drowsy—monks practice *zazen* meditation. Meditation is combined with early rising, little sleep, and hard daily work in the regimen of Zen monasteries.

Left: One of the more spectacular austerities practiced by Buddhist monks on Mount Takao, near Tokyo, is early springtime immersion in an icy waterfall.

Right: A woman undergoes the water purification that is also pictured on the facing page. Unlike Shintō water, which ritually cleanses the body, the icy chill of this Buddhist austerity is meant to freshen and purify the mind as it strengthens the will. The boy in the foreground of this woodblock print is a Buddhist

TALISMANS

Taxi drivers attach them with suction cups to the windshields of their Toyotas; children tie them to their bookbags alongside their train or bus passes; shopkeepers install them in the entryways to their establishments. Inscribed with the characters *kotsu anzen* (traffic safety), *gakugyo seikyo* (success in schoolwork), or *josai shofuku* (dispel misfortune, welcome good luck), all are forms of *omamori*, protective talismans dispensed by temples and shrines throughout Japan. The income from such sales, hardly insignificant, helps to support these religious institutions, which receive little or no government aid since the separation of church and state was instituted after World War II.

Omamori come in many shapes, sizes, and materials. Those made of paper, wood, or fabric are most common, but plastic is fast replacing these traditional materials. Some are little more than pieces of folded paper inscribed with the name of a deity or a Buddhist mantra. According to ancient belief, great spiritual power resides in words—beautiful ones can bring about good, ugly ones can cause evil. Others are wooden slips or plaques whose power derives from physical association with a shrine. Ise, the most highly venerated shrine in the nation, is rebuilt every twenty years, and the wood from the old structure is used, among other things, for *omamori*. Most common, however, are the little brocade bags bearing the name of the shrine or temple where they were made and a suitable prayer. These are purchased by the hundreds by Japanese school children as souvenirs of their annual class excursion.

Omamori are a form of preventive medicine,

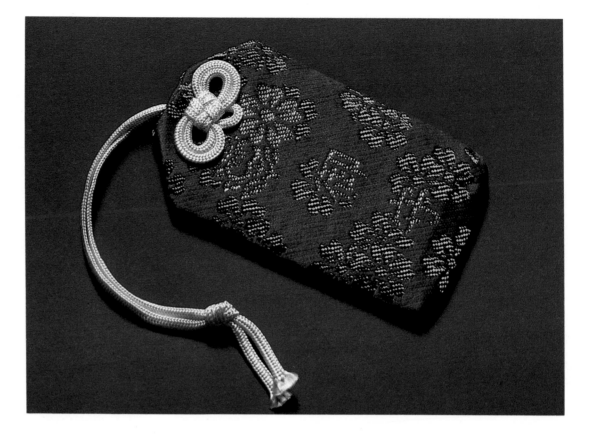

ema a remedy. The word *ema* literally means horse picture: in ancient times it was customary to present shrines with a black horse when petitioning the *kami* for rain and a white one for clement weather. In time the living animal was replaced by a wooden plaque with a picture of one, and individuals dedicated them when petitioning the *kami* for anything—from a cure for compulsive gambling (a widespread problem among both men and women), to a girlfriend's fidelity. The subjects depicted on *ema* have expanded accordingly. A picture of an octopus, believed to be the messenger of Yakushi, the Buddha of Healing, figures on *ema* with prayers for recovery from a variety of ailments. A kneeling woman with milk flowing profusely from her breasts is another common theme, giving explicit expression to a mother's desire for abundant milk. Fear of upcoming

exams motivates many young students to leave plaques with their likenesses at the shrine of Kitano Tenjin, the patron saint of literature.

Ema are sold primarily by shrines, and those available today are mass produced for popular consumption. Having inscribed his name, the date, and a prayer, the petitioner hangs his *ema* on a special rack before the sanctuary, or in a covered hall or *emado* provided for this purpose. Because space is at a premium, *ema* are periodically removed to make room for new ones. In recent years, with the increasing interest in folk art, many old *ema*, which may be as much as several square feet in size, have found their way into museums in Japan and abroad. The Peabody Museum in Salem, Massachusetts, for example, has an exceptionally fine collection.

Left: The most common type of *omamori,* sold in a temple or shrine, is a small brocade bag on a cord. The talismans, which come in many forms, are purchased to help insure traffic safety, success in school examinations, and general good luck.

Above: Thick, twisted straw rope *(shimenawa)* is used to mark off sacred space in Shintō. Attached to a building or *torii,* it indicates a festive occasion.

Above: This cheerful chaos of cheap decorations welcomes the New Year. Traditional symbols like the face of Daikoku (god of wealth) are mingled with lucky dice, *shogi* (Japanese chess) pieces, and flags.

Left: Ema come in all shapes and sizes, but the most common are mass-produced wooden boards with a slight peak on the upper edge. Dedicated at a shrine, the *ema* bear petitions of all sorts. On the plaque at the upper right corner of the photo, Kiyomizu Mitsuru invokes the god's aid to help some college friends find mates.

12 · THEATER

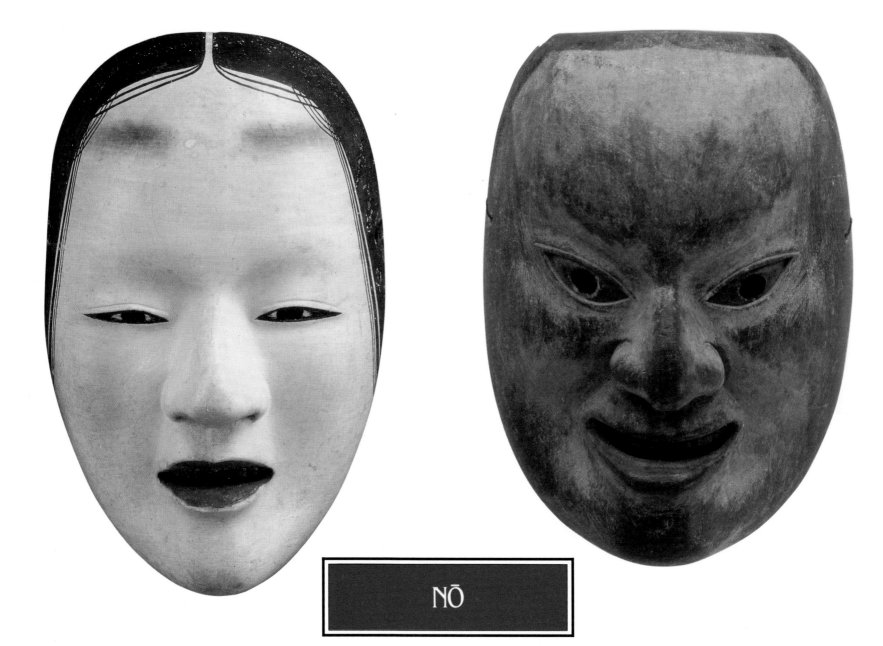

NŌ

It isn't easy to picture turbulent temple festivals, with jugglers and performing animals or boisterous harvest-time music-making in the paddy mud when we watch a performance by one of today's five major schools of Nō, Japan's aristocratic theater. What we see and hear is a spectacle that combines brilliant color and costume, droning chant, and an otherworldy slowness of pace. In a culture that has produced masterpieces of both understatement and overstatement, the Nō is the flower of the former attitude.

Nevertheless, the esthetic of restraint that typified the Nō after its patronage by the fourteenth- and fifteenth-century military nobility is only one element in a composite form that, like the motion picture five hundred years later, sums up the whole artistic and popular culture of its time and place.

Kanze Kan'ami and his son Zeami were the alchemists who completed the blending of the

Above: This festival dancer in a demon mask is keeping alive traditions of public dance and music-making which, in medieval days, contributed to the birth of the Nō. A few pieces of the Nō repertoire, such as the dance-drama *Okina*, retain a folkloric dimension that predates the literarization of Nō.

Far left: The *waki-onna* Nō mask, the idealized face of a classical court lady, allowed sculptors to achieve some of their finest effects. The expression changes subtly as the actor moves his head. The *waka-otoko* (young man) mask at left displays a vigor that links it with the masks of *gigaku,* one of the many medieval performance arts that contributed to Nō.

disparate elements: *sarugaku,* a lively vaudeville with Chinese roots, which could include diabolo-tossing and wrestling as well as protothetrical burlesque and mime; *dengaku,* a general term for temple and shrine plays in the countryside; the *kouta* (popular song), a sort of ancient blues, and many other things. By Kan'ami and Zeami's time, both *dengaku* and *sarugaku* had reached a high level of professionalism. It remained for the father and son to turn these diversions into high art.

Kan'ami's central contribution was making a lively narrative song and dance (the *kusemai*) the focus of the Nō performance. Zeami was a consummate esthetician, equally interested in powerful mimetic acting *(monomane)* and an overall mood of mysterious profundity *(yūgen).* As Matsuo Bashō took a diverting, frivolous subgenre of poetry and crafted the *hokku* as we think of it, Zeami's insistence on the seriousness of this "higher vaudeville," and his interest in classical literature, placed Nō securely within high culture.

Nō is essential theater, in that it unfolds between two figures mainly, the protagonist *(shite)* and deuteragonist *(waki).* It is also a poem of unveiling, of revelation. The essential dramatic business of a Nō play is not a conflict resolved, but the revealing of the true identity of the *shite.* Encountered by the *waki,* the *shite* first appears as an insignificant person, perhaps a temple attendant or a nondescript old woman. The *shite* reappears transformed, and in dancing the crucial *kusemai,* relives his or her former life, and especially the pivotal moment when the *shite's* karma is determined. For the *shite* is really a spirit, a happy or hungry ghost. In the happy, felicitous plays, the *shite's* self-revelation hallows the place, and the *waki* continues his journey in joy. If the protagonist is a defeated warrior or a spurned court lady, doomed to endless remorse, then the *waki* (who is typically a traveling priest) vows to pray for the release of the

BEST TEN NŌ PLAYS

■

ATAKA Flight and loyalty. Adapted as the Kabuki play *Kanjinchō.*

SANEMORI Death of an old warrior.

KAYOI KOMACHI (Wandering Komachi). Loves of Japan's greatest poetess.

TAKASAGO Felicitous dance-play about married love.

HAGOROMO (Robe of Feathers). A timeless folktale.

AOI NO UE (The Lady Aoi). An episode from *The Tale of Genji.*

SUMA GENJI (Genji at Suma). The hero in exile.

KAGEKIYO The failed hero.

KINUTA (The Filling-Block). The sorrows of parting.

NISHIKIGI (Brocade Wand). A marriage after death.

shite's soul into the Western Paradise of the Buddha Amida.

The magnificent Nō masks, worn by the *shite* in his two manifestations, are great works of Japanese sculpture in their own right, vigorous but human, no matter how "possessed" or otherwise demonized the visage may be. The slow steps of the *shite,* in his brilliant costume and enigmatic mask, moving to the burden of the chorus chant and the vivid punctuation of drum and flute, induce in the theatergoer a mesmerized attention that is very much a journey into another world. The Nō enthralls because it goes beyond *imitating* the spirit world: its stagecraft actually casts a spell. And "spell" is one of the more interesting translations of the word "play."

KABUKI

When a brilliant merchant culture arose in Osaka and Edo (Tokyo) after the unification of the country in 1600, the center of Japanese cultural gravity shifted from the military elite (who were the patrons of the slow, exquisitely understated Nō theater) to the mercantile downtowns of Japan's great cities. People there wanted a theater that excited, not an art of mysterious reticence. They patronized the puppet theater, with its contemporary emphasis, but the time was also ripe for an actor's art so that highlighting the human body could turn into memorable theater.

Kabuki arose as if to meet this need. Like all of Japan's theater arts, it began in the milieu of shrine and temple entertainment. To be more precise, an enterprising young woman by the name of Okuni, a priestess of the Izumo Shinto shrine at Kyoto, began doing a provocative song-and-dance act in the dry riverbed of the Kamo River. She mimed a drunken male pleasure-seeker, a slumming samurai, and even a Portuguese priest with cross and rosary. And she displayed her own charms. No wonder people dubbed this new thing Kabuki, from a verb that means to carry on in an eccentric, provocative, yet stylish way. Contemporary black English translates it perfectly: "to get freaky."

The national administration, careful to control sexual energy lest it end up as political insurgency, banned Okuni's "woman Kabuki," which was, admittedly, mostly a sexual advertising service for the women involved. "Young men's Kabuki," which followed, emphasized other tastes. "Men's Kabuki" was the last form this theater took, and it has remained a male monopoly, with women being portrayed by

One of the most remarkable resources of the Kabuki is the stage itself. An indoor stage built on the scale of an outdoor one, the Kabuki performance space demands color, spectacle, and outsize gesture if the actors are not to appear dwarfed and insignificant. Kabuki stagecraft developed in spectacular directions as well; the revolving stage of the eighteenth-century Japanese playhouses became a permanent feature of theaters in the West.

preternaturally skilled female impersonators *(onnagata)*. Inadvertently, the old sex laws helped heighten the stylization of Kabuki and raise its dignity as a theater art. By the early twentieth century, the *onnagata* were the greatest and most dignified virtuosos of all, and it was a while before even the modern theater and the movies gave up female impersonators.

After about 1750, Kabuki began to overshadow the puppet theater. And why not? Here was a theater that was full of life. The Nō, with its bare cedar-wood stage, suggests scenery and properties, when it has to, in the extreme abstract. A boat is a cloth-covered circle of rope. And *Nō* music is an astringent combination of three drums, a single flute, and chorus. When the black, brown, and green Kabuki curtain is rolled away, however, you might see a grand panorama of downtown Edo, painted with the exaggerated vanishing-point perspective that "Dutch" art studies brought to Japan. A scene change will be accomplished by a grand swing of the revolving stage, bringing another bright, detailed, and oversize set into view. The music is a dense texture of *shamisen*, enriched by a huge battery of offstage percussion.

Yet it is with the arrival of a star actor upon the *hanamichi* (the main runway that runs from the rear of the theater to the stage) that Kabuki comes into its glory. Stopping at the "seven-three" point (three-tenths of the distance from the stage), the actor turns to face the audience and strikes a pose. The house erupts with shouts, and for an instant the Japanese theater sounds like a stadium.

The play that ensues will be either a *jidaimono* (historical play) or *sewamono* ("talk-of-the-town" or contemporary life play). In the former, the *aragoto* or "rough-stuff" performance style will dominate. *Aragoto* heroes made up in brilliant red and white, traditionally popular in the rawer, newer city of Edo, perform

BEST TEN KABUKI PLAYS

■

NARUKAMI (The Thunderer). Boisterous, folkloric dance piece.

SUKEROKU The pinnacle of urban machismo and style.

SHIBARAKU (Wait a Minute!). The favorite *aragoto* (rough-stuff) play.

KANJINCHŌ (The Subscription List). The Nō play *Ataka* in Kabuki guise.

SUGAWARA DENJU TENARAI KAGAMI (The Sugawara Teachings: Mirror for Training the Hand). Immense play about Japan's greatest calligrapher and his exile.

MUSUME DŌJŌJI (Woman of the Dōjō Temple). Dance of demonic transformation.

YOTSUYA KAIDAN (Yotsuya Ghost Stories). Immortal tales.

BENTEN KOZŌ (Benten the Thief) by Mokuami. Lowlife play by the last great Kabuki playwright.

IZAYOI SEISHIN (Izayoi and Seishin) by Mokuami. A nineteenth-century love story.

NEZUMI YOZŌ (The Rat Boy) by Mokuami. A domestic tragedy.

bravura feats of choreographed violence. The gentler *wagoto* (peaceful business) style dominates the domestic dramas that Osaka playwrights contributed. These include a generous number of adaptations from the great puppet playwright Chikamatsu. Kabuki also adapts Nō plays, and a comparison of the two treatments of the same material is a fascinating theatergoing experience.

Whatever the genre, however, Kabuki is an actor's theater first and foremost. Modern productions under the auspices of the Shōchiku entertainment empire are often mere collages of the histrionic highlights of long plays, series of set pieces for actor-heroes.

Although Kabuki-trained actors have been prominent in Japan's various modern theater forms, modern playwrights and directors found this more a curse than a blessing, and labored to free their new art from the influence of what once had been a vibrant avant garde.

For dance plays and pieces adapted from the puppet theater, a full musical ensemble and a group of chanters perform onstage, and offstage percussion is also employed. This is a familiar piece from the dance repertoire, called *Renjishi*, in which a pair of lions are beset by playful butterflies (at left).

For the Westerner, the essence of the Bunraku has always been its miraculous puppets. Half human size, dressed and coiffed as meticulously and colorfully as human actors, and manipulated by three men (one for the body and right hand, another for the left hand alone, a third for the feet), men whose coordination and subtlety of control are little short of magical, these cloth and wood creatures seem to think, to feel, to live, perhaps more intensely than you and I.

Still, the real heart of the "doll theater" is elsewhere: It, or rather he, sits to the audience's right, his mobile face contorted with shifting emotions—pain, grief, fear, tense nobility. His voice, vocal cords tensed, shifts from a resonant chant to the falsetto notes of stage femininity, to rough masculine growls. The *shamisen* player who sits next to him punctuates the flow of his voice with the instrument's special combination of near-vocal and percussive sounds. This is the *gidayū* chanter, the man in charge of the text, the one who plays all the roles, delivers all the narration, and unifies the performance.

In its essence, Bunraku is a literary and vocal genre supplied with magnificent "illustrations." The *gidayū* chanter is the descendant of the blind monks who sang the epics of medieval Japan, and his art is perhaps the noblest living example of Japan's many traditional arts of storytelling.

Indeed, Japan's greatest dramatist, Chikamatsu Monzaemon, was drawn to the doll theater precisely because of its verbal integrity; unlike the Kabuki, where the actor always ruled and texts were sometimes crudely carpentered together or freely altered, the doll plays enshrined the text as written and allowed Chikamatsu to develop a textual art to match the virtuosity of the master of *gidayū*.

Although he also proved himself a master of the sort of bombastic historical drama—complete with wild animals and other special

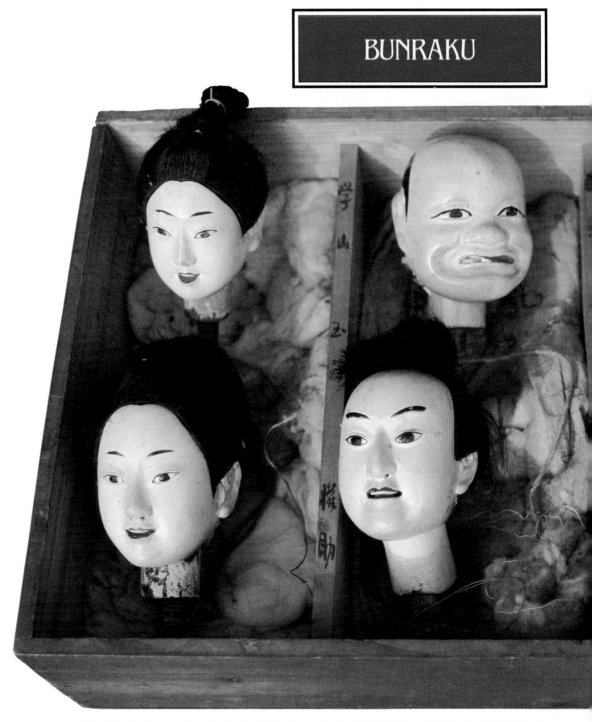

BUNRAKU

Bunraku puppet heads lie in a box, ready to be attached to bodies and make their entrances. As the puppet theater grew in popularity, the puppets grew in size and complexity. The three-man puppet was introduced in 1724, and the designers of heads developed movable eyebrows and jaws (see head at bottom left.)

BEST TEN PUPPET PLAYS

■

KOKUSENYA KASSEN (Battles of Coxinga) by Chikamatsu. Adventures of a Sino-Japanese pirate hero.

SONEZAKI SHINJŪ (Love Suicide at Sonezaki) by Chikamatsu. The first great love-suicide play.

SHINJŪ TEN NO AMIJIMA (Amijima Love Suicides) by Chikamatsu. The author's greatest play.

SHUSSE KAGEKIYO (Kagekiyo Victorious) by Chikamatsu. A dark melodrama. (See Nō play *Kagekiyo*.)

ONNAGOROSHI ABURA JIGOKU (The Woman Killer: Hell of Oil) by Chikamatsu. The great playwright's only murder mystery.

KANADEHON CHŪSHINGURA (Alphabet Book: Storehouse of Loyalty). The revenge drama about the 47 Rōnin.

HADESUGATA ONNA MAIGINU (Dancing Robe of the Woman of Fashion). A later love-suicide play, composed collectively.

SHINREI YAGUCHI NO WATASHI (Miracle at Yaguchi Ferry) by Hiraga Gennai. Historical drama by a great scholar.

IMOSEYAMA ONNA TEIKIN (Household Teachings for Women at Imo and Se Mountains) by Chikamatsu Hanji.

ICHINOTANI FUTABA GUNKI (War Chronicle of Young Sprouts at Ichinotani). Classical battles and dazzling language tricks.

effects—that puppets can bring off so well, we remember Chikamatsu today mainly for his *sewamono* (talk-of-the-town plays), melodramas of love and duty among Osaka's merchant class. These plays, often based on current news, represent the first attempt in Japanese literature to invest the lives of Japan's economically powerful but politically powerless middle class with the heroic dignity the medieval war tales had reserved for the bearers of swords.

If the noble warrior was all duty, then the ordinary pleasure-loving Osaka urbanite could typify the struggle, rife with dramatic potential, between duty (to family, boss, friends) and the lawless joys of the licensed brothel quarter. Chikamatsu's plots almost always resolved this struggle in a spirit of "all for love: or, the world well lost"; the handsome retail shop employee finally elopes adulterously with his courtesan lover. The price of love's victory is, of course, death, in the form of a double suicide and prayers for rebirth together on the same lotus in Paradise.

In Chikamatsu's day, the puppets were not nearly so remarkable as they are today. They were simple affairs operated by one puppeteer apiece, and the manipulators remained out of sight.

Clearly, the chanter's art stood out even more than it does today. In 1724, however, the puppeteer Yoshida Bunzaburō stood up for his craft by developing the three-man puppet, operated with all three humans in plain view. It was a good move, one that ushered in two decades of phenomenal popularity for the doll theater. The Kabuki was hard put to compete, and had to wait until the second half of the eighteenth century for its heyday.

Today's government-subsidized Bunraku is a frozen form, redoing Chikamatsu classics and other plays of the best years. The chief puppeteer, who bears all of the forty-pound weight of the puppet, is regularly allowed the privilege of showing his naked face, while his assistants are veiled in black gauze.

Finally, in our day, the art of the puppet master announces itself coequal with that of the master of the text. The art may have stopped evolving, but it is still vital.

MODERN THEATER

Japan's first halting steps toward a modern theater were taken against the background of the turbulent politics of the Meiji period. The *sōshi shibai* (political-enthusiast plays) dramatized and popularized the struggle for a representative national assembly during the 1880s, establishing a strong tradition of political theater. Japan's smashing successes in the Sino-Japanese War made this genre nationalistic and warlike. The much greater sense of national and cultural self-confidence that followed Japan's victory over Russia in 1905 gave rise to *shimpa,* or "new school" drama, an updating of the Kabuki that featured works by new writers, translations of foreign plays, and a partial breakdown of the taboo against actresses.

Despite its forays into modernity, *shimpa* stagecraft and acting were close stepchildren of the Kabuki. When the great critic and theorist Tsubouchi Shōyō, a professor of English at Waseda University, decided to try to create a modern Japanese musical theater, he envisaged a dynamic blend of the values of Kabuki and the spirit of the new European stage, whose spokesmen were Ibsen and George Bernard Shaw. He was determined to learn and teach this new spirit in its own terms, and so he and his Waseda students bravely studied and rehearsed elocution, modern stage movement, and the plays of these modern masters. In 1911, the Waseda dramatic club had considerable success touring with plays like *John Gabriel Borkman, A Doll's House,* and *Julius Caesar.* (Shōyō's beautiful prose translations of Shakespeare were standard until after World War II.) Shōyō's ultimate goal, toward which his own distinguished plays were written, was

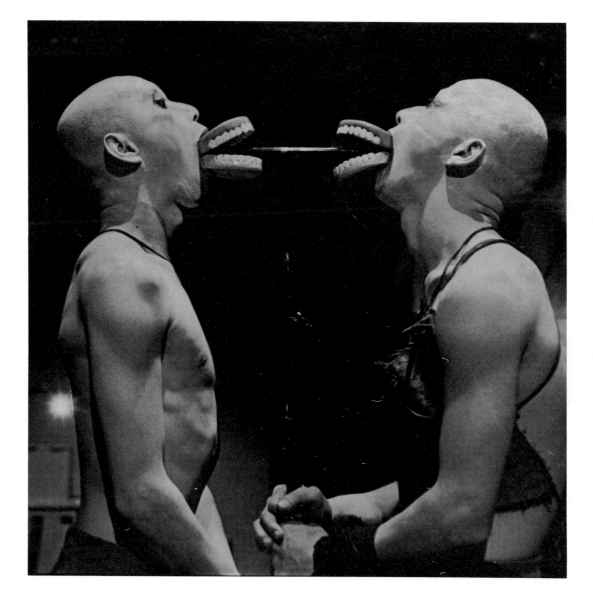

an Eastern-Western synthesis; his efforts were soon outdistanced, however, by more aggressively cosmopolitan efforts.

In 1909, Osanai Kaoru founded the Free Theater (Jiyū Gekijo) as a showcase for the determinedly modern views he held. A formidable authority on the latest European trends, Osanai had visited Russia, Scandinavia, Germany, France, and England in 1912–13, the magic years of European modernism. By the

A matched pair of bald-headed servants flash their teeth at one another in Terayama Shūji's theater piece *Nuhikun* (Instructions to Servants), from 1977. The late Terayama was a multitalented writer, filmmaker, essayist, and poet whose *Tenjosajiki* (Gallery) troupe gave Japanese avant-garde theater international exposure.

time he founded the Tsukiji Little Theater as a permanent home for the Free Theater troupe in 1924, he was a devotee of Stanislavsky and committed almost exclusively to producing European works in translation. Modern theater *(shingeki)* in the twenties had a body of sophisticated theorists, some excellent performing facilities, but undertrained actors, unreliable translations, and an orientation that discouraged young Japanese playwrights.

One place, however, where Japanese plays were in demand was on the political Left. Closely tied with labor unions, troupes like the Japan Labor Theater and the Zen'ei (Vanguard) troupe looked for stories of the Japanese proletariat to mount along with Soviet plays and the work of radicals like Upton Sinclair. This sophisticated updating of the *sōshi shibai* dominated the modern theater movement between 1925 and 1940, and although nonpolitical troupes like the Bungaku-za (Literary Theater) did distinguished work, the *shingeki* movement as a whole was so identified with political unorthodoxy that it nearly expired under wartime repression.

The freer postwar climate saw the revival of the Bungaku-za and the Haiyū-za (Actors' Theater), the latter led by Senda Koreya, Japan's most distinguished modern actor and a Brecht authority. Nineteen forty-seven, a banner year for postwar liberalization, marked the founding of the Mingei (Popular Arts) troupe, inheritor of a strong tradition of Russian-influenced Japanese humanism, and the Budō no Kai (Grapes Club), a showcase for the folklore-flavored work of the playwright Kinoshita Junji.

The real powerhouse of modern *shingeki*, however, appeared in the first postwar "boom" year, 1953. This troupe, Shiki (Four Seasons), has moved from Anouilh and Giraudoux to *Applause, Mame,* and *Jesus Christ Superstar,* achieving a popularity and profitability rivaling Japan's commercial industry of all-girl revues and other light entertainment.

All that Shiki stands for underwent a powerful challenge at the hands of experimental theater beginning in the mid-sixties. University troupes and other youthful conclaves revived the scandalous, carnival spirit and raw sexuality of early Kabuki, and wedded it with modern absurdism, Theater of Cruelty theory and the love of the perverse and grotesque one can find everywhere in the modern Japanese arts. Terayama Shūji's Gallery troupe and Kara Jurō's Situation Theater in its red tent explore modern avenues of expression from a position of romantic cultural nationalism, as they dig for Japanese roots that run deep into national psychology, normal and—especially—abnormal. These troupes have succeeded in putting modern Japanese theater into the international mainstream, confirming, in their raucous way, the wisdom of that careful nationalist, Tsubouchi Shōyō.

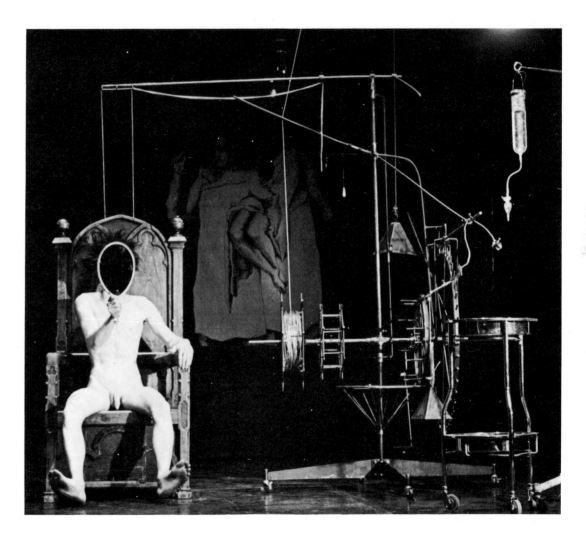

In the opening scene of *Nuhikun,* a naked man is approached by the "Saint-Master Machine," which gives him a wig and a mustache and makes him Master. Terayama's wild parable, loosely based on Jonathan Swift, follows the carryings-on of a group of servants who discover the symbols of mastership but who create Hell when they try to use them.

DANCE

Dance in all its forms flourishes in today's Japan. Eager mamas buy their little daughters pointe shoes and tutus so that the little ones can be stars in the gala ballet school recital. Earnest, respectful young ladies learn to handle fans and roll their heads in the best *Nihon buyō* (Japanese classical dance) manner. Other, but equally earnest, women study Graham and Cunningham modern dance technique for a sense of freedom and physical fitness. The dance pieces within Kabuki *(shosagoto)* are the most popular elements of the contemporatry commercial revival of Japan's spectacular middle-class theater. And throughout the country, in shrines, temples, department-store theaters, and on NHK public TV, the old dance forms survive.

Japanese dance has always been something like Japanese poetry—artful and tradition-bound to be sure, yet simple and spontaneous at the same time, a direct expression of powerful emotion and, in its refusal of the leaps and pirouettes of Western ballet, a celebration of the body's dependence upon the earth. The founding myth of dance in Japan is the story of Ama no Uzume (The Heavenly Startling Female), who did a startling dance upon an overturned washtub to lure the sulking Sun Goddess out of the Rock Cave of Heaven. When Uzume lifted her skirts, the hooting and whistling and laughter accomplished her purpose: A jealous Sun Goddess returned light and warmth to the world. Sacred Shinto music and dance has ever after preserved the spirit of Uzume's performance: It summons the gods to earth, where they caper and play with humans.

More sophisticated dances, called *bugaku,* arrived in the seventh and eighth centuries, when Japan was the easternmost outpost of a brilliant international Buddhist culture that reached all the way to Iran and Afghanistan. Korea and Central Asia contributed elegant line and circling dances *(mai)* that were adopted at court, and considerably influenced not only Shinto performance *(kagura)*, but popular dance as well. *Bugaku,* the official dance form of the imperial court, is still performed today. Along with the solemn music called *gagaku* that accompanies it, this constitutes the oldest continuous performance tradition in the world. By the late eleventh and twelfth centuries, Japanese dance was entering upon one of its most colorful and creative ages. Popular evangelical Buddhism encouraged public dancing, especially during the summer Obon festival. These ecstatic chant-dances forsook the sweeping lateral and circular movements of the *mai* in favor of jumping and stamping,and the other major pattern of dance movement, the *odori,* came into history.

In the fourteenth century, the great aristocratic dance-drama, the Nō, was born as a complex synthesis of courtly *mai,* clerical Bud-

Dancers with spears perform the Bugaku dance called *Embu.* Bugaku choreography is highly symmetrical, very slow, and nobly solemn, as befits the oldest continuous music and dance tradition in the world. The *gagaku* orchestra is at the rear.

The dance is *Bairo Hajinraku,* and the costumes are stylized versions of the clothing of eighth-century warriors on the Asian continent. Bugaku dances derive from Central Asian, Chinese, Korean, and native Japanese sources.

dhist dance, open-air vaudeville, folkdance, and the women's *kusemai,* in which the dancer told a tale as she danced and mimed. Patronized by wealthy military aristocrats, the Nō soon took on the characteristics they favored: refinement, suggestiveness, and classical culture.

But the sexual energy, the sense of fun, and the cheerful egalitarianism of the folkdance and the *Bon-odori* remained potent, and gave birth to the Kabuki. Significantly, Okuni of the Izumo Shrine, who ''invented'' the form, was a Shinto shrine dancer also skilled in the Buddhist open-air *odori.* As Kabuki matured, dance's position within it was strengthened and elaborated. The earliest Kabuki dance pieces were tours-de-force for female impersonators *(onnagata).* Dance was especially favored for creating an eerie mood for ghost scenes. As the narrative and mime element in dance (always important in Japan) grew stronger, however, challenging pieces for men developed, increasingly complex dance-plays were written, and dramatic dance scenes were inserted into nondance plays. Kabuki dance in the mid-nineteenth century was spectacular, dominated by the *hengemono,* one-man revues in which slick costume changes allowed an actor to adopt several roles.

Dance-plays, including adaptations from the Nō and Kyōgen (comic interludes between Nō plays), have come to be mainstays of Kabuki's continuing appeal. Kabuki dance also fathered what is called *Nihon buyō,* (Japanese classical dance), which despite its name is really a product of the twentieth century, a refined version of stage dance dominated by women teachers and students, although a number of contemporary Kabuki actors are also the heads of *buyō* schools. Together, Kabuki (on the stage) and *buyō* (in the performance hall, private home, or banquet room) gather in and sum up elements of every previous dance tradition in Japan—everything from the grace of the *mai* to the earthiness of the *odori.*

The *hohin* dancer's headgear—lacquered *kammuri* hats decorated with blossoms—bespeaks the Shintō origin of the dance.

13 · TRAVEL

CULTURAL TRAVEL

The Japanese have always been avid tourists. Possibly something in the tribal blood stirs them, for their long-ago ancestors voyaged—and perhaps beyond the distant shore they marched—from places far away to reach these islands.

The figure of the traveler excites the Japanese imagination: lonely perhaps, but free, as stay-at-homes are not. The poetry and prose of travel are important in the literary tradition. The travel diary is an honored mode of expression; an old family storehouse will likely yield a forebear's account of a journey. Almost invariably the journey is more important than the destination.

"If you love your son let him travel," says a Japanese proverb, and another follows like a corollary: "A traveler is without shame." The son—any traveler—may kick up his heels as he cannot do at home. But the license to misbehave is not generally considered a valid excuse for travel. A more plausible reason must be offered: religion, health, business, or a cultural pursuit in the nature of self-improvement. In the early centuries, when tribes were battling for supremacy, it was exploration and conquest that put men in motion.

Travel by boat came first, of course, but highways quickly became a concern. At first the aim was to connect the imperial capital, today's Kyoto, with distant provinces; later, to tie the rest of the country to the shogun's capital, Edo, which became Tokyo. Of the five great highways and several lesser ones, the most important during the long reign of the Tokugawa shoguns, 1603–1868, was the Tokaidō, the Eastern Sea Route that runs close to the Pacific coast; it linked Edo with Kyoto and,

by extension, Osaka, the commercial capital. The Tokaidō is still Japan's busiest corridor; along it are the nation's industrial heartland and almost half of its population. The old Tokaidō Road, immortalized in its latter days by the woodblock prints of Hiroshige, has been overlaid by wide concrete. The country's main trunk railroad was built near it, and now the Shinkansen (the bullet trains) and an express highway follow the same route. Almost nothing remains to suggest the old road, its picturesque stages, and its views.

But father inland was the Nakasendō or Kiso-Kaidō, the Central Mountain Road that

also linked Edo and Kyoto. Several miles of it still exist, and those seeking the flavor of the old highways can walk those stretches and can stay at the forty-third and forty-fourth of its sixty-nine post towns, Tsumago and Magome. When the central railroad was built these mountain villages were bypassed, which wreaked economic distress on them but saved them from the onslaughts of modernization and preserved the heritage that is now their asset. Both villages summon thoughts of Shimazaki Tōson, a literary giant of the late nineteenth and early twentieth centuries. Tōson was born and spent his boyhood in Ma-

Left: From the entrance of the inn named Matsushiro-ya, one can catch a glimpse of the old Nakasendō highway as it winds through the village of Tsumago. The Nakasendō linked Kyōto and Edo (present Tokyo) via a mountainous inland route.

Above: Inns and shops along the Nakasendō in Tsumago village present an aspect almost unchanged since the days when the Nakasendō was an important national highway (1603–1868).

where he paused along the way to compose memorable haiku. Such a place is Hiraizumi, where there was once a provincial capital so grand it rivaled Kyoto and where Japan's most loved hero, Yoshitsune, met his tragic end; there Bashō was moved to write: ''The splendors of the three generations of Hiraizumi now comprise the briefest of dreams, . . . there are only faint remains stretching out for two and a half miles. . . . Yoshitsune and his brave adherents took refuge in this citadel, but the most famous names claim the world only a little while, and now the level grass covers their traces . . . .

> *The summer grasses:*
> *The high bravery of men at arms,*
> *The vestiges of dream.''*

And so authorities lead tours to eminent Buddhist temples and Shintō shrines and to noted gardens; to Sado Island, where unruly emperors and religious leaders were exiled; and to places like Dazaifu, near Fukuoka on Kyushu, an ancient headquarters for regional government. In 901 Dazaifu was the place of banishment for Sugawara Michizane, litterateur and prime minister who was undone by conspiracy; after his death he was deified as Tenjin, the god of learning. He is worshiped throughout the country at Shintō shrines dedicated to him. The chief of those shrines stands at Dazaifu, where he lived out his exile, loyally offering daily prayers for the well-being of the emperor who had exiled him. The god of learning is earnestly worshiped in Japan, and not just by students hoping to pass their examinations. Veneration of cultural heroes like him provides a valid and worthwhile excuse for travel.

gome; drawn back by nostalgia, he used the two villages and their people again and again in his fiction. Tourists interested in literary landmarks walk the narrow winding street that was the post road in both villages. They savor the worn and weathered deep-eaved old buildings and lodge at inns like the Matsushiroya in Tsumago, a structure 180 years old, lovingly maintained and operated.

The legacy of Kyoto and Nara draws hordes of tourists, but other Japanese follow the footsteps of cultural heroes who wandered far from those old capitals. Few would attempt to trace Bashō's entire course on his journey to the north, but a good many join tours to visit spots

RITUAL TRAVEL

The Japanese long ago found that ritual makes everything more bearable. In their ancient civilization ritual orchestrates much of life, as it does travel.

Ritual occasions periodically set the Japanese in motion in what one writer has called "human wave travel." The last days of the year see a concerted effort to go "home" for New Year, to join the rest of the family where the roots are. And because recent decades have seen mass migration from country to city, this greatest of all Japanese holidays brings mass movement from the cities to the country.

Although most Japanese are reluctant to use the vacation days granted to them (authorized or not, taking days off seems to indicate the wrong attitude), there is a frantic rush to take advantage of Golden Week, when a few days' holiday can be put together with minimum absence from work. The seven days from April twenty-ninth through May fifth usually offer spring at its most beguiling, and they are studded with three holidays plus, of course, a weekend. Companies don't fight it: blue-collar workers generally get five days off in a row and their white-collar counterparts, three. The National Police Agency annually predicts that half the population will dash to resort areas and exhorts travelers to keep the accident rate down.

The crush that ushers in the New Year recurs in summer. The Bon festival honors the dead, and homeward-bound travel to the family gravesite jams every means of transportation. Again, many businesses close and railroads hire extra men to push a few more bodies into the cars, but the compacted crowd, squeezed and shoved, remains good-humored.

There is nothing unique to Japan about the ritual of honeymoon travel, but it does seem remarkable that nowadays more than half the couples go abroad, and about as many travel to Europe (14.5%) as to nearby islands like Guam and Saipan. Ten years ago only ten percent of the newlyweds left Japan.

Ritual travel begins early—few Japanese forget their school trips. The many daylong outings blur in memory but the four- or five-day trips remain vivid. Built into the curriculum and eagerly anticipated, these trips come during sixth grade (the last year of elementary school), ninth grade (the last year of junior high school), and eleventh grade (the next-to-last year of senior high school; university entrance examinations or job-seeking make the last year too busy). The school administration decides where the students will go; the parents pay the bill. For a year or two prior to each trip students bring to school a monthly deposit.

Consider the trips a Tokyo girl has taken. In her school district, sixth-graders always go to the same place: Lake Yamanaka at the foot of Mount Fuji, where they lodge in a hostel owned and operated by the school board (each ward of the city has its own school board). The several elementary schools in the district are scheduled one after another. "Before the trip we studied Fuji-san and planned our activities. We were divided into groups—the sixth grade might have from three hundred to five hundred students—and each group excitedly devised a program to present at campfire: a play or songs and skits.

"In junior high school we went to Kyoto and Nara. We stayed for three days at a huge inn in Kyoto that specialized in lodging student tours, and each morning we were bundled into buses to see the sights with our tour guides. Trouble was, after we went to bed we talked half the night so that we saw all those temples with very sleepy eyes.

"We used to envy the rich girls at some of the private schools; they'd go to Hawaii or sometimes even to Europe. But our senior high school trip was good. We went to the west—to Hiroshima, and the old castle town of Hagi (so rich in history!), and Kurashiki (so rich in art!), and the great castle at Himeji (beautiful!). That trip was most fun because we were permitted to form small groups—three or four friends—and do our sightseeing on our own; we had to make our plans in advance and submit them for approval.

"Students from other parts of Japan often come to Tokyo. I have a friend from the

Above: Primary-school students on a day trip from ranks. When these youngsters reach sixth grade, they will take their first extended trips.

Left: A tour group lines up for a *kinen shashin* (commemorative photo) before the Great Buddha at Kamakura. Domestic tourism peaks during the New Year, the Bon Festival holiday, and spring's Golden Week.

northern part of the country who did that. He told me he will never forget the thrill when he first saw the ocean.''

And so while still young the Japanese experience the cozy security of group travel, an example of a tendency much commented on by those attempting to analyze Japanese society: that throughout life most Japanese find fulfillment and assurance not in individualism but by merging into the groups they belong

to—family, the organization that employs them, classmates (it is not unusual for men in their eighties to attend reunions of their elementary school class). It is natural that these feelings should extend to travel. But one should remember that in Europe, for example, American tour groups are at least as conspicuous as Japanese; the big difference is that the Japanese are willing to conform and move as their tour guide wishes.

FANTASY TRAVEL

In every city and frequently along the highways between them travelers will note a special kind of hotel. Most are instantly recognizable: they are as flamboyant as a circus band. They may look like a fairy tale castle or a turreted citadel from the days of chivalry or a mysteriously beached ocean liner; or they may be a basic boxlike building but with arched windows, sinuously spiralled columns, and pedestals supporting sculptures of scantily clad Aphrodite. At night these eloquent facades glow with pink or purple neon. The sign near the entrance quotes prices by the hour. Some of these establishments have occupancy rates of two hundred percent or more. How do they do it?

These are the love hotels, the *avec* hotels, for it is assumed that only *with* a partner would one check in. In the districts where they cluster everyone seems to be *avec*: couples, mostly young, blithely purposeful and unself-conscious (the middle-aged may seem a bit furtive). A third to a half of them are married couples seeking private pleasure denied to them in their small homes, where their children or their in-laws lie on the other side of a paper door.

Each twosome has a choice to make, for every hotel offers a variety of rooms at a wide range of prices. It might be assumed that their customers are already in the mood, but these places leave nothing to chance. Musically inclined? You might like a bed set in a huge model of a grand piano. Do automobiles excite you? Choose a bed shaped like a car, with real wheels and tires. A Turkish harem? There are also beds that elevate and rotate and mirrored ceilings that lower.

You may, of course, settle for a basic, uncomplicated room, but even that will likely be lush with cushiony scarlet carpeting, mirrored walls, a bed that pulses to the tempo of your choice, a big tub in a bathroom that suggests a tropical bower, and the standard accessories: heady perfumes, fragrant soap and bath scents, sexual attachments and electric vibrators (the ones advertised in current magazines), and a television set with a selection of pornographic films. Chances are you can tape your own performance in bed; the instructions assure you that when you view the tape it will automatically erase, but there have been reports of cases where the hotel made a copy, later sold and distributed to the considerable chagrin of the performers.

Incidentally, one canny traveler has written that when he arrives in a city only to be told that every hotel is jammed, he shrugs and finds a love hotel, secure in the knowledge that if a room isn't available at the moment one will be soon, and it will be comfortable, clean, quiet

and, rented for the whole night instead of at hourly rates, not overly expensive.

There are about 25,000 love hotels in Japan but only one Disneyland, the latter's singularity being guarded by patents, copyrights, and ironclad contracts.

Tokyo's is the newest, largest, and costliest (to build) of the Disneylands and the first overseas. The unfortunates who enter or leave Japan at Narita—one of the world's most mislocated airports—may blink when, on the long, slow trip into Tokyo, they see Disney spires across the drab dockyards that ring Tokyo Bay. Disneyland stands on a landfill, on land that didn't exist twenty years ago, but even earlier than that the Japanese promoters (a high-powered team of Mitsui Real Estate and the Keisei Electric Railroad, which serves the area) were courting the Disney organization. After years of tortuous negotiation they struck a deal. Disney planned it all, supervised its construction, polices its operation to keep it up to Disney standards, and in return gets a percent-

Above: The Mikado love hotel in Ōsaka offers couples privacy behind a rather bewildering Italianate-Moorish-Miami Beach façade. Palm trees add a romantic, tropical touch.

age of the take; the Japanese supplied the land, the money (more than $650 million), and are sole owners.

Devotees of Anaheim and Orlando need have no qualms; from the moment they enter the gate they are in Walt's world. The landscaping may have a subtle Japanese touch, one or two of the many eating places offer Japanese dishes, and one show truncates 1,500 years of Japanese history in sixteen minutes, but everything else is as familiar as big-eared Mickey himself; even the signs and the greetings—''Have a Nice Day''—are in English.

This is as the Japanese want it. They are the most numerous foreign visitors to California's Disneyland, they know the genuine product, and they want no tampering with it. Tokyo's Disneyland encapsulates the Japanese dream of what America ought to be, which happily coincides with the America fantasized by Walt Disney: Anglo-Saxon, orderly, efficient, squeaky-clean, and smiling. Fantasies in synch make both parties happy.

Left and above: Inside and outside views of one of Japan's unique modes of fantasy travel: the Cable Car Bath at Arita *onsen* in Wakayama Prefecture. From the warmth of their little individual tubs, patrons can gaze out at a dramatic (and chilly) seascape, proving definitively that the bath is meant as pure pleasure.

Stone markers guide pilgrims along the famous circular pilgrimage path around the island of Shikoku.

Pilgrims enter the *hondō*, or main hall, of a temple on the Shikoku itinerary of holy places.

PILGRIMAGE

Ascetics have wandered through the Japanese landscape from time immemorial, but it was the aristocracy who ritualized pilgrimage in Japan. In the tenth century the nobility of the imperial court began to journey from Kyoto to the Shintō shrines and Buddhist temples that cluster where the mountains meet the sea at Kumano on the southern tip of the Kii (Wakayama) Peninsula. Pilgrimage to Kumano became such a fad that in the twelfth and thirteenth centuries one retired emperor performed it twenty-one times, another thirty-one times, and a third, thirty-three times. Travel offered an escape from the duress of ceremony at the court, and Kumano was a powerful magnet: among its gods are two of Buddhism's most popular deities, Amida and Kannon. In the mists of Kumano's waterfalls and behind them in the depths of the peninsula's rugged mountains, Japanese religion was shaped as native Shintō and imported Buddhism met and melded. Eventually this pilgrimage was ex-

panded in the other direction to meander across the waist of the main island, linking thirty-three temples dedicated to Kannon. Two similar pilgrimages developed farther north. By performing all three, the truly devout could, and still can, offer prayers to Kannon at one hundred temples.

Pilgrimage in every part of the world has in it an element of tourism, and Japan is no exception. One must not minimize the religious urge, but from its aristocratic beginnings up to the present, pilgrimage has been an excuse for a journey; and until the end of the Edo period just about every Japanese needed a good excuse in order to get a travel permit.

Pilgrimage was seldom haphazard. Usually pilgrims were led by *sendatsu*, leaders who both guided the pilgrims on their way and instructed them in their worship. *Sendatsu* also promoted the organization of pilgrimage *kō*, clubs whose members contributed a coin or two each month and every year by lottery

chose a member or members who would get the treasury and the chance to make the pilgrimage. There still are some *sendatsu*, but today tour companies are the chief promoters.

It was only with the Edo period that peace, security, and general economic well-being made it possible for the common people to do much traveling. Throughout this long period the most popular pilgrimage by far was that to the sacred Shintō shrines of Ise. Ise's outer shrine is dedicated to the goddess of bountiful harvests and the prosperity they bring; the inner shrine is dedicated to the sun goddess Amaterasu, the ancestral deity of the imperial family. Fundamental in the role of the emperor is his position as the chief priest of the Ise shrines.

It was commonly said that every Japanese should worship at Ise at least once in his lifetime, and many made it. Not only were the Ise shrines preeminent in the nation, but the trip could be one long revel. (As already noted, a journey can be the excuse for a spree.) Ordinary traffic was heavy, but about every sixty years a kind of spell swept the land: then hundreds of thousands of men, women, and children dropped what they were doing and joined a human wave sweeping towards Ise.

Pilgrimage to Ise had political overtones, for worshipers were paying homage to the imperial line in times when the emperor was politically subordinate to the shogun. Although the sentiment evoked was usually latent, it was exploited in the late Edo period by plotters scheming to topple the shogun in the name of the emperor. They instigated mass pilgrimage to Ise and used it to fan passion for their cause.

Still, most pilgrimage has been Buddhist rather than Shintō. Or perhaps more accurately, it was overtly Buddhist with a mingling of Shintō, for few Japanese compartmentalize their faith and as pilgrims they worshiped at the altars of both. That was certainly true of the pilgrims whose avowed aim was to visit each of the country's sixty-six provinces and the notable Buddhist temples and Shintō shrines in each. Other magnets for pilgrimage are headquarters temples of the major Buddhist sects and of the ''new religions,'' each being indelibly associated with the founder.

The pilgrimage to the eighty-eight sacred places of Shikoku (fourth largest of Japan's main islands) is unique in the world because it is essentially circular. It thus typifies certain Buddhist concepts: it has no beginning and no end; like the quest for enlightenment it is unending. What is important is the striving rather than the destination, the going rather than the goal. The benefits come from the asceticism while completing the mountainous circuit of almost a thousand miles: the essence of the pilgrimage lies in the physical, mental, and spiritual demands made on the pilgrim and the physical, mental, and spiritual rewards.

This Shikoku pilgrimage is undertaken in faith in Kōbō Daishi. Kōbō Daishi is the posthu-

In this print by the nineteenth-century landscape master Andō Hiroshige, pilgrims pause on their journey. It was in the Edo period (1603–1868) that the country as a whole became wealthy enough to allow ordinary people to go on pilgrimages in large numbers. The Ise Grand Shrine became a favorite goal of Edo-period pilgrims.

mous title of the priest Kūkai (774–835). Kūkai founded the Shingon sect, but over the centuries he has been transformed from the great master he was into a saint and a deity, a nonsectarian figure who is venerated all over Japan. Faith and ascetic exercise can work miracles and—as with other pilgrimages—the Shikoku pilgrimage and the figure who inspires it are credited with innumerable cures and other marvelous happenings.

The Shikoku pilgrimage, probably the most

arduous of the pilgrimages, was still one of the most popular from the early 1600s well into the twentieth century. Today it attracts more pilgrims than ever before, well over a hundred thousand each year. Promotion by the bus companies has been a factor in this—they offer two-week tours of a route that in the old days took two months to walk—but it is religious sentiment that leads people to choose pilgrimage over more mundane tours. All over Japan there is a revival in religious pilgrimage.

Japan has a magnificent transportation system. Railroads push into every region, buses pick up where the railroads leave off, domestic airlines serve the key cities, ferries link the many islands.

The heart of the system is the railroads, both the JNR (the government owned and operated Japanese National Railways) and the fourteen private lines; the latter are primarily commuter lines, but they also run to resort areas. For the most part Japan's railroads are in good health. It is true that JNR has for two decades been piling up staggering deficits, but that sickness seems curable (JNR main lines make money) and is being treated. The private railroads are very profitable.

To one inured to American railroads, Japan's railroads are a marvel. On most routes

GETTING THERE

the service is fast, frequent, and on time. You can set your watch by the trains, and you can stand at a position marked on the platform in full confidence that a door will open in front of you. And JNR's bullet trains—the Shinkansen—have shown the world what modern trains can do.

The Shinkansen story is phenomenal. Its roadbed is all new, frequently tunneled through mountains, much of it elevated; there are no grade crossings. The normal schedule on the most heavily traveled route—Tokyo to

Racing through the rice-growing plains of the Tōhoku district, Japan's newest Bullet Train heads north. The Tokyo to Morioka route is a showcase for Japanese National Railways' fastest trains and a boon to the northern region, which has long lagged behind the rest of the nation economically.

Osaka—is 220 trains during a day that begins at 6 A.M. and ends shortly before midnight. In peak seasons up to 255 trains a day are operated: a train every four and one quarter minutes *on average*, although the schedule is denser during peak hours. Every train consists of sixteen cars that run at speeds up to 130 miles (210 kilometers) per hour. (The newest route, Tokyo to Morioka, is built for faster speeds, and JNR is working to regain the honor of running the world's fastest trains, which the French snatched when they built their new railroad.) Yet one rides with no impression of great speed, even while gazing out the window as paddy fields, wooded hills, or factories and towns appear and disappear. As one rolls along, operations are controlled from a center in Tokyo Station by a system that sets a maximum speed for each train running, based on the location of the train in front of it and other factors affecting safety; in two decades there have been no fatalities. Shinkansen trains are not luxurious, but they provide a reasonably comfortable seat and a smooth, swift ride from city center to city center.

For that matter, one does not board any Japanese transport—train, airplane, bus or ferry—in expectation of great comfort. The emphasis is on utility, a solution to the need to move many people efficiently. During rush hours more commuters stand than sit, and they stand tightly packed. (The most comfortable trains in Japan are the special expresses run by the private railroads to the resorts they serve.)

The bullet trains radiate from Tokyo and travel Japan's busiest and most heavily populated corridors. Yet, along with burgeoning industry and vibrant cities, one does see traditional farms and rugged mountains—including, if the weather cooperates, a glorious view of Fuji-san itself.

To probe deeper into Japan one takes other lines and perhaps changes to a bus. The bus system of Japan is sensibly designed to supplement the railroads. Bus terminals are almost invariably located on the plaza in front of the railroad station; from there buses go where trains cannot: along roads that twist into the mountains or along jagged coasts; to quiet villages, old temples, rustic hot springs; to great gorges whose gigantic walls of rock are made glorious in the autumn by the maple trees that cling there.

Trains tunnel under the Kammon Strait to connect Honshu and Kyushu, but to get to

Shikoku or Hokkaido one must change to a ferry, emphasizing that this is a country of islands—more than 3,300 of them big enough to count, of which about 440 are inhabited. It follows that the Japanese do a good deal of island hopping. There are some one thousand scheduled shipping lines and many more that operate when and if. There are slow boats and fast, vessels ranging from chugging little launches to hydrofoils and car and truck ferries. Some of the long-distance boats offer

A large hydrofoil plies the Inland Sea near Imabari. Long a major avenue of commerce and conquest, the Inland Sea is also part of a huge industrial zone.

fairly luxurious accommodations, but at their cheapest rates (folksy second class, where passengers sprawl in carpeted areas in a big cabin), boats are the least expensive way to travel, short of hitchhiking; they offer a leisurely and relaxing alternative, often with memorable seascapes as a bonus.

Travel in Japan can be fun.

LODGING

Japan offers an extraordinary variety of lodgings for the night. Tokyo's Okura Hotel has been justly praised as one of the world's finest, and others have their spirited partisans. Many major hotels and a number of smaller establishments offer tasteful public and private rooms, fine restaurants, and the facilities a traveler needs whether pleasure-bent or on business, with attentive, gracious service by a staff dedicated to putting the guest at ease. And these pleasures come at rates below those in comparable cities around the world.

Still it is doubtful that any luxury hotel can enfold a guest in the luxury offered by a superlative *ryokan*, a Japanese inn. Take, for example, Harihan: spread on a hilltop in Nishinomiya, between Osaka and Kobe, everything about it is traditional Japanese at its best—the architecture, the cuisine, the pampering service, the serenity of it all. A mountain stream winds through the gardens that beckon guests from their rooms; cherry blossoms appear in the spring, glowing maples color the fall, and a thatch-roofed teahouse stands beside a lawn large enough to accommodate the thousand devotees who cluster around red-draped tables for an annual New Year's tea ceremony.

Such a *ryokan* is not for everybody. Harihan does not advertise and accepts no reservations from the big agencies that book most travelers (and exact a commission from the establishment); and Harihan is expensive, though still a bargain when one compares its rates with the upper tariffs of a fine hotel. Moreover, not everyone today wants what a *ryokan* offers. The guest at a fine inn must surrender to its ways. No menu will be offered: dinner, served

in the privacy of one's suite, will be as the chef has planned it (though nowadays a guest may be asked his preference for breakfast). The guest must welcome the personal service: the same maids who greet one on arrival will help one settle in, sit and chat as they serve meals, lay the beds on the *tatami*, be always on call, and wave one off on departure. Today the greater impersonality of a hotel appeals to many Japanese (they are classified as "dry" personalities; those who respond emotionally to the old ways are "wet").

Of course not all inns are posh—far from it. There are some ninety thousand of them and they range widely in quality and price; generally one gets what one pays for, though there can be surprises, pleasant and unpleasant, up and down the line. Somewhat less expensive are *minshuku*; these are family-operated inns with a homey atmosphere (a friend has defined a *minshuku* as an inn where you can overhear the family quarreling), but the term has speedily blurred as many less expensive *ryokan* adopted the name. *Kokumin shukusha*, "People's Lodges" are publicly and privately operated in national parks; their settings may be their best feature, for most are bleakly institutional. There are also a few Western-style *minshuku*, called "pensions," and, of course, youth hostels. Finally, many Japanese have access to guest houses operated by the company they work for—or that a cousin works for.

Western-style hotels vary as widely, and the falling off in quality is more abrupt than among *ryokan*.

A fairly recent development is the "business hotel," designed specifically for the short stay of the typical Japanese businessman, who travels light, often making do with a briefcase. The business hotel offers little in the way of personal service: as in a motel, the guest carries his own bag. The rooms, mostly single, are truly small, and if there is a closet it will be minimal; a couple of pegs on the wall may

The mistress of Harihan *ryokan* arranges flowers in one of the suites. *Ryokan* not only offer the traveller traditional architecture but also the sort of highly attentive service many Japanese prefer.

substitute. But most of these hotels are new and clean, the bed is comfortable, and the bathroom is gleaming molded plastic—two or three large pieces fitted together so compactly that it is easy to reach the towel from the tub. An adequate restaurant is usually at hand.

Business hotels aim to be inexpensive, but their rates have crept up. The answer to this rise is the latest phenomenon: the capsule hotel. One of the newest, largest, and most elaborate is the Green Plaza in Tokyo's Shinjuku district, a major business, transportation, and entertainment center. The Green Plaza comprises eleven brightly lighted stories

aboveground plus two below. It boasts a Japanese restaurant, a sushi bar, a Chinese restaurant, and a coffee shop that serves Western food; three saunas, three swimming pools, and an exercise room; and several lounges. The top floor is a reception hall and the roof accommodates a wedding chapel (weddings are big business for Japanese hotels) with stained-glass windows and a crosstopped belfry—a snappy blend of New England and Las Vegas. The hotel "rooms" are tucked in the middle of the building, 660 of them in a space that would accommodate about 100 small rooms in a business hotel. Each consists of a molded plastic capsule about five feet high and wide and six feet seven inches deep—something like a sleeping berth on an American train but equipped with television, AM/FM radio, read-

ing light, writing desk, and intercom connected to the front desk. The guest crawls in from the end (other models open from one side), and uses a curtain for privacy (the units are not individually air-conditioned so a door is not feasible). The units are stacked two high, with ladders to the uppers.

The Green Plaza suggests that one reason for checking in is to watch a favorite television program undisturbed. One patron said he stayed there one night a week in order to catch up on essential reading away from the distractions of his family in their small home. Some use capsule hotels simply to save money. But it is no accident that the Green Plaza is located in an entertainment district near busy railroad stations: most of its guests check in because they have missed the last train home after an

Here is another reason to stay in a fine *ryokan:* the scenery around the Harihan and the *ryokan's* own garden. A large wooden bridge crosses a mountain stream below the buildings of the inn.

evening of drinking. In the early evening the capsule area and its washrooms and toilets are spotless and quiet; a few men, wearing the robe provided by the hotel, are reading or watching a large television screen in a comfortable lounge. This may change when the revelers roll in. Television monitors scan the passages, and the management says it tolerates no offensive behavior, but most drunks are noisy and some get sick.

One might think that with the capsule the Japanese have pushed miniaturization of the hotel room to its ultimate, but that is not a safe bet.

MOUNTAIN AND SEA

Mountain and sea: the Japanese feel the pull of both. There are few places where one cannot see the mountains (even in Tokyo, now that the air has been cleaned up, Fuji is visible), and not much of the country is more than fifty miles from the sea.

The Japanese are an island people whose prehistoric ancestors crossed the sea to get here. The sea is in their blood and a definite presence in their lives. It is a rare meal that does not include food from the sea; its waters beget the snow that buries the northwestern regions in winter and the torrents unleashed by typhoons in summer; it is the barrier that insulates them and makes them different from the people of the continent, and at the same time it is the limitless avenue that beckons them to reach out to the rest of the world.

The mountains are so central in their lives that they became sacred long ago. They are the source of life, for from their depths well the streams that water the valleys, and the destination in death—the refuge of ancestral spirits, the dwelling places of the gods. The sense of awe in the face of mountains permeates Japanese religion and Japanese life.

Visitors may encounter stereotypes that have some truth in them. It is said that the people of the mountains are taciturn, phlegmatic, introspective; that the people of the coasts are outgoing, gregarious, adventurous. They complement each other, these two types;

The village of Bō-mura near Mt. Hiei in the vicinity of Kyōto offers a view of a classic Japanese landscape: rice fields on the lowlands, thatch-roofed farmhouse protected by trees, and in the background, steep, forested uplands and mountains. This pattern is repeated in countless places throughout Japan.

the tensions between them are invigorating.

Mountain and sea: the juxtaposition is dramatic where coastlines plunge from dizzying heights into the ocean. It is insistent in the Inland Sea; one is never out of sight of some of its hundreds of islands, each a mountaintop. On these usually placid waters one can sail from peak to peak.

Many of those peaks are scarred, a reminder that at times the Japanese seem determined to level the mountains and dump them into the sea. Since history began they have struggled to enlarge the narrow limits that can be tilled and lived on. Vast areas that were once ocean now hold homes and factories, paddy fields, and ports—and amusement parks. Cities push out their coastlines farther and farther.

Even in deep mountains one sees this struggle. Heights are terraced to grow fruit, peaks are sliced off and hotels rise in their stead, "skyline drives" are carved out for a mobile population's ceaselessly multiplying automobiles. Nature retaliates with landslides.

Yet the mountains and sea remain: the mystical feelings of reverence, of wonder, of fear inspired by the mountains, the intuitive feelings of separateness, of uniqueness, of destiny aroused by the sea.

Where shall we travel, to the mountains or to the sea? Both call, both are at hand—hiking? swimming? skiing? sailing? hunting? fishing? Pleasant dilemma.

Right: Ise Bay, at the south end of Mie Prefecture, is both a workshop and national park. In this photo, some of the commercial pearl beds and their associated buildings can be seen. Ise-Shima National Park offers spectacular marine scenery and islands covered with subtropical plants.

Above: The unearthly beauty of Matsushima on the northern Pacific coast has inspired poets and painters for hundreds of years. Over 260 pine-clad islands of all sizes dot Matsushima Bay, offering breathtaking views in all weather. Strong wind and wave action has sculpted the islands into shapes full of the beauty and mystery of monochrome ink landscapes.

179

遊び

14 • CHILD'S
PLAY

Above: Two young stalwarts pose with a plastic statuette of the comic-book hero Astro-Boy. The insects on this and the facing page were drawn by Hokusai.

GAMES

At the turn of the century, a group of Japanese children might huddle on a streetcorner for a few moments, then send one of their number on his mission: to approach a Western gentleman and ask the time of day. Unaware of being observed, the man would pull out his timepiece, and the children would shriek and scatter. The object of this game was to guess what kind of watch the patsy would be carrying.

Rock, paper, scissors (*jankenpon*) is the classic way to decide who will be "it" in Japan. Grownups play this game too at geisha parties, where "it" must down a cup of sake.

Rhythmical chanting appears to be part of children's games all over the world. "Deer, deer, how many horns?" goes one, and the children must guess how many fingers the "deer" is holding up behind his back. *Kagome, kagome* is the name of another game in which one child crouches in the middle of a circle while the others march around singing a chant that ends: "Who is right behind you?" Folklorists postulate a religious origin to *kagome* and similar chanting games, seeing in them ancient rituals that have been relegated to the sphere of child's play.

During the Meiji period (1868–1912), interest in things of the West touched everything from politics to children's toys. The first decade of Meiji saw handmade playthings lose favor to commercially produced ones, often imitations of Western toys. By the second decade of Meiji, Japanese-made toys were being exported all over the Far East. At the

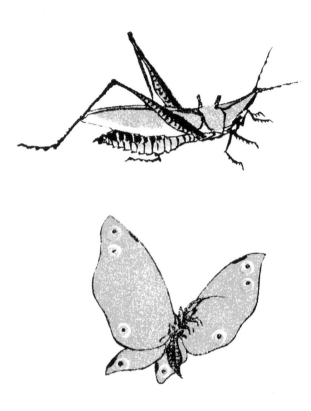

contests. These carefree groups became more structured in the early teen years when farm boys joined village youth groups, and young men in the cities gathered on the streets to engage in competitive sports or gambling.

Girls' play has always had a more practical flavor. Playing house, in particular, was never very far from actually keeping house if you were a farmer's daughter. For children of the urban merchant class, one game in particular was thought useful for both sexes—*karuta*, poetry matching cards. The object of the game is to pair up halves of classic poems written on separate cards; but the social object, when young men and women played, was to judge the opponent's reactions for clues regarding his or her character. This was a popular game when marriage negotiations were under way.

Among the things Japanese children do for amusement, catching insects has a classical resonance lacking in such pastimes as building with tinkertoys. Little boys have always loved to capture bugs, especially ones of fierce appearance like the three-inch-long, pincer-jawed *kabuto mushi*. Named "helmet beetle" because its horns resemble the decorative metal flanges on a samurai's helmet, the *kabuto mushi* is common in early summer, even in suburbs close to the heart of Tokyo. Occasionally it may be found in pet stores or, more likely, at a shrine fair, hawked by a peddler. But children usually prefer to hunt their own. The aggressive male insects are prized by little boys, who groom their small warriors for battle against the beetles kept by their friends. A circle of excited kneeling boys, intent on action in the dirt, is very likely to be engaged in a beetle match—the ponderous movements of mortal combat in miniature are endlessly fascinating to nine-year-olds.

Chasing fireflies *(hotaru)* is a more gentle pursuit, and one that has classically been associated with young girls. A maiden with fireflies bespangling the long sleeves of her kimono at dusk is an ancient summer poetic cliché. In rural areas, children fashion crude cages of dry grass for their captives and carry their booty like natural torches. There is a description of a firefly-hunting expedition in Tanizaki's novel *The Makioka Sisters* which Japanese readers must find wonderfully reminiscent: The city-dwelling sisters visit a relative in the countryside and indulge in a poetic firefly hunt, remarking all the while at their rare opportunity. Today, the encroachment of urban development on its habitat has made the once-common firefly an exotic insect as far as most Japanese children are concerned.

By far the most esthetically developed form of insect amusements is the keeping of various members of the cricket family, primarily for the sounds they produce. In the same way that potted plants were kept as ornamental nature, pleasing to the eye, caged crickets were kept as ornamental nature for the ear. A keen appreciation of insect song is found throughout Japanese literature, from the earliest known collection of poetry, but it seems that the practice of maintaining insects in cages became popular only in the seventeenth century.

Insect aficionadoes hunted their own or bought from the insect seller. By the late eighteenth century, the demand for fine chirping crickets was so great that an itinerant dumpling vendor named Chūzō found fame and fortune by discovering a way to breed the beloved *suzumushi* (bell cricket) in captivity. In their natural state, crickets hatch around mid-July and begin to sing in October. When bred in a warm room, they can be hatched in April and ready for market by late May. Described by Japanese as resembling a watermelon seed, the *suzumushi's* tintinnabulation is rendered as a soprano *ri-i-i-in.* Grosser insects such as the *kirigirisu*, which looks like a grasshopper, and the locustlike *umaoi* (horse driver) have correspondingly deeper voices: *zu-i-in-tzo.*

Columbian Exposition held in Chicago in 1893, visitors to the Japanese pavilion were astounded at a flying mechanical butterfly produced by an Osaka toymaker.

In the traditional rhythm of social life, children passed through different stages of play activities. Babies of course remained in the house, under parents' watchful eyes. Toddlers and slightly older children were allowed to play on the porches under the eaves, or even in the garden or courtyard. Here they could at least be heard if not seen. This was the last stage of childhood where the sexes mingled.

At about age four, little boys suddenly disappeared from the immediate vicinity of the house in order to be with their peers. Groups of boys between the ages of four and eight were their own best friends. They would walk on stilts, spin tops, play hide and seek, tag, hopscotch, and of course have rock throwing

ORIGAMI

Several years ago, a ten-year-old girl from Columbia, Missouri, won the All-America Origami Competition with her creation: a praying mantis playing the piano. Origami has come a long way from the rote folding of "a thousand cranes."

In Japan, the art of folding paper became child's play sometime in the fourteenth century. Considered an amusement for girls in particular, the frivolity of fashioning squares of colored paper into replicas of cranes, frogs, helmets, and paired birds was excused as discipline for training little fingers in preparation for sewing. Until the early twentieth century, young girls could practice their dexterity by folding the predefined set of approximately one hundred fifty foldable clichés. Free-form origami appeared in the 1920s and since then has enveloped the world, with Tokyo as headquarters of the International Origami Research Center.

Mindful of the underlying seriousness with which many seemingly ephemeral pastimes are treated in Japan, one suspects that origami too has deep roots; that the folding of paper into different two– and three–dimensional shapes was not originally a rainy afternoon's activity for bored children. Indeed, paper was a precious commodity when it first became available from China: "Draw on silk, it will last 500 years; draw on paper, it will last 1000 years," as a proverb has it.

When Genji, the Shining Prince, received a poem from a lady, he judged it first by the texture and fold of the paper. The manner of folding expressed as much about the lady's character as did the sentiments she enfolded. Special forms of folded paper are attached to

The most familiar origami shape of all is the lucky crane *(tsuru),* often found in a vast paper "flock" of a thousand. The gift of a thousand cranes *(sembazuru)* denotes a heartfelt wish for luck for the recipient and is often given to invalids as a prayer for their recovery. Modern origami has progressed far beyond this type of over-familiar, if beloved, imagery, and is now a minor art alive with experimentation and humor.

the straw ropes hung before a sacred place in Japan, be it tree, shrine, or rock. The Shinto priest shakes a stick bristling with folded papers in the rite of purification; and in traditional methods of exorcism, the sufferer's soul was represented by a piece of folded paper that was meant to absorb the evil influences before it was burned or floated down a river. It is probably not by accident that the spoken term *origami* (folded paper) is homonymous with ideographs meaning "descent of the deity."

Various ways of folding paper were once an important part of the bureaucratic lives of warriors and nobles. Different schools of etiquette prescribed ways to fold the paper that accompanied gifts or the paper used for written orders to subordinates. Ceremonial origami is best seen today at a Japanese wedding in the "male butterfly," "female butterfly" folded paper decorations on the sake containers for the bride and groom.

Paper folding took on a rather different social function around the turn of the twentieth century when educational origami became a part of the kindergarten and grade school curriculum in Japan. In 1913, standardized packets of colored paper, fifteen centimeters square, were marketed all over Japan with great success. Although some educators disapproved of the rote and repetitive nature of folding the traditional origami shapes, their misgivings were dismissed by the creators of the new origami, who argued that the manipulation of shapes gave children a basic ground-

A little girl stands next to a solemn display of origami cranes. The scene is the main memorial to the dead in Hiroshima, and many strings of *sembazuru* (see opposite page) have been offered for the repose of their souls. Folded paper has long had religious significance in Japan, where it is employed in rites of purification, exorcisms, gift-giving and in the demarcation of sacred space. The very word origami is homonymous with the phrase "descent of the deity."

ing in the principles of plane geometry. Origami as work therapy has more than a few proponents in Japan and elsewhere.

Origami today has clearly broken away from its traditional fixed forms. Enthusiastic hobbyists vie with one another in the creation of new shapes and combinations. Practically the only rules left are that the paper cannot be cut or the figure colored after folding.

KITE FLYING

A cluster of carp kites flies proudly over homes on Boys' Day. Families display one kite—of appropriate relative size—for each son. The carp, which swims upriver, is an emblem of health and intrepidity; colorful kites bearing its image are nearly as familiar as Mt. Fuji and the *torii* gate as symbols of Japan. At festival time Japanese skies are alive with many different fanciful animal kites; lucky creatures like the crane and the tortoise are joined by squid *(ikanobori)*, swallows, and manta rays. Ideographs and images of actors and samurai also decorate kites.

Kites are child's play in Japan, but a great deal more as well. In many regions of the country, adults stage grand kite competitions between villages. Warrior kites of paper and bamboo carry razors on their strings to cut down their equally armed opponents. For over three hundred years, villagers in Saitama Prefecture have been building monster kites three times a man's height for such contests.

Today these activities are carried on as sport, but originally kites evoked deeper meanings. Kites are associated with Japanese New Year festivities because of their role in auguring the fortunes of the upcoming year. People in some regions fly kites to bear their prayers for health and worldly success. Kites also hover to rout evil spirits from home or village.

The first use of a kite in Asia is attributed to the Chinese general Han Xin in the second century B.C. He purportedly used one to measure his army's distance from the enemy camp. Kites are also called "wind harps" in China, from the practice of attaching trailing strips of cloth to split bamboo, which then vibrate with the breeze. As with so many objects of material culture, the kite came to Japan from China in the eighth century. Kite flying during the medieval period was a noble pastime—one of the gentlemanly arts of a Japanese courtier. Flying kites just for fun apparently was uncommon before the seventeenth century. Around 1620, the chief magistrate of the city of Nagasaki was reported to have somehow affixed candles to bamboo and paper structures and flown them through the night, so great was his passion for kite flying. By that time, Europeans too had discovered the fun of flying kites, and Dutch traders had brought Chinese kites home to Holland for their children.

Tako is the common term for kite, written as a single ideograph composed of the elements "cloth" and "wind." As an instance of nomenclature convergent with English and yet totally coincidental, an early Japanese term for these light constructions was paper kite *(shien),* referring to the bird. The use of the

falconid term presumably came from the aerial acrobatics both perform. Squid banner *(ikano-bori)* is another frequently heard name, no doubt because of the resemblance of tentacles to tails. As with the better-known *koinobori,* or carp banners raised on poles for Boys' Day, kites carry aloft peoples' wishes for strong and vigorous little boys.

The elongated diamond is but one possible

shape among Japanese kites. Crane kites and tortoise kites, manta rays, jelly fish, and migratory birds in a row crowd festival skies. Kites in the shape of auspicious ideographs are popular, as are those with faces of Kabuki actors and samurai warriors. For the incorrigible aficionado, there are even sparrow-sized pocket kites—just the thing for that odd moment when the right puff of breeze happens along.

Above: The staff of a carp-kite shop shows off a giant piece of merchandise. The Japanese kite comes in all dimensions, from pocket-size to the giant kites of Hoshubana Village— forty-eight by thirty-six feet. There is even a legendary kite one-quarter-inch square that is flown with a line invisible to the naked eye.

Left: The face of a classical court lady decorates a kite. This is a relatively demure image; many kites bear grimacing, howling, or scowling faces—and all employ vigorous designs and brilliant color contrasts to startle the earthbound onlooker.

MODERN TOYS

"We do not remember the world of Vaiston Weir. Our memories were suppressed when we were born on planet Earth. We have only one hope—the earthling Shō Zama who discovered how to utilize the energy of his own body aura to combat the Aura Battlers, the fearsome monster robots who destroyed Vaiston Weir. Transforming himself into Crusader Dunbine, Shō Zama engages in battle with his enemies Drumlo, Virunvee, and Dana O'Shee."

Japanese children can watch the science fiction exploits of the Aura Battlers on television, and they can buy their favorite monsters, die-cast or plastic, in toy stores. There are action models that shoot missiles, like Denjiman Daidenjin (made by Popi, one of the largest manufacturers of science fiction toys), and there are stationary models that can assume various poses in a home-built georama. The principle is the same as playing with a doll house, except that the scene is fantastic rather than domestic.

A molded plastic Tyranosauruslike Godzilla with wheels in his feet was one of the earliest Japanese *monsutaa* toys, and the dinosaur motif continues to be strong. Super-robot SanKanOh is accompanied by sidekick Tokyū Manmosu (special mammoth). Robots have been in the ascendancy since the 1970s. Current models are less boxy than their predecessors, and many have decidedly arthropodish features: crablike carapaces, beetle-wing capes, antennae, claws, and horns.

The phrase "change model" is frequently emblazoned on the colorful boxes containing these SF fantasy figures. For example, Go-Daikin Daltania, a super-robot, can be manipulated with a few twists to change into a lion.

Leopaldon has removable legs and streamlines into a spaceship with a sphinxy top turret. There is a line of cars that metamorphose into robots: Space Cobra Psychoroid, a Porsche, and a fire truck that turns into Fiya-Robo.

The names of these fantastic monstrosities are often terribly un-Japanese. The language of science fiction is strongly English-flavored, but a poster proclaiming: "Fight! Dougram to save independency of the deloyer!" would hardly stir the soul of an American grade-schooler.

Kaijū, literally "strange beast," is the original Japanese term for monster, but *monsutaa* is probably the generic term for the creatures now. Some *monsutaa* represent law and order, such as Techroide Vigorus, model 210 of the Technopolice. To the untutored eye, all robot-type *monsutaa* look basically the same: armor-plated thorax, hands as weapons, stony expression. Yet upon closer examination of *monsutaa* as a group, there is a clear spectrum of good versus evil, primarily indicated by the degree of the creature's anthropomorphism. The set of the arms, the extent to which the head emerges from the shoulders, and the proportions of the chest are all cues to the creature's character.

Monster toys belong to the world of little boys, although the fantasy romance comics and TV programs favored by girls often feature robotic heroes and villains. A set of perky teenybopper super-heroettes known as the Urusee Yatsura, or "noisy brats," are available as model kits to be assembled and painted. These Kewpie-faced cuties are probably made to appeal to girls, but their leopardskin-bikini-clad bodies may be as much fantasy figures to boys as any *monsutaa*.

Right: When he debuted in the 1950s, Godzilla was in every sense a villain in Japanese monster movies. Since the 1960s, however, he's been on the side of the angels, defending Japan against the likes of Megalon and the Smog Monster.

Left: Among the many masks for sale in this toy stall are robot and monster faces, in which the small science-fiction fan can impersonate the superheroes and megavillains that appear on television and in the toy shops.

15 · AFTER
HOURS

THE BAR

Japanese men are identified by what they drink. The *mizuwari*, ''with water'' (Scotch being understood), is the liquid equivalent of the ubiquitous dark blue business suit. Individual preference may be expressed in the choice of brand; once decided, a man sticks to his brand with unswerving loyalty. Rémy Martin, *onzarox,* is what a neatly suited executive is likely to order. Like so many things in Japan, liquor brands jockey for place in a hierarchy. Rémy Martin has toppled Johnny Walker Black from its long-held postwar preeminence, and Rémy will doubtless yield in its turn.

On the whole, Japanese are unadventurous drinkers—no martinis, no whiskey sours, no margaritas. Mixed drinks, primarily sweetish ones, are the preserve of ladies over thirty, on the rare occasions when they drink in public.

Social drinking is by and large an activity of men in Japan. This cultural fact is the middle-class manifestation of a feudal urban tradition of separating men's and women's activities. Socially, wives are confined to the sphere of domesticity. The after-hours world of bars and nightclubs can be thought of as an emotional ''safety valve'' for the hard-working Japanese businessman. Constrained by rules of hierarchy and propriety in his job, he can let loose (in a socially condoned manner) with his cronies in a bar.

There is no necessity to find a date either, because women known as hostesses are as much a commodity in the bar as is the liquor. Management chooses ladies whose looks and style fit with the decor and carefully planned ambience of the establishment. More of a companion than a cocktail waitress, the hostess sits with groups of customers (drinking is

seldom a solitary activity in Japan) and entertains them with her egregiously feminine presence. She chatters on, encouraging guests to keep their glasses filled, providing a willing ear for the boasting and occasionally a willing knee for the caresses of the ordinarily proper businessman. Although the tone of the conversations is often salacious, after-hours assignations with hostesses are rare.

The very classiest bars and nightclubs of Tokyo's Ginza and Akasaka areas are the playgrounds of Japan's business and government elites. Often only as large as an American home's living room, they are as elegantly appointed as the inside of a jewel box. Customers are generally on expense accounts, and the expense can be phenomenal. Would-be

patrons without proper introduction are gently turned away at the doors of these places.

But there are any number of bars for the common man as well, and even those without hostesses do a flourishing business. Many bars operate under the management of one mama-san. After age thirty, a hostess will find herself on a rapid road to retirement. If she is smart and lucky, she will have planned all along to parlay her hostess earnings, with the aid perhaps of a patron's capital, into her own establishment. Hostesses and mama-sans are the heiresses to the geisha tradition of feminine companionship for men. Outnumbering geisha by at least fifty to one, they smooth the Japanese male ego back into shape, ready for another day of attempting economic miracles.

Left: A forest of signs for bars on a Tokyo street. Japanese drinking places run the gamut from tiny "stand-bars" to enormous, brassy nightclubs. The highest toned establishments, however, are small and splendid. Often located on the upper floors of buildings in the entertainment districts, they cater to a select clientele.

Above: Three old friends from southern Japan have a chance reunion in Tokyo and go to a friendly neighborhood bar to reminisce in this scene from *Tokyo Story*. In many of his films, the late Yasujiro Ozu used bar scenes to evoke the wistfulness and the courage of middle-aged men living in a time of rapid change.

GEISHA

Geisha are exotic, even in Japan. This community of female entertainers has survived into the twentieth century largely because of an unlikely metamorphosis: A century ago, geisha were society's fashion innovators; now they are curators of tradition. The thousand or so geisha remaining in Tokyo and Kyoto are highly conscious of their role in preserving the arts of classical music and dance.

Yet although these arts are respected and admired by society at large, geisha occupy an ambivalent position in the public mind. The recherché glamour of the geisha does not appeal to everyone, especially the modern youths. A geisha whitens her face with nightingale droppings while Japanese teenagers oil their skins to tan. A geisha's kimono reveals the nape of her neck—a traditional erotic focus—while movie stars adopt plunging décolleté. Most important, unlike 98 percent of Japanese women, geisha do not marry. Geisha symbolize the ultimate exotic Oriental woman to the West—yet, strange as it now seems, the first geisha were men.

From about 1600, Japan had an elaborate system of licensed prostitution, confined by law to specific enclosed areas of the cities. In the brothels lived the *yūjo* (women of pleasure), known for their sexual expertise. Of the numerous hours that men spent in the pleasure quarters, however, only a few were devoted to sex. Most of the time was spent in

Left: The geisha still wears her kimono pulled back to reveal the nape of the neck and a hint of shoulder. The white powder she wears on face and neck has been a symbol of refinement since classical times.

partying. The lure of the pleasure quarters was the romance, elegance, and excitement of the one place in feudal society where money, charm, and wit made more of an impression than social class.

Geisha were called in to these parties of the *yūjo* and their customers to entertain with music, dance, and chatter. The notion of female geisha gained popularity in the mid-eighteenth century and by 1800, they had completely overshadowed their male counterparts. Forbidden to sleep with the *yūjo*'s customers, geisha were recognized by the authorities as distinct from prostitutes. Geisha were supposed to be ladies of the evening, not ladies of the night. The distinction remains in effect today—which is why being a geisha is a legal occupation, though prostitution was made illegal in Japan in 1957.

A geisha party today can be considered a business expense. The president of a company engages a room at a teahouse, knowing that the food ordered and the geisha summoned by the proprietress will make a suitable impression on his client. Rarely are guests women. This is because wives are not included in business-related socializing, and because few women have as yet established a toehold in Japanese upper management. The engaging of geisha is a very limited activity these days. Most Japanese have never even met a geisha, and young people dismiss geisha parties as expressions of the nostalgia of the rich and elderly. Still, for the connoisseur, there is something about the atmosphere of a gathering with attendent geisha that can be found nowhere else in Japan. Geisha, like caviar, are an acquired taste.

Above: A prosperous gentleman has his picture taken with three apprentice geisha *(maiko)* in Kyōto.

Right: Although she is not wearing her full finery, this off-duty Kyōto geisha is still a model of elegance as she hurries on an errand. Postwar geisha are conservers of tradition rather than style-setters.

Above: Two apprentice geisha cross a Kyōto street. Although viewed as precious cultural symbols, geisha live on the margin of the respectable working Japanese world and do not marry.

YOSHIWARA

Be prepared for the fact that in Japan
there is no sin, original or otherwise.
Bernard Rudofsky in *The Kimono Mind*

In the seventeenth century, when Edo was the new capital of a Japan at last united after centuries of civil war, there developed a culture of pleasure the like of which has perhaps never been seen in the West. It was called Yoshiwara (the Reed Moor) for the swampy ground on which it was first built, but by a simple substitution of homophonous Chinese characters, it was soon known as Yoshiwara, (the Joyful Moor). Sex—abundant and delicious—was at the heart of this remarkable *demimonde*, but it was sex seen in the context of pleasure, not the other way around.

Founders of the gay quarter insisted upon its salubrious effects. Claimed one: "Virtuous men have said, both in poetry and classic works, that houses of debauch, for women of pleasure and for streetwalkers, are the worm-eaten spots of cities and towns. But these are necessary evils, and if they be forcibly abolished, men of unrighteous principles will become like raveled thread." This was an ominous warning, apparently, for by 1626, the Yoshiwara was in operation as a self-contained pleasure quarter. Though it moved several times and burned down repeatedly, it remained a feature of Edo culture for more than two centuries. Samurai, merchants, actors, performers, writers, wrestlers came through the Omonguchi (the mouth of the Great Gate) and strolled along the the main street and into

Left: Geisha of the Yoshiwara dance in an eighteenth-century print. While sex was the basic commodity of the licensed quarter, all manner of other elegant pleasures were also available: music, dance, *sake*, fine food, and the enjoyment of woodblock art.

Right: A Yoshiwara courtesan refuses to see a client. The city of pleasure contained women of all degrees of availability; the highest-class ones could be imperiously selective, while the bedraggled "night hawks" *(yoru no taka)* were simple streetwalkers.

side streets with names like Gojukken machi (the Street of Fifty Houses).

Ritual was well established for entrance to the houses. First, the guests went to a *hikite-jaya*, a teahouse where they were served food and drink, entertained with dancing, music, stories, and shown books picturing the courtesans they could choose. Books picturing amorous couples in all sorts of embraces were also popular. The *shunga*, or erotic prints, varied in

quality as much as did the courtesans themselves, but the finest are executed in a style both fascinating and strange, the women with limbs totally elastic, the sex organs of both partners terrifically enlarged and drawn in a flowing style so they look for all the world like a river entering a pond, and both clothed in sinuous robes that part just where wanted. After a party that usually lasted hours (at least in the better houses), the guest would be led to the courtesan's house, where he could take the final pleasures in the flesh. For as Mark Twain is supposed to have said, "You can't beat sex when it comes to pleasure."

In the West, artists often frequented similar quarters—Degas in Paris's Latin Quarter, E. J. Bellocq in New Orleans's Storyville. But Yoshiwara gathered the finest artists and writers of the day. Virtually all the great printmakers—Utamaro, Hokusai, Kunisada—made works showing the courtesans, geisha, waitresses, actors, and street crowds. The greatest prose writer of his day, Ihara Saikaku, wrote almost all his works about denizens of Osaka's equivalent of the quarter. And the wonderful playwright Chikamatsu, known especially for works for the puppet theater like *The Love Suicides at Sonezaki,* wrote several of his best-loved plays about runaway courtesans and their lovers. The culture of love and pleasure penetrated to the heart of that first Japanese urban culture, a way of life that came to be characterized as The Floating World.

Daybreak in the Yoshiwara was like the end of everything. One visitor noted, "Mornings the floating world of Joyful Moor sleeps, weary, drugged by *sake* and other bought pleasures. Along the main center street, the *naka no cho,* flowering cherry trees, scent the morning. The bright blossoms are already falling from the trees, trees that never bear fruit. Behind the high fences that separate the establishments, nodding fawn-pink and peach-pink blossoms contrast brightly with the weathered timber."

16 • LANGUAGE

LEARNING JAPANESE

léarn·ing [-iŋ] *n*. Ⓤ 学ぶこと；学問，学識，知識；博学: a man of ～ 学者.

Jap·a·nése [dʒæpəníːz] *a*. 日本の，日本人 [語]の: ～ beetle 〖虫〗まめこがね / ～ ivy つた 《Boston ivy ともいう》/ a ～ lantern 岐阜じょうちん (Chinese lantern) / ～ paper 和紙 《Japan paper ともいう》/ ～ persimmon かき(の木・実) (kaki) / ～ quince びわ (loquat)；ばけ (Japonica) / ～ river fever つつが虫病. ——*n*. **1** (*sing*. & *pl*.) 日本人. **2** Ⓤ 日本語.

The words above are entries in Kenkyūsha's New Pocket English-Japanese Dictionary. The English-speaking student of Japanese has many fine dictionaries at his disposal, the result of the devoted labor of Japanese lexicographers. In addition, the teaching of Japanese in America is a lively field, with many competing textbooks and theories of instruction.

How the times do revolve. Ten years ago, fresh out of college in Boston, I applied for a position in a chic little boutique. The proprietor asked me what I had studied in school, and I said, "Japanese." He laughed so hard he choked. The same fellow, if he is still in business, probably gets Japanese customers every day now, and like many Americans, is considering picking up a little of the mysterious language that gave us *kimono*, "just a skosh," and *kamikaze.*

Good for him, and good for you too if you are thinking about it. Although Japanese never expect a foreigner to know the smallest scrap of their language, it's an act of great politeness to try out a little Japanese in their presence. But remember: Knowing a *little* Japanese is astonishingly different, in every respect, from knowing a lot.

Japanese is unrelated to languages we Westerners know. Since it is something of a universe unto itself, beginning to learn the language is like learning to drive a beautiful, odd car with the steering wheel on the ceiling, twelve extra pedals, and no speedometer or turn signals. Your ability to back this amazing contraption out of the driveway and put it into gear will make you proud, fascinated, and eager for more.

After a year or so of Japanese, however, a great existential question arises: Shall I go on? Because now you are getting a sense of the enterprise. The writing system looms. Beyond that, another barrier: the highly idiomatic and thoroughly socialized quality of Japanese expression. Japanese was never meant to be anybody's international language. It is of, by, and for a particular people, and you must walk their walk, to an unusual extent, if you want to talk their talk. And beyond that barrier... but wait.

The great eighteenth-century philologist Kamo no Mabuchi once registered a memorable complaint, since echoed by all students, Japanese and foreign, about Japanese writing: "Can anyone, even if he devotes himself earnestly, learn all these many Chinese characters? What a nuisance, a waste of effort, and a bother!" Mabuchi, a nationalist, was criticizing China, which bequeathes its elegant, ancient system of thousands of ideographs to the eastern islanders. The problem, *pace* Mabuchi, is not so much learning to write the characters as such. The system is not based on "one picture for one idea;" rather, it is a web of some two hundred elements combined in various, but eminently learnable and almost al-

ways exciting, ways. It is not easy to learn them, but the system is not illogical.

The Japanese twist is that a single character is likely to have a minimum of two pronunciations (some have five or more), corresponding to the dual vocabulary elements (Chinese-derived and native) in Japanese. It is as if a single character rendered our English terms "with," "con-" and "para." The first half of words like "withholding," "concept," and "parallel" would be the identical character, you see. So learning a character becomes rather difficult, requiring a certain acquired "feel," an ability to guess... you get the idea, don't you? Yes, Japanese is a language that must be *lived.* To really communicate in it requires a real commitment, fueled by a real love.

There is a further problem. Suppose you feel the love and make the commitment and learn the language. You'll delight the Japanese, right? And they will reward your efforts. Well, not exactly. You'll delight one in twenty. Others may feel invaded and threatened by your knowledge of their national secret code. At the very least, they will feel the sort of embarrassment we feel when a Hungarian says something like "catch you later, bro'" in a thick accent. They may refuse to speak to you in anything but their own broken English.

So why do it at all? Why commit to Japanese?

The big answers are the best. For the delights of a rich tradition of expression. In order to have all your ideas about language turned on their heads. To enter another universe of thought. To insist on the possibility of human communication across vast cultural and linguistic barriers. To toast a friend correctly. To transform your life.

GLOSSARY OF ENGLISH LOANWORDS IN JAPANESE

■

One more delight and/or terror of learning the language is the large number of non-Japanese words that have been adopted into Japanese.

■

APPU Up. Used in many compounds like *imēji-appu* (to improve one's appearance) and *raifu-appu* (to improve one's way of life).

BAIKINGU Viking. The name for any sort of smorgasbord or buffet, as in *chūka-baikingu* (Chinese buffet).

BĀSUKON Birth control.

BESUTO-TEN Best ten or top ten.

BIJITĀ Visitor at a club. Or as in *bijitingu-chīmu* (visiting team).

BŌI Waiter. Or in compunds like *bōi-hanto* (boy hunting) or *shisutā-bōi* (sister-boy, an effeminate man).

CHENJI Change. But limited in meaning to change of inning in baseball; *menbā-chenji* is a substitution in baseball or other sports.

DERAKKUSU Deluxe. Used figuratively in slang, as *derakkusubaka*, a deluxe, or total, idiot.

EKISAITO SURU To become excited or excite. Used in reference to sporting events or popular music concerts.

ERO Short for *erochikku* (erotic). A very common loan word.

FAITO Fighting spirit.

GETTSŪ "Get two." Used when calling for a double play in baseball.

GORĪN-PISU Green peas.

GŌRUNDEN AWĀ "Golden hour" or prime time on television.

HAI-MISU "High miss" or old maid.

HAPPĪ-ENDO Happy ending.

HOTTOKĒKI Hotcakes.

KANNINGU "Cunning." Means cheating on an examination.

KISSU Kiss.

KONE An influential acquaintance. Short for *konekushon* (connection).

MAI-KĀ A car belonging to an individual. Literally, "my car."

MAITO-GAI A very strong man. Derived from "dynamite guy."

MASU-PURO Mass production. Short form of *masu-purodakushon.*

MERIKEN Used today chiefly in compounds to indicate American origin of a product. Once meant a punch in the nose.

NAU NA FĪRINGU The now feeling; up-to-date.

NO-KA-DĒ No car day. A day on which traffic is prohibited in a given part of town.

NŌ-KOMENTO No comment.

Ō-ERU O.L. Stands for office lady or woman employed in an office.

ON-EA On the air.

ŌRU-BAKKU "All back." To comb the hair straight back.

RABU Love. Used most frequently in compounds like *rabu-hoteru* (love hotel, a hotel for trysts) and *rabu-retā* (love letter).

RASUTO-HEBI "Last heavy." Means a big last effort.

REJĀ-BŪMU Leisure boom or increased leisure time.

RIMOKON Short for *rimōto-kontorōru* (remote control). Used in slang to refer to a henpecked husband.

ROMANSU-GURĒ "Romance grey." Refers to the attractive grey hair of a middle-aged man.

RON-PARI Literally, "London-Paris." A slang word for describing a cross-eyed person, who appears to see London with one eye and Paris with the other.

SARARĪMAN A white collar worker. Literally a salary man.

SENSU Sense. Means good taste or good sense.

SUKOTCHI-ROKKUSU Scotch on the rocks.

SURIRU Thrill.

SWEAT Name of a popular soft drink.

TAFU Tough, meaning strong.

TORE-PAN Sweat pants for athletes. Short for *torēningu-pantsu.*

UETTO "Wet." Refers to a soft-hearted or sentimental person.

VSOP Very Special One Pattern. In university slang, refers to anything made according to formula, such as James Bond movies.

YŪZĀ User or consumer of goods.

LEVELS OF POLITENESS

Every language in the world uses honorifics—that is, maintains rules for the expression of deference to others and awareness of one's own place in a social or moral or familial hierarchy. My choice of the word "nice" instead of "dynamite" or "terrific" when I am speaking to elderly Aunt Edna is one example of the way we make honorific language in English—by a choice of adjectives. One will also, of course, strictly limit slang of whatever sort. I will choose a euphemistic verb for an unpleasant action. I will not—because I cannot—alter the way I form a past tense, or the term by which I refer to myself: "I."

Japanese, which is often and erroneously called a "vague" or "imprecise" language, has a very precise and useful array of exact substitutions you can make when you want to "upgrade" your language for talking to Aunt Edna, your professor, a cabinet minister or, most usefully, someone you've just met. Your vocabulary and the grammatical form of your utterance change rather markedly when you do this, and so it is sometimes felt that honorifics are a form of circumlocution, of saying a lot of fancy and insincere nonsense. But the Japanese language is not to be indicted here. Status differences invite "cleaned up" speech in any language; the fact that Japanese *keigo* (honorifics) are explicit and generally obligatory may indeed mean that they are taken for granted if observed, and less time is spent by speakers warily watching for signs of correct behavior in one another. After all, wouldn't it be a relief to have a more or less cut-and-dried speech style for Aunt Edna? Hearing the right verb endings would put her at her ease, and you might have to put up with a little less nagging.

Of course, Japanese honorifics go beyond this sensible scenario in a number of ways. You adjust your speech level to accord with the nature of your relationship with your interlocutor; ("I" is *watakushi* for Edna, *boku* with a friend; "to see" is *mimasu* at the tea party and *miru* in the corner bar)—but forms also change along what one eminent American scholar of Japanese calls "the axis of reference." If in a group of friends you refer to professor X or

another high-formal type person in your life, you are allowed a plain verb ending, but should choose a higher-class verb, of which there are several for basic actions. It goes without saying that if you are talking *about* professor X *with* professor Y in the latter's office, both the axis of address (to professor Y) and the axis of reference should be honorific.

Another difference is along the gender line. Japanese girls and women simply use more

Above: In this scene from Yasujirō Ozu's film *Tokyo Story,* three friends chat over *sake.* These middle-aged former classmates speak in an abrupt, plain style without circumlocutions; their language is Japanese at its most down-to-earth and egalitarian. At right, in another scene from the same film, an elderly couple relaxes with their daughter-in-law. In this situation, formality levels are at issue. The man may use plain forms in addressing both women, while his wife's speech to him will be more formally respectful. The daughter-in-law will be deferential to both elderly people. Needless to say, these speech issues do not affect the cheerfulness and ease of the party.

honorifics more of the time. Old-fashioned ladies never used informal verbs except with children and servants; today young urban women, talking among themselves, sound more or less like their male counterparts. Women's traditional speech differs so markedly from men's in so many ways, however, that it can't really be seen as a merely impoverished and subjugated version of a freer male mode. It is ambivalent, like so many of the products of ancient sexism—both a mark of women's "other" status and a separate idiom.

Naturally, honorifics are variable, and their use a matter of choice to a certain degree. This means that they can be expressive. Once Edwin O. Reischauer, the historian and former ambassador to Japan, was taking questions after lecturing at a large Japanese university. A student stood up and demanded, in a deliberately provocative plain form studded with slang and topped off by the plainest of plain verbs: "Hey Reischauer, what about Hiroshima? You got something to say about that?" Reischauer replied with an equally slangy crack about Pearl Harbor. The point was made, though. A people brought up to know their place in a sometimes hypocritical and stifling system of obligations and deferences are also natural experts at using the power of straight speech to break through the web.

CHARACTERS

There is a long-standing myth in the West that Chinese characters are "pictures of ideas," little drawings expressing abstract concepts directly, without the intervention of spoken language. It's a wonderful idea, and has excited first-class minds from Bacon to Leibniz to Ezra Pound. If it were only true, the Japanese might have had an easier time of it.

Truth to tell, the Chinese character is correctly described as an *ideograph;* It stands for a spoken word in the Chinese language. The thousands of Chinese characters are made up of two hundred or so meaningful elements that, long ago, were pictographic—they have

pictographic *etymologies*, so to speak. But most of these elements no more look like what they originally depicted than the Roman letter *A* recalls the oxhead from which it descended.

True, a handful of ideographs do strongly suggest what they represent. Another group operate like the parts of a rebus puzzle, and another group is made up of combinations of two or more significant elements that together suggest another concept—"fire" plus "rice-field" to mean "dry field fertilized by burning." The overwhelming majority, however, are combinations of a semantic, or meaning-bearing, element with a phonetic element, or pronunciation hint. Thus a character with the "speech" element on the left and on the right an element meaning "ancestral temple" (and pronounced *shih* when it is by itself) stands for the Chinese word *shih*, meaning "poem." It would be nice if this combination suggested

something about the holiness of poetry. It doesn't. It just alerts you: "This is the word having to do with language or speech that is pronounced *shih.*"

Obviously, to learn Chinese characters is to plunge into both the semantic field and the soundscape of the Chinese language. This is what the Japanese did in the sixth century when, following the only high-civilization example available to them, they borrowed both a learned language and a writing system for their native speech.

Chinese characters, as we saw, always bear both sound and meaning. Japanese is full of little syllables used only functionally to inflect verbs, indicate grammatical function, and so on. Japanese pioneers were in a quandary: We can use Chinese characters for meaning (agreeing to pronounce them as if they were Japanese), but we also have to use them

The four characters above are read *shūji nyūmon*, which may be translated as "introduction to calligraphy." (*Shūji* actually refers to the correct, as opposed to the artistic or expressive, writing of the Sino-Japanese characters.) The little numbers indicate the invariable stroke order in which each character must be written. The two-stroke character directly above (*ru* in modern Chinese) conveys the idea of entering and may be read as *nyū, ju, iru, hairu,* or *ireru* in Japanese, depending on context.

somehow for these little functional particles, for mere sound. Yet the characters insist on bearing meaning, and a page of writing partly semantic and partly phonetic will produce confusion. Just how do we know when a character is to be read of meaning (as if it were Japanese) and when for pure sound (in its Chinese pronunciation, to stand for a functional Japanese syllable)? Eventually, a limited body of Chinese characters habitually used for their sound value alone solidified into a syllabary *(kana)* that could handle the inflections and other little jobs, while characters in their full glory bore the main meanings, both the transcription of native Japanese words and the direct writing of the thousands of Chinese words that were enriching the Japanese vocabulary.

To say that the result was a rich, difficult system is to understate the case. The lateral complexity of character plus *kana* was matched by the vertical complexity embodied by each character, which could easily have both a Japanese reading and a Chinese one, or many Chinese ones, since the Japanese re-imported words at different moments of Chinese speech history.

Given these special values, it's no wonder that the Japanese have an almost superstitious respect for the written word. But then the written word has always had profound artistic and talismanic significance in the Chinese-influenced world. Calligraphy is not only the highest art form, with a stylistic range as wide or wider than any other art, but also the training ground and toolkit of the ink painter. The brush strokes that form ideographs are the bases for the ones that make rocks, clouds, birds. Hence when we see ideographs on landscape scrolls, we're not just seeing a painting somebody has written on; we see a juxtaposition of sister arts, each announcing its involvement in the truth and beauty of the other.

Beautiful writing was a romantic obsession in the classical world of Genji. The grace with which a lady traced out her soul's promptings on paper was a far more potent spur to love than a mere glimpse of her face—which, powdered paper-white and decorated with painted black eyebrows, was a calligraphic work itself.

The courtiers of classical Japan were intelligent, tasteful people, and they were right about the power of the brush to move us. A taste for calligraphy is easily acquired by looking at it as powerful abstract design, and not worrying about our inability to read it. What is vital to our appreciation of Sino-Japanese writing, however, is an awareness that it is the cornerstone of a great civilization, and a useful treasure whose establishment and furtherance has always required ingenuity and heroic discipline.

BIBLIOGRAPHY

Adachi, Barbara. *Living Treasures of Japan.* New York: Kodansha, 1973.

Allen, Ellen G. *Japanese Flower Arrangement: A Complete Primer.* Rutland, VT: C.E. Tuttle, 1963.

Beasley, W.G. *The Meiji Restoration.* Palo Alto, CA: Stanford University Press, 1972.

————. *The Modern History of Japan.* New York: St. Martins, 1981.

Boxer, C.R. *The Christian Century in Japan: 1549–1650.* Berkeley: University of California Press, 1974.

Castile, Rand. *The Way of Tea.* New York: Weatherhill, 1971.

Chandler, Billie T. *Crafts and Trades of Japan with Doll and Flower Arrangements.* Rutland, VT: C.E. Tuttle, 1964.

Chiba, Reiko, ed. *Down the Emperor's Road with Hiroshige.* Rutland, VT: C.E. Tuttle, 1965.

Chibbett, D.G. *The History of Japanese Printing and Book Illustration.* New York: Kodansha, 1977.

Dalby, Liza. *Geisha.* Berkeley: University of California Press, 1984.

Detrick, Mia. *The Sushi Book.* San Francisco: Chronicle Books, 1981.

Dotzinko, Grisha. *Enku: Master Carver.* New York: Kodansha, 1976.

Dower, John, ed. *Origins of the Modern Japanese State: Selected Writings of E.H. Norman.* New York: Pantheon, 1975.

Draeger, Donn F., and Warner, Gordon. *Japanese Swordmanship: Technique and Practice.* Rutland, VT: C.E. Tuttle, 1983.

Evans, Mary A., and Evans, Tom. *Shunga: The Art of Love in Japan.* London: Paddington, 1979.

Fujiwara, Yuchiku. *Rikka: The Soul of Japanese Flower Arrangement.* Translated by Norman Sparnon. Rutland, VT: C.E. Tuttle, 1976.

Gibney, Frank. *Japan: The Fragile Superpower.* New York: New American Library, 1980.

Gorham, Hazel H. *Japanese and Oriental Ceramics.* Rutland, VT: C.E. Tuttle, 1970.

Griffin, Stuart. *Japanese Food and Cooking.* Rutland, VT: C.E. Tuttle, 1955.

Gunji, Masakatsu. *Kabuki.* New York: Kodansha, 1965.

Hall, John, and Beardsley, R.K. *Twelve Doors to Japan.* New York: McGraw-Hill, 1965.

Hauge, Victor, and Hauge, Takako. *Folk Traditions in Japanese Art.* New York: Kodansha, 1978.

Haydock, Yukiko, and Haydock, Bob. *Japanese Garnishes.* New York: Holt, Rinehart & Winston, 1980.

Hibbett, Howard. *Contemporary Japanese Literature: An Anthology of Fiction, Film, and Other Writing Since 1945.* New York: Knopf, 1977.

————. *The Floating World in Japanese Fiction.* Rutland, VT: C.E. Tuttle, 1974.

Hihara, Koho, et al. *Ikebana in Quick and Easy Series.* Rutland, VT: C.E. Tuttle, 1978.

Itoh, Joan. *Japanese Cooking Now: The Real Thing.* New York: Warner Books, 1980.

Japan Graphic Designers Association. *Graphic Design in Japan,* 3 vols. New York: Kodansha, 1983.

Japanese Woodcut Book Illustrations, 4 vols. New York: Abaris Books, 1980.

Johnson, Margaret K., and Hilton, Dale K. *Japanese Prints Today: Tradition with Innovation.* Rutland, VT: C.E. Tuttle, 1980.

Keene, Donald, ed. *Anthology of Japanese Literature: Earliest Era to Mid-Nineteenth Century.* New York: Grove Press, 1955.

The Kodansha Encyclopedia of Japan, 9 vols. New York: Kodansha, 1983.

Lee, Sherman E. *The Genius of Japanese Design.* New York: Kodansha, 1981.

Masatoshi. *The Art of Netsuke Carving.* New York: Kodansha, 1981.

Michener, James A. *Japanese Prints: From the Early Masters to the Modern.* Rutland, VT: C.E. Tuttle, 1963.

Miyoshi, Masao. *Accomplices of Silence: The Modern Japanese Novel.* Berkeley: University of California Press, 1975.

Morris, Ivan. *The Nobility of Failure.* New York: Holt, Rinehart & Winston, 1975.

————. *Tale of Genji Scroll.* New York: Kodansha, 1971.

Murase, Miyeko. *The Arts of Japan.* New York: McGraw-Hill, 1977.

Narazaki, Muneshige. *The Japanese Print: Its Evolution and Essence.* New York: Kodansha, 1966.

Omae, Kinjito, and Tachibana, Yuzuru. *The Book of Sushi.* Translated by Richard Gage. New York: Kodansha, 1981.

Ortiz, Elisabeth L., and Endo, Mitsuko. *The Complete Book of Japanese Cooking.* New York: M. Evans, 1976.

Paine, Robert T., and Soper, Alexander. *The Art and Architecture of Japan.* Gretna, LA: Pelican, 1980.

Perrin, Noel. *Giving up the Gun: Japan's Reversion to the Sword. 1543–1879.* Boston: G.K. Hall, 1979.

Practical Karate Series, 6 vols. Rutland, VT: C.E. Tuttle, 1983.

Reischauer, Edwin O., and Craig, Albert M. *Japan: Tradition and Transformation.* Boston: Houghton-Mifflin, 1978.

Statler, Oliver. *Modern Japanese Prints: An Art Reborn.* Rutland, VT: C.E. Tuttle, 1956.

————. *Japanese Inn.* New York: Jove (BJ Publishing Group), 1962.

————. *Japanese Pilgrimage.* New York: William Morrow and Co., Inc., 1983.

Tanaka, Sen'o. *Tea Ceremony.* New York: Kodansha, 1973.

Tsuji, Shizuo. *Japanese Cooking: A Simple Art.* New York: Kodansha, 1980.

Yamada, Chisaburoh, et al., eds. *Japonisme in Art: An International Symposium.* New York: Kodansha, 1981.

SOURCES
AND
INDEX

CANADA

GENERAL ORGANIZATIONS

JAPAN SOCIETY OF CANADA
Apt. #105
320 Thompson Blvd.
Montreal, Quebec
H4N 1C1
(514) 729-4327

THE JAPAN TRADE CENTRE (1957)
151 Bloor Street West
Toronto, Ontario
M5S 1S8
(416) 962-5050

THE JAPANESE CANADIAN CENTENNIAL SOCIETY
Nu-Mode Dress Co.
530 Adelaide Street West
Toronto, Ontario
M5V 1T5
(416) 363-8162

JAPANESE CANADIAN CULTURAL CENTRE OF METROPOLITAN TORONTO
123 Wynford Drive
Don Mills, Ontario
M3C 1K1
(416) 429-0676

JAPANESE SWORD SOCIETY OF CANADA
2345 Keele Street
Toronto, Ontario
M6M 4A2
(416) 241-4603

ARTS

THE RISING SUN
234 Queen Street East
Toronto, Ontario
M5A 1S3
(416) 368-1410

STUART JACKSON GALLERY
119 Yorkville Avenue
Toronto, Ontario
M5R 1C1
(416) 967-9166
prints

BOOKS, RECORDS & FILMS

FURUYA TRADING CO.
460 Dundas Street West
Toronto, Ontario
M5T 1G8
(416) 366-5451

JAPAN SPECIALTIES TRADING CO.
463 Eglinton Avenue West
Toronto, Ontario
M5N 1A7
(416) 489-8611

SANKO TRADING
221 Spadina Avenue
Toronto, Ontario
M5T 2E2
(416) 862-1082

CRAFTS

ENTERPRISE SALES AND DISTRIBUTORS
146 Front Street West
Toronto, Ontario
M5J 1G2
(416) 593-7407

GARCO TRADING CO.
100 Brydon Drive
Rexdale, Ontario
M9W 4N9
(416) 742-5270

IMPORT & DOMESTIC TRADING
1800 Beulac Street
Montreal, Quebec
H4R 1W8

THE JAPAN PAPER PLACE
966 Queen Street West
Toronto, Ontario
M6J 1G8
(416) 533-6862

JAPAN SPECIALTIES
463 Eglinton Avenue West
Toronto, Ontario
M5N 1A7
(416) 489-8611
satsuma; *kutani*; Imari

R. MADESKER & SON LTD.
565 Alness Street
Downsview, Ontario
M3J 2T8
(416) 661-3456
pottery

MASA CRAFTS
170 Finchdene Square
Scarborough, Ontario
M1X 1B3
(416) 292-8961
shoji

MITSUKO ADACHI
515 Mt. Pleasant Road
Toronto, Ontario
M4S 2M4
(416) 484-2881
Imari; *satsuma; kutani;*
hibachi; kimono

GARDEN DESIGN

BANAWE LTD.
211 Telson Road, Unit 1
Markham, Ontario
L3R 137
(416) 495-1377
bonsai

CATALINO TRADING LTD.
110 Torbay Road, Unit 4
Markham, Ontario
L3R 1G5
(416) 495-6905

FUJI LANDSCAPE & GARDENERS
3164 East 23rd Avenue
Vancouver, B.C.
V6L 1P6
(604) 434-7527

HIRO LANDSCAPE & GARDENING
5827 Inverness Street
Vancouver, B.C.
V5W 3P6
(604) 325-2833

HIRO TSUJIMOTO LANDSCAPING
5745 Laurel Street
Burnaby, B.C.
V5G 1N4
(604) 294-0518

KATZUO LANDSCAPING LTD.
3912 Albert Street
Burnaby, B.C.
V5C 2C9
(604) 299-5414

LAKESIDE LANDSCAPING
3353 East 28th Avenue
Vancouver, B.C.
V5R 1T2
(604) 438-1421

MILLARD LISTER DISTRIBUTING LTD.
206 Dolomite Drive
Toronto, Ontario
M3J 2N2
(416) 661-0671

PACIFIC RIM LANDSCAPING LTD.
23080 Dyke Road
Richmond, B.C.
V6V 1E1
(604) 524-2622

ROY HARADA LANDSCAPE & GARDENING
540 Queensbury Avenue
North Vancouver, B.C.
V7L 4M7 (604) 980-5840

7-5-3 GARDEN ENTERPRISES LTD.
1 Burleigh Heights Drive
Willowdale, Ontario
M2K 1Y6
(416) 225-7836

TAKU LANDSCAPING
3641 East Pender Street
Vancouver, B.C.
V5K 2E4
(604) 298-5311

TORIZUKA LANDSCAPING CO.
2124 Gerrard Street East
Toronto, Ontario
M4E 2C2
(416) 699-3277

VALLEYVIEW GARDENS
3112 Kennedy Road
Scarborough, Ontario
M1V 1T1
(416) 291-1270
bonsai

MS. TOSH OIKAWA
1082 Pape Avenue
Toronto, Ontario
M4K 3W7
(416) 425-3161
origami

OKAME
46 Kensington Avenue
Toronto, Ontario
M5T 2K1
(416) 593-8879

SAKURA CRAFT CENTRE
Suite 511
45 Sheppard Avenue East
Willowdale, Ontario
M2M 5W9
(416) 223-3424
wood box making

SANKO TRADING
221 Spadina Avenue
Toronto, Ontario
M5T 2E2
(416) 862-1082

SHELAGH'S OF CANADA
43 Hazleton Avenue
Toronto, Ontario
M5R 2E3
(416) 924-7331

TINSEL MANUFACTURING LTD.
5600 Finch Avenue East
Agincourt, Ontario
M1B 1T1
(416) 293-1211

WILLIAM SMITH & SONS, LTD.
20 Voyageur Court South
Rexdale, Ontario
M9W 5M7
(416) 675-2755

YOSHI
58 Rusty Crestway
Willowdale, Ontario
M2J 2Y4
(416) 492-7880
Japanese hand-made paper

GIFTS AND HARDWARE

BAZAAR & NOVELTY CO. LTD.
1185 Caledonia Road
Toronto, Ontario
M6A 2X1
(416) 787-1803

BELGO CANADIAN MANUFACTURING CO. LTD.
500 King Street West
Toronto, Ontario
M5V 1L7
(416) 366-2241

DUNDAS UNION STORE LTD.
173 Dundas Street West
Toronto, Ontario
M5G 1C7
(416) 977-3765
ceramics

FURUYA TRADING CO.
460 Dundas Street West
Toronto, Ontario
M5T 1G9
(416) 977-5451

GIFT CRAFT LTD.
373 Front Street East
Toronto, Ontario
M5A 1G4
(416) 366-8901

GOLDCO IMPORTERS
461 King Street West
Toronto, Ontario
M5V 1M1
(416) 366-2835
toys

INTERNATIONAL GAMES
CANADA LTD.
2337 Lenworth Drive
Mississauga, Ontario
L4X 2G6
(416) 625-0131

NIPPON IMPORTING CO. LTD.
30 Duncan Street
Toronto, Ontario
M5V 2C2
(416) 364-4646

NORITAKE CO. INC.
90 Nugget Avenue
Agincourt, Ontario
M1S 3A7
(416) 291-2946

ORIENTAL ARTS TRADING CO.
2257 Bloor Street West
Toronto, Ontario
M6S 1N8
(416) 767-6233

PARAMOUNT GIFT STORE
733 Danforth Avenue
Toronto, Ontario
M4J 1L2
(416) 463-3426

PARAMOUNT TRADING CO.
229 Yonge Street
Toronto, Ontario
M5B 1N9
(416) 363-2886

SAKURA GIFTS
60 Bloor Street West
Toronto, Ontario
M5S 1M1
(416) 928-3385

INSTRUCTION

EAST YORK BOARD OF EDUCATION
Continuing Education
520 Cosburn Avenue
Toronto, Ontario
M4J 2P1
(416) 425-9435

ETOBICOKE BOARD OF EDUCATION
Administration Office
.1 Civic Centre Court
Etobicoke, Ontario
M9C 2B3
(416) 626-4360

HATASHITA JUDO CLUB
131 Queen Street East
Toronto, Ontario
M5C 1S1
(416) 364-8670

JAPAN KARATE ASSOCIATION OF MANITOBA
52 Albert Street
Winnipeg, Manitoba
R3B 1E8
(204) 942-1521

JAPAN MARTIAL ART CENTRE
681 Markham Street
Toronto, Ontario
M6G 2M2
(416) 535-5914

JAPANESE CANADIAN CULTURAL CENTRE
123 Wynford Drive
Don Mills, Toronto
M3C 1K1
(416) 429-0676

SENECA COLLEGE
Newnham Campus (Main campus)
1750 Finch Avenue East
Willowdale, Ontario
M2J 2X5
(416) 491-5050
ikebana; calligraphy; karate

MRS. TERRY SHIN
8 Dallington Drive
Willowdale, Ontario
M2J 2G3
(416) 493-6776
tea ceremony (cha no yu)

TORONTO JAPANESE GARDEN CLUB
1 Burleigh Heights Drive
Willowdale, Ontario
M2K 1Y6
(416) 225-7836
ikebana

TSURUOKA KARATE INC.
2200 Yonge Street
Toronto, Ontario
M4S 2C6
(416) 481-4760

UNIVERSITY OF BRITISH COLUMBIA
Continuing Education
2075 Westbrook Mall
Vancouver, B.C.
V6T 1W6
(604) 228-2181

UNIVERSITY OF MANITOBA
Continuing Education
541 University Centre
Winnipeg, Manitoba
R3T 2N2
(204) 261-5760

MEDIA

THE CANADA TIMES
291 Dundas Street West
Toronto, Ontario
M5T 1G1
(416) 593-2777

THE NEW CANADIAN
479 Queen Street West
Toronto, Ontario
M5V 2A9
(416) 366-5005

THE NIKKA TIMES
720 Spadina Avenue
Suite 508
Toronto, Ontario
M5S 2T9
(416) 923-2819

MEDICINE

MR. KENICHI SAITO
822 Broadview Avenue
Toronto, Ontario
M4K 2P7
(416) 466-8780
shiatsu

MR. K. KAMIYA
2993A Bloor Street West
Toronto, Ontario
M8X 1C1
(416) 326-1349
shiatsu

KIKKAWA SHIATSU
2444 Bloor Street West
Toronto, Ontario
M6S 1R2
(416) 762-4857

SHIATSU CENTRE LTD.
177 College Street
Toronto, Ontario
M5T 1P7
(416) 979-2824

UNITED KINGDOM

GENERAL ORGANIZATIONS

FAR EAST CENTER
St. Anthony's College
Oxford
0865 59651

JAPAN ASSOCIATION
Regis House
43-46 King William St.
London EC4
01 623 5320

JAPAN FOUNDATION
35 Dover St.
London W1
01 499 4726

JAPAN INFORMATION CENTER
9 Grosvenor Square
London W1X 9LB
01 493 6030

JAPAN NATIONAL TOURIST OFFICE
167 Regent Street
London W1
01 734 9638

JAPAN RESEARCH CENTER
School of Oriental Studies
Malet Street
London WC1
01 637 2388

JAPAN SOCIETY OF LONDON
656 Grand Buildings
Trafalgar Square
London WC2
01 839 1697

JAPANESE CHAMBER OF COMMERCE AND INDUSTRY
c/o Mitsubishi Corp.
Bow Bells House
Bread Street
London EC4
or
c/o Sitsui & Company
Temple Court, 11 Queen Victoria
London EC4

JAPANESE EMBASSY
46 Grosvenor Street
London W1X 0BA
01 493 6030

OPUS
12 Sutton Row
London W1V 5FH
01 734 5867
club for cultural exchange

ROYAL SOCIETY FOR ASIAN AFFAIRS
42 Devonshire Street
London W1
01 580 5728

GROCERIES & COOKWARE

FURUSATO FOODS
67a Camden High Street
London NW1
01 388 3979

J. A. CENTRE (Supermarket):
348 Regents Park Road, Finchley
London N3 2LJ
01 349 0011

529a Finchley Road, NW3
01 794 7018

250 Upper Richmond Road, SW15
01 789 3980

5 Warwick Street, W1
01 434 2030

70 Coney Hall
West Wickham, Kent
01 462 3404

NINJIN JAPANESE FOOD SHOP
244 Great Portland Street
London W1
01 388 2511

NIPPON FOOD CENTRE:
61 High Street, Wimbledon
London SW19
01 947 5872, 946 0495

483 Finchley Road, Hampstead
London NW3
01 794 2933

193 Upper Richmond Road
Putney, London SW15
01 788 3905

INSTRUCTION

**CENTRE OF JAPANESE
STUDIES**
University of Sheffield
Sheffield

MEDIA

ASAHI SHIMBUN
Room 247, "The Times"
New Printing House Square
Gray's Inn Road, London WC1X
8EX
01 837 0934, 3554

TV ASAHI
Deghardt House
31 Foley Street
London, W1P 7LB
01 580 4825

BBC JAPAN SECTION
Bush House, Strand, London WC2
01 240 3456 Ext 2503

CHUNICHI-TOKYO SHIMBUN
Suite 6-26, London International
   Press Centre
76 Shoe Lane, London EC4A 4BL
01 353 5991

FUJI TV
83 Farringdon Street
London, EC4A 4BL
01 353 0377, 9560

HOKKAIDO SHIMBUN
Suite 6-26, London International
   Press Centre
76 Shoe Lane, London, EC4
01 353 5991

JIJI PRESS
10 Salisbury Square, London EC4
01 353 5417, 3902

KYODO NEWS SERVICE
Communications House
Gough Square, London EC4
01 353 3470, 7557

MAINICHI SHIMBUN
8 Bouverie Street, London EC4
01 353 3477

NHK (Nippon Hoso Kyokai)
Visnews House, Cumberland
   Avenue
London, NW10 7EH
01 961 3040, 3096

NIHON KEIZAI SHIMBUN
c/o "The Financial Times"
Bracken House, Cannon Street
London, EC4
01 248 4019, 7694

NISHI-NIPPON SHIMBUN
Suite 6-26, London International
   Press Centre
76 Shoe Lane, London, EC4
01 353 5991

**NTV (Nippon Television
Network)**
Visnew House, Cumberland Avenue
London NW10 7EH
01 965 3282, 2905

SANKEI SHIMBUN
c/o Associated Press
83 Farringdon Street
London, EC4A 4BL
01 583 0689

**TOKYO BROADCASTING
SYSTEM INC.**
Suite 6-14, London International
   Press Centre
76 Shoe Lane, London EC4
01 353 5508/9

YOMIURI SHIMBUN
c/o "Daily Mail"
Northcliffe House, Room 40
London, EC4Y 8HJ
01 353 6952

UNITED STATES

GENERAL ORGANIZATIONS

ASIA SOCIETY
3414 Milam
Houston, TX 77002
(713) 520-7771

THE ASIA SOCIETY
725 Park Ave.
New York, NY 10021
(212) 288-6400

**CONSULATE GENERAL OF
JAPAN**
909 West 9th Ave.
Anchorage, AK 99501
(907) 279-8428

400 Colony Square Bldg.
1201 Peachtree St., NE
Atlanta, GA 30361
(404) 892-2700

Federal Reserve Plaza
14th floor
600 Atlantic Ave.
Boston, MA 02210
(617) 973-9772

625 N. Michigan Ave.
2nd floor
Chicago, IL 60611
(312) 321-9000

1742 Nuuanu Ave.
Honolulu, HI 96317
(808) 536-2226

504 First National City Bank Bldg.
1021 Main St.
Houston, TX 77002
(713) 652-2977

250 East First St.
Los Angeles, CA 90012
(213) 624-8305

1538 International Trade Mart
2 Canal St.
New Orleans, LA 70130
(504) 529-2101

One Citicorp Center
153 East 53rd St.
44th floor
New York, NY 10022
(212) 986-1600

2400 First National Bank Tower
1300 SW Fifth Ave.
Portland, OR 97201
(503) 221-1811

1601 Post St.
San Francisco, CA 94115
(415) 921-8000

3110 Rainier Bank Tower
Seattle, WA 98101
(206) 682-9107

EMBASSY OF JAPAN
2520 Massachusetts Ave., NW
Washington, DC 20008
(202) 234-2266

**GARDENA VALLEY JAPANESE
CULTURAL INSTITUTE**
16215 S. Gramercy Pl.
Gardena, CA 90247
(213) 324-6611

**HOLLYWOOD JAPANESE
CULTURAL INSTITUTE**
3929 Middlebury St.
Los Angeles, CA 90004

**INTERNATIONAL CENTER OF
INDIANAPOLIS**
1050 W. 42nd St.
Indianapolis, IN 46208
(317) 923-1468
Japanese festivals, origami

**INTERNATIONAL INSTITUTE OF
YOUNGSTOWN**
661 Wick Ave.
Youngston, OH 44502
(216) 743-5189
cultural exhibits, festivals

JAPAN CENTER
Post & Buchanan
San Francisco, CA 94115
(415) 346-3242   922-6776
collection of shops, restaurants,
   hotel, spas, theater

JAPAN CULTURE CENTER
1275 Space Park Dr.
Houston, TX 77058
translation services, tea ceremony,
   ikebana demonstration

**JAPAN NATIONAL TOURIST
ORGANIZATION**
333 North Michigan Ave.
Chicago, IL 60601
(312) 332-3975

1420 Commerce St.
Dallas, TX 75201
(214) 741-4931

2270 Kalakaua Ave.
Honolulu, HI 96815
(808) 923-7631

624 South Grand Ave.
Los Angeles, CA 90017
(213) 623-1952

45 Rockefeller Plaza
New York, NY 10020
(212) 757-5640

1737 Post St.
San Francisco, CA 94115
(415) 931-0700
books, pamphlets, travel
   information

JAPAN SOCIETY OF BOSTON
22 Battery March St.
Boston, MA 02109
(617) 451-0726

JAPAN SOCIETY OF NEW YORK
333 E. 47th St.
New York, NY 10017
(212) 832-1155
language instruction, excellent film
   and lecture programs, gallery,
   library

**JAPAN SOCIETY OF
SAN FRANCISCO**
312 Sutter St.
Room 406
San Francisco, CA 94108
(415) 986-4383

JAPAN SOCIETY OF VERMONT
c/o Allan Andrews
Department of Religion
University of Vermont
Burlington, VT 05405

**JAPANESE AMERICAN
ASSOCIATION**
7 W. 44th St.
New York, NY 10036
(212) 840-6942
classes in cooking, *ikebana*,
sumi-e, and tea

**JAPANESE AMERICAN CLUB
OF COLUMBUS**
2120 Haverford Rd.
Columbus, OH 43220
(614) 457-6742

JAPANESE AMERICAN CULTURAL & COMMUNITY CENTER
244 San Pedro St., #505
Los Angeles, CA 90012
(213) 628-2725
instruction in painting, *ikebana*, *koto*, *buyō*, *shamisen*, and *nagauta*

JAPANESE ASSOCIATION
Ohio University
Scott Quad
Athens, OH 45701

JAPANESE EDUCATIONAL INSTITUTE OF HOUSTON
14133 Memorial Dr.
Houston, TX 77079
(713) 493-0840

KEN ZEN DŌJO
152-8 W. 26th St.
New York, NY 10001
(212) 741-2281
classes in cooking, *sumi-e*, *ikebana*, tea, martial arts

MINYŌ CLUB
Mrs. Etsuko Oba
2237 Silver Maple Ct.
Indianapolis, IN
(317) 632-7315
classes in tea ceremony, *sushi*, cooking, calligraphy, origami, kite-making

PEOPLES AND CULTURES
1330 Old River Rd.
Cleveland, OH 44113
(216) 621-3749

US-JAPAN CROSS-CULTURE CENTER
244 San Pedro St.
Los Angeles, CA 90122
(213) 617-2039
language instruction and study tours

US-JAPAN CULTURE CENTER
2139 Wisconsin Ave., NW
Washington, DC 20007
(202) 333-6760

ARTS

ALBERTS-LANGDON, INC.
126 Charles St.
Boston, MA 02108
(617) 523-5954
antiques

ANTIQUES KAYOKO
13006 Woodland Ave.
Shaker Heights, OH 44120
(216) 795-0113
ceramics, Imari, prints, kimono, *obi, tansu*

ARTS & DESIGNS OF JAPAN
Carmel, CA
(408) 624-0820
antiques

ASAKICHI ANTIQUES
1730 Geary Blvd.
San Francisco, CA 94115
(415) 921-2147

ASIA HOUSE GALLERY
Salem, MA 01945
(617) 745-8257
by appointment

ASUKA ANTIQUES
25-A Tamalpais Ave.
San Anselmo, CA
(415) 459-4026

AZUMA GALLERY
142 Greene St.
New York, NY 10012
(212) 925-1381

MARY BASKETT GALLERY
1002 St. Gregory St.
Cincinnati, OH 45202
(513) 421-0460
prints

BERNHEIMER'S ANTIQUE ARTS
52C Brattle St.
Cambridge, MA 02138
(617) 547-1177

BIJUTSU
1528½ California St.
San Francisco, CA
(415) 673-7880
antiques

BIWA-HŌSHI ORIENTAL ANTIQUES
5041 Oroville-Quincy Hwy.
Oroville, CA
(916) 589-1071

BIZEN
3314 Sacramento
San Francisco, CA
(415) 346-3933
antiques

BROWN-BAUMANN FINE ARTS
336 North Ave.
Weston, MA 02139
(617) 893-2731

CHINOH GALLERY
69 Fifth Ave.
New York, NY 10003
(212) 255-0377

EASTERN ACCENT, INC.
237 Newbury St.
Boston, MA 02116
(617) 266-9707
art, antiques, furniture

T. EBIHARA, INC.
91 Grand St.
New York, NY 10013
(212) 431-4562
art dealer

GARENDŌ GALLERY
12955 Ventura Blvd.
Studio City, CA 91604
(213) 783-1861

GIFU ORIENTAL ANTIQUES
335 Bleecker St.
New York, NY 10014
(212) 255-9484

HURST & HURST
53 Mt. Auburn St.
Cambridge, MA 02138
(617) 491-6888
art, fine books

ISSHIN-DŌ
341½ E. First St.
Los Angeles, CA 90012
(213) 623-2927
kakemono, other art, antiques, china

JAPANESE ART & ARMS
11764 W. Pico Blvd.
West Los Angeles, CA 90064
(213) 479-2901

JAPAN GALLERY
1210 Lexington Ave.
New York, NY 10022
(212) 288-2241

KABUTOYA GALLERIES
Ghirardelli Sq.
900 North Point
San Francisco, CA
(415) 776-2800
prints of all periods

BETTY KILLIAN ORIENTAL ARTS
122 Middlebury Turnpike
Chester, CT
(203) 526-2967
tsuba, porcelain, prints

KIMURA GALLERY
1933 Ocean Ave.
San Francisco, CA
(415) 585-0052
prints

D. G. KOLB
North Hampton, NH
(603) 964-8813
prints

KONISHI ORIENTAL ANTIQUES
8325 Beverly Blvd.
Los Angeles, CA 90048
(213) 651-0368

KURA GALLERY
Rockrimmon Rd.
Stamford, CT
(203) 322-1028
house in Japanese style, prints on exhibit for sale

KYŌYA
248 East First St.
Los Angeles, CA 90012
(213) 617-1072

MATSUKI ANTIQUES & GIFTS
1951 Union St.
San Francisco, CA
(415) 922-3102
new and antique kimono, art, furnishings

MICHIKO'S GIFTS & ART
1841 Solano Ave.
Berkeley, CA
(415) 525-2707
antiques, *tansu*, screens, vases, Imari, kimono

THE MITERED CORNER
5225 Hill Ave.
Toledo, OH 43615
(419) 531-6789
prints

MITSUKOSHI GALLERY
465 Park Ave.
New York, NY 10022
(212) 753-5580

MIZUNO GALLERY
210 E. Second St.
Los Angeles, CA 90012
(213) 625-2491

NAKAMURA ANTIQUES
San Francisco
(415) 391-6694

ORIENTAL ANTIQUES
1303 Park Western Dr., #6
San Pedro, CA 90732
(213) 519-1504

ORIENTAL ART GALLERY
692 Madison Ave.
New York, NY 10021
(212) 688-0931

ORIENTATIONS
16 Maiden Lane
San Francisco, CA 94108
(415) 981-3972

PROVENANCE GALLERY
Biltmore Plaza Hotel
Kennedy Plaza
Providence, RI 02903
(401) 751-5800

PUCKER/SAFRAI GALLERY
171 Newbury St.
Boston, MA 02116
(617) 267-9473
art

RONIN GALLERY
605 Madison Ave.
New York, NY 10022
(212) 688-0188

SERVICE-KNOLLE ANTIQUES
480 Vallejo
San Francisco, CA
(415) 981-7717

SHIBATA'S ART STUDIO
3028 Fillmore
San Francisco, CA
(415) 567-1530

SHIOTA, T. Z.
3131 Fillmore
San Francisco, CA
(415) 567-5428
arts

SUMIDA GALLERY
129 Japanese Village Plaza
Los Angeles, CA 90012
(213) 680-0394

TOKYO ARTS SALON
32-50 70th St.
Jackson Heights, NY 11370
(212) 898-4347

YAMANAKA FINE ARTS
2500 Wilshire Blvd. #1030
Los Angeles, CA 90057
(213) 383-0253

YESTERYEAR ANTIQUES
776 W. Whittier St.
Columbus, OH 43206
(614) 444-0054

YOKO ANTIQUES
2557 Colorado Blvd.
Los Angeles, CA 90041
(213) 257-6011

ZENIYA
18039 Crenshaw Blvd. #205
Torrance, CA 90504
(213) 324-6275
art gallery

BOOKS, RECORDS & FILMS

AMERASIA BOOKS
338 E. Second St.
Los Angeles, CA 90012
(213) 680-2888

ASIA BOOKSTORE
2100 W. Redondo Beach Blvd.
Torrance, CA 90504
(213) 538-4619

ASIAN BOOKSTORE
12 Arrow St.
Cambridge, MA 02138
(617) 354-0005

CAMERA ONE THEATRE
366 S. First St.
San Jose, CA 95112
(408) 295-6308
films

CHENG & TSUI CO.
25 West St.
Boston, MA 02111
(617) 426-6074
books on Japan

EAST-WEST BOOK SHOP
1170 El Camino Real
Menlo Park, CA 94025
(415) 325-5709

EAST-WEST BOOKS
2026 Sawtelle Blvd.
West Los Angeles, CA 90025
(213) 479-8929

EAST & WEST SHOP
4 Apple Blossom Lane
Newtown, CT
(203) 426-0661
books

FUTABA RECORDS & GIFTS
109 N. Lincoln Ave.
Monterey Park, CA 91754
(213) 283-9535

ISHIDA BOOK STORE
41-12 Main St.
Flushing, NY 11355
(212) 445-6288

1088 Central Ave.
Scarsdale, NY 10583
(914) 723-6408

JAPAN BOOKS & RECORDS
3345 N. Clark
Chicago, IL 60657
(312) 248-4114

JAPAN FILM CENTER
333 E. 47th St.
New York, NY 10017
(212) 832-1155

JAPANTOPIA BOOKS
69 W. 10th St.
New York, NY 10011
(212) 477-9002

KINOKUNI-YA BOOKSTORES OF AMERICA
110 Los Angeles St.
Los Angeles, CA 90012
(213) 687-4447

KONIKUNI-YA
123 S. Weller St.
Los Angeles, CA 90012
(213) 687-4480

KINOKUNI-YA BOOK STORE
10 W. 49th St.
New York, NY 10020
(212) 765-1461
records too

KINOKUNI-YA BOOKSTORES OF AMERICA
1581 Webster
San Francisco, CA 94115
(415) 567-7625
English and Japanese language
books on Japan

KODANSHA INTERNATIONAL
10 E. 53rd St.
New York, NY 10022
(212) 393-7050
major publisher

KOKUSAI THEATRE
3020 Crenshaw Blvd.
Los Angeles, CA 90016
(213) 734-1148
films

KOKUSAI THEATRE
Post & Buchanan St.
San Francisco, CA 94115
(415) 563-1400
films

LINDALEA THEATRE
251 S. Main St.
Los Angeles, CA 90012
(213) 624-5648
films

MAGIC RADIO
139 Japanese Village Plaza
Los Angeles, CA 90012
(213) 625-8485
records

MELODY RECORDS
16127 S. Western Ave.
Gardena, CA 90247
(213) 321-6892
records

PACIFIC FILM ARCHIVE
2626 Bancroft Way
Berkeley, CA 94720
(415) 642-1437
splendid collection of films

SHAMBALA BOOKSELLERS
2482 Telegraph Ave.
Berkeley, CA 94704
(415) 848-8443
Asian philosophy and religion

TAIYŌ-DŌ RECORD SHOP
Japan Center
Kintetsu Bldg.
1737 Post St. #11-A
San Francisco, CA 94115
(415) 885-2818

TOKYO BOOK STORE ("ZEN ORIENTAL")
521 Fifth Ave.
New York, NY 10017
(212) 697-0840
records too

TOKYO BOOKSTORE
1562 Lemoine Ave.
Fort Lee, NJ 07024
(201) 947-8917

TSUTSUMI-DŌ BOOKS
Pear Tree Center
2801 W. Ball Rd.
Anaheim, CA 92804
(714) 527-2065

CHARLES E. TUTTLE, INC.
28 South Main St.
P.O. Box 140
Rutland, VT 05701
(802) 773-8930
major publisher on Japanese topics

WEATHERHILL
Charles E. Tuttle Company
28 S. Main St.
Rutland, VT 05701
(802) 773-8930

CRAFTS

BECKLEY-CARDY-KIGER CO.
4869 W. 38th St.
Indianapolis, IN 46254
(317) 299-8040
Japanese kites

DAIKOKU
Japan Center
1737 Post St.
San Francisco, CA 94115
(415) 563-4550
mingei

FIVE EGGS
436 West Broadway
New York, NY 10012
(212) 226-1606
mingei, clothing

FUTON BED WEST
9420 Reseda Blvd.
Northridge, CA 91324
(213) 701-0677

HAKATA CHINA & IMPORTS
4505 Centinela Ave.
Los Angeles, CA 90066
(213) 832-4731
ceramics

HANKYŪ, INC.
707 Wilshire Blvd. #4770
Los Angeles, CA 90017
(213) 629-4305
china, ceramics

HASHIMOTO/PLATZ DESIGN
404 Park Ave., S.
New York, NY 10016
(212) 685-3718
interior carpentry

HOKAMA CUSTOM WOOD CRAFT AND REPAIR
1631 W. Carson St.
Carson, CA 90501
(213) 328-5345
(213) 324-4420

HOUSE OF SWORDS
1762 Buchanan
San Francisco, CA
(415) 929-0989
swords and antique arts

IRONHORSE COMPANY
1705 Solano Ave.
Berkeley, CA 94707
(415) 528-3302
Japanese science-fiction-toy
specialty shop

IWASAKI IMAGES
19330 Van Ness Ave.
Torrance, CA 90501
(213) 328-7121
plastic food

IWASHIRO ASSOCIATES
450 West Broadway
New York, NY 10012
(212) 677-7100
carpentry

KATSURA CONSTRUCTION
389 Broom St.
New York, NY 10013
(212) 925-5641
carpentry

KEWPIE CHILDREN'S
BOUTIQUE
Honda Plaza, 448 E. Second St.
Los Angeles, CA 90012
(213) 617-3057
toys

KIYOSHI SHINTŌ
1249 E. Sixth St.
Los Angeles, CA 90021
(213) 622-6624
carpentry

KURATA SHOTEN
2422 W. Jefferson Blvd.
Los Angeles, CA 90018
(213) 734-3913
futon

KUROMATSU
722 Bay St.
San Francisco, CA 94109
(415) 474-4027
mingei

LONG'S BOOKSTORE
1836 N. High St.
Columbus, OH 43201
(614) 294-4674
origami supplies

MANEKEE CHILDREN'S
VILLAGE
127 Japanese Plaza
Los Angeles, CA 90012
(213) 628-5919
toys

MASHIKO
Japan Center
1581 Webster St.
San Francisco, CA 94115
(415) 346-0748
mingei

MATSUYAMA INTERIORS
131 W. 21st St.
New York, NY 10011
(212) 757-1444
carpentry

MICHI TOYS
342¼ E. First St.
Los Angeles, CA 90012
(213) 626-7522

MINGEI JAPANESE FOLK ART
398 West Broadway
New York, NY 10013
(212) 431-6176

MINAMI CUSTOM WOODCRAFT
1224 W. 256th St.
Harbor City, CA 90710
(213) 534-4135
fusuma, shoji, Japanese furniture,
   sushi bars, cabinets, etc.

MITSURU CHILDREN'S SHOP
107 Japanese Village Plaza
Los Angeles, CA 90012
(213) 628-2921

MIYA SHOJI & INTERIORS
107 E. 17th St.
New York, NY 10011
(212) 243-6774

MYTHOLOGY UNLIMITED
370 Columbus Ave.
New York, NY 10024
(212) 874-0774
toys, design books, posters

NEW MOON
932 Massachusetts Ave.
Cambridge, MA 02139
(617) 492-8262
futon, furnishings

NIPPON BIKEN CONSTRUCTION
628 W. 52nd St.
New York, NY 10019
(212) 757-1444
carpentry

NIPPON-TO JAPANESE
SWORDS
5019 Santa Monica Ave.
San Diego, CA 92106
(619) 222-6918

NORITAKE CO., INC.
2050 E. Vistabella Way
Compton, CA 90220
(213) 537-9601
china

OHTA STUDIO
159 Mercer St.
New York, NY 10012
(212) 966-1782
carpentry

ORIENTAL PORCELAIN
GALLERY
2702 Hyde St.
San Francisco, CA 94109
(415) 776-5969

ORIGAMI CENTER OF AMERICA
31 Union Square, W.
New York, NY 10003
(212) 255-0469

ŌZORA
238 E. Sixth St.
New York, NY 10003
(212) 228-1325
carpentry

PETER'S VALLEY
Rte. 615
Layton, NJ 07851
(201) 948-5200
Japanese Anagama kiln

SHINTO OF AMERICA
2808 Oregon Court
Unit J-3
Torrance, CA 90503
(213) 320-0867
plastic food

SHOJI WORKSHOP
20-10 31st Ave.
Astoria, NY 11106
(212) 274-9351

SUZUKI CARPENTRY
284 Lafayette St.
New York, NY 10022
(212) 431-4147

SUZUKI FUTON MFG.
810 E. Chestnut St. #A
Glendale, CA 91205
(213) 243-2754

TACONY
38-25 Woodside Ave.
Woodside, NY 11377
(212) 478-2424
carpentry

TAJIMI POTTERY (U.S.A.), INC.
2029 Sawtelle Blvd.
West Los Angeles, CA
(213) 473-3946

TAMURA WOOD CRAFT
1605 E. First St.
Los Angeles, CA 90033
(213) 269-9673
cabinetry

TANYA JAPANESE SWORD
SHOP
Honda Plaza
402 E. Second St.
Los Angeles, CA 90012
(213) 620-9963

TOKUSAN
2639 Loganrita Ave.
Arcadia, CA 91006
(213) 446-6361
carpentry

UNIVRON INTERNATIONAL
555 Madison Ave.
New York, NY 10022
(212) 755-1390
carpentry

WOODLINE
1731 Clement Ave.
Alameda, CA 94501
(415) 521-1810
mail-order carpentry supplies and
   tools

WORLD WIDE GAMES
Box 450
3527 West S.R. #37
Delaware, OH 43015
(614) 369-9631
Japanese games

YABE, YASUKO
(617) 623-5427
textile arts, dyeing, lectures,
   demonstrations

DESIGN

ABE, SHIN
29 Garrison Ave.
Somerville, MA 02144
(617) 625-5211
gardens

ASANO DESIGN STUDIO
104 E. 40th St.
New York, NY 10016
(212) 687-3545
graphics

BLUEFINGERS
101 Charles St.
Boston, MA 02108
(617) 523-8774
kimono

BONSAI GALLERY
6086 Busch Blvd.
Columbus, OH 43229
(614) 885-4376
bonsai, gifts

CHIKUGO-EN BONSAI
NURSERY
18110 S. Western Ave.
Gardena, CA 90248
(213) 323-4011

EAST-WEST FURNITURE
2929 W. Ball Rd.
Anaheim, CA 92804
(714) 827-8410

EBIHARA, YOSHIKO
91 Grand St.
New York, NY 10013
(212) 431-4562
textile design

FUJI BONSAI NURSERY
13170 Gleanoaks Blvd.
Sylmar, CA 91342
(213) 367-5372

FUJI TRADING
340 E. Arlight St.
Monterey Park, CA 91754
(213) 723-0161
Japanese room materials

FUJUTARŌ COMPANY
306 N. Baltimore Ave.
Monterey Park, CA 91754
(213) 573-3354
Japanese room materials

S. GOI, INC.
246 E. Second St.
Los Angeles, CA 90012
(213) 624-4546
kimono

HOASHI STUDIO
310 Madison Ave.
New York, NY 10017
(212) 697-7208
graphic design

I. S. DESIGN
57 E. 11th St.
New York, NY 10003
(212) 473-7400

IKEDA BONSAI GARDEN
6522 Stanton Ave.
Buena Park, CA 90621
(714) 521-6576

JAPAN DESIGN CENTER
40 E. 49th St.
New York, NY 10017
(212) 838-6803

JAPAN LANDSCAPING
9311 Kramer Ave.
Suite N
Westminster, CA 92683
(714) 531-4888
(714) 839-2242
gardens

JAPAN NURSERY
Route #1
Box 60-M
Dey Glove Rd.
Englishtown, NJ 07726
(201) 446-2186
bonsai

JAPAN NURSERY, INC.
135 W. 28th St.
New York, NY 10001
(212) 947-6953
bonsai

JAPAN TRADING CO.
1762 Buchanan
San Francisco, CA
(415) 929-0989
shoji, furnishings, garden
  ornaments

**JAPANESE GARDEN DESIGN &
ART CENTER**
2618 Meadow Lark Lane
Escondido, CA 92027
(619) 743-2424

K. I. DESIGN & DEVELOPMENT
1336 E. Katella Ave.
Anaheim, CA 92805
(714) 750-7005
oriental design specialist

KANAI, KIYOSHI
115 E. 30th St.
New York, NY 10016
(212) 679-5542
graphic design

KAWASE ORIENTAL SHŌJI
724 E. First St.
Los Angeles, CA 90012
(213) 629-4174

10954 Warner Ave.
Fountain Valley, CA 92708
(714) 962-6616
(714) 545-5803

KOJIMA, KENJI
41 W. 89th St.
New York, NY 10024
(212) 580-4807
graphic designer

KUCHIBA, KUNIHIKO
121 Dubbin St.
Brooklyn, NY 11222
(212) 389-8274
interior design

KURAGAMA NURSERY
Weller Court #205-B
123 S. Weller St.
Los Angeles, CA 90012
(213) 617-0005

KURAGAMI NURSERY
2547 Rainbow Valley Rd.
Rainbow, CA 92028
(619) 728-6882
bonsai

KUSUMOTO BONSAI NURSERY
750 W. 157th St.
Gardena, CA 90247
(213) 324-1806

KYOSHIGE INTERNATIONAL
4154 Marathon St. #1
Los Angeles, CA 90029
(213) 669-0404
kimono

KYOTO LANDSCAPING
1617 Ponderosa
Costa Mesa, CA 92626
(714) 546-0464
gardens

LANDSCAPE DESIGN, INC.
P.O. Box 2112
Duxbury, MA 02332
(617) 934-5200
gardens

MARUHACHI, USA
3856 Cerritos Ave.
Los Alamitos, CA 90720
(213) 598-9691/9693
kimono

**MARUMIYA STONE LANTERN &
BONSAI NURSERY**
16819 S. Normandie Ave.
Gardena, CA 90247
(213) 327-8826
garden design

MATSUSHITA LANDSCAPING
33411 Ocean Hill Dr.
Dana Point, CA 92629
(714) 493-3465
gardens

MURATA BONSAI GARDEN
13631 Beach Blvd.
Westminster, CA 92683
(714) 894-4919

**NAKAMAKI GROUP
(LANDSCAPE ARCHITECTS)**
438 S. Camino Del Rio St.
San Diego, CA 92108
(619) 291-4401

NICHI-BEI BUSSAN
1715 Buchanan
San Francisco, CA 94115
(415) 346-2117
kimono

OHTA STUDIO
159 Mercer St.
New York, NY 10012
(212) 966-1782
interiors

OKAMURA, MASAO
Brooklyn Botanic Garden
1000 Washington Ave.
Brooklyn, NY 11225
(212) 622-4433
bonsai

OTA BONSAI NURSERY
3221 E. Chapman Ave.
Orange, CA 92669
(714) 771-0866

SAIKI DESIGN
185 Madison Ave.
New York, NY 10016
(212) 679-3523
graphics

**SATSUMA NURSERY &
LANDSCAPING**
4906 La Cuenta Dr.
San Diego, CA 92124
(619) 560-9155
gardens

SAWANO & ASSOCIATES
Architects
12872 Valley View St. #7
Garden Grove, CA 92645
(213) 430-5473
(714) 895-1340

SOKO INTERIORS
1672 Post St.
San Francisco, CA 94115
(415) 922-4155
tansu

**STONE WORKS—DANIEL
BLAIR**
131 Union St.
New Bedford, MA 02740
(617) 992-1338
gardens

SUZUKI CARPENTRY STUDIO
284 Lafayette St.
New York, NY 10012
(212) 431-4147
carpentry & interior design

TAKAHASHI DESIGN
12 W. 37th St.
New York, NY 10018
(212) 695-6863

TAKUMI DESIGN GROUP
1406 W. 178th St.
Gardena, CA 90248
(213) 516-7990
Japanese room materials

TOKYO NURSERY
4238 S. Sepulveda Blvd.
Culver City, CA 90230
(213) 397-0941
gardens

WATANABE GARDEN ART
4521 N. Walnut Grove Ave.
Rosemead, CA 91770
(213) 285-3724
gardens

YAMAGUCHI BONSAI NURSERY
1905 Sawtelle Blvd.
West Los Angeles, CA 90025
(213) 473-5444

YAMASHIRO, HARUO
18411 Evelyn Ave.
Gardena, CA 90248
(213) 323-4476
gardens

GIFTS, HARDWARE &
-COOKWARE

ANZEN HARDWARE
232 E. Second St.
Los Angeles, CA 90012
(213) 613-0415

220 E. First St.
Los Angeles, CA 90012
(213) 628-2068
Japanese tools, housewares

DRAGON TRADING
943 Dopler
Akron, OH 44303
(216) 836-8877

EAST WEST IMPORTS
249 Broad St.
Manchester, CT
(203) 649-6939

EAST-WEST TRADING CO.
68 Howe St.
New Haven, CT
(203) 777-2117

HAGI
360 E. First St.
Los Angeles, CA 90012
(213) 624-8370
dolls, china, lacquerware

HASTINGS HOUSE
River Rd.
Essex, CT
(203) 767-8217

HŌRAI-SAN
242 Washington St.
Brookline, MA 02146
(617) 277-4321
gifts, home furnishings, kimono,
  books

IMPERIAL KAMADO
350 Paseo Sonrisa
Walnut, CA 91789
(714) 594-9558/9
(213) 333-6086
hardware

INTERNATIONAL TRADING
340 E. Azusa
Los Angeles, CA 91101
(213) 628-7473
Imari, *satsuma*, *kutani*, lacquer

**KONGO COMPANY GIFTS &
ART OBJECTS**
319 E. First St.
Los Angeles, CA 90012
(213) 628-8472
china, ceramics

KOTOBUKI GIFT CENTER
743 S. Vermont Ave.
Los Angeles, CA 90055
(213) 380–1052
china, ceramics

KOTOBUKI ORIENTAL GIFT
193½ S. Beverly Dr.
Beverly Hills, CA 90212
(213) 275–9887

KOTOBUKI GIFTS
2269 Chestnut
San Francisco, CA 94123
(415) 922–0548

MARUYA U.S.A.
18220 S. Western Ave.
Gardena, CA 90248
(213) 516–7674
china, ceramics, rice cookers,
    wooden and iron goods,
    kitchenware, toys, lacquerware,
    carpentry tools, knives

MEIJI-YA
1569-F W. Redondo Beach Blvd.
Gardena, CA 90247
(213) 770–4677
china, ceramics

MIKASA CHINA
20633 S. Fordyce Ave.
Carson, CA 90749
(213) 636–2301
china, ceramics

NANIWA CORPORATION
327 Japanese Village Plaza
Los Angeles, CA 90012
(213) 624–1015
cookware specialty shop

ORIENTAL CONCEPTS
125 Main St.
Westport, CT
(203) 226–9948
gifts

ORIENTAL GIFT, INC.
Washington Square Shopping
    Center #91
Indianapolis, IN
(317) 897–6400

**ORIENTAL TEA & MERCANTILE
CO.**
2940 Locust St.
St. Louis, MO
(314) 535–4713

ORIENTAL TRADE CENTER
3986 Monroe
Toledo, OH 43606
(419) 472–1739
food, handcrafts

OTAFUKU GIFT SHOP
14775 Jeffrey Rd.
Irvine, CA 92714
(714) 552–4271
general gifts, china, cosmetics

SATSUMA ORIENTAL IMPORTS
2029 Sawtelle Blvd.
West Los Angeles, CA 90025
(213) 473–3946
china, kimono

**T & A INTERNATIONAL
TRADING**
2808 Oregon Court, Unit J-1 & J-2
Torrance, CA 90503
(213) 320–9711
kitchen equipment, ceramics, gifts

TREE'S PLACE
Junction Routes 6-A & 28
Orleans, MA 02653
(617) 255–1330
crafts, furniture

TSUTSUMI-DŌ
2801 W. Ball Road
Anaheim, CA 92804
(714) 527–2065
gifts

UEDA DEPARTMENT STORE
350 E. First St.
Los Angeles, CA 90012
(213) 687–4812
gifts

UWAJIMA-YA
6th South & South King
Seattle, WA 98104
(206) 624–6248
department store

WOODLINE
1731 Clement Ave.
Alameda, CA 94501
(415) 521–1810
mail-order kitchen knives

**YAMAGUCHI DEPARTMENT
STORE**
2057 Sawtelle Blvd.
West Los Angeles, CA 90025
(213) 479–9531

**YOKOHAMA OKADAYA CO.,
LTD.**
123 S. Weller St. #107-9
Los Angeles, CA 90012
(213) 620–9330

INSTRUCTION

ARTS, CRAFTS, &
POETRY

**AMERICAN INSTITUTE OF
TEXTILE ARTS**
Pine Manor College
400 Heath St.
Chestnut Hill, MA 02167
(617) 731–7133
classes in Japanese textile making

ARASE DOLL MAKING
1785 E. First St.
Los Angeles, CA 90033
(213) 264–5435
            267–0240

KAJI ASO STUDIO
40 St. Stephens St.
Boston, MA 02115
(617) 247–1719
classes in *sumi-e*, calligraphy,
    ceramics, tea ceremony

ATELIER TOKYO
321 E. Second St.
Los Angeles, CA 90012
(213) 617–3595
art school

BEIKOKU SHODŌ KENKYŪ-KAI
(American Calligraphy Study
    Group)
Ikuta Kanshu, Director
15725 Raymond Ave.
Gardena, CA 90247
(213) 321–9405
Japanese calligraphy classes

BUNKA SHODŌ
Hattori Kosen
244 S. San Pedro St. #302
Los Angeles, CA 90012
(213) 389–9615
Japanese calligraphy classes

**CROSS-CULTURAL
COMMUNICATIONS**
239 Wynsum Ave.
Merrick, NY 11566
(516) 868–5635
English-language *haiku* club

ENDŌ ARTS
9691 Colony St.
Anaheim, CA 92804
(714) 774–5975
sumi-e classes

HAIKU SOCIETY OF AMERICA
c/o Japan Society
333 E. 47th St.
New York, NY 10017
(212) 832–1155

IGARASHI JAPANESE ART
224 San Pedro St. #302
Los Angeles, CA 90012
(213) 633–6996

INDIANAPOLIS ART LEAGUE
820 E. 67th St.
Indianapolis, IN
(317) 255–2464
sumi-e classes

ITAGAKI, AYA
14 Curtiss Rd.
Hanover, NH 03755
(603) 643–3539
calligraphy classes

**JAPANESE DOLL-MAKING
ASSOCIATES**
2109 E. Third St.
Los Angeles, CA 90033
(213) 269–1441

KYOTO KIMONO ACADEMY
312 E. First St. #500-B
Los Angeles, CA 90012
(213) 617–0044
kimono-making classes

NEW CHINA GIFTS
1994 N. High St.
Columbus, OH 43201
(614) 299–5190
calligraphy supplies

**NIPPON KYŌIKU SHŪJI
REMMEI**
(Japan Educational Calligraphy
    Union)
965 S. Hudson Ave.
Los Angeles, CA 90019
(213) 931–2441
calligraphy classes

OI, MOTOI
2450 95th St.
East Elmhurst, NY 11369
(212) 478–5418
sumi-e classes

PIONEER ART CLUB
244 S. San Pedro St.
Los Angeles, CA 90012
(213) 680–1656
sumi-e classes

**RADCLIFFE COLLEGE
CERAMICS PROGRAM**
245 Concord Ave.
Cambridge, MA 02138
(617) 495–8680
ceramics classes

RAFU SHODŌ KAI
(Los Angeles Calligraphy Club)
Kato Kosen
700 E. Sunset St.
San Gabriel, CA 91776
(213) 286–7608

SAGA, MASAE ART CLASS
18003 Crenshaw Blvd. #A
Torrance, CA 90504
(213) 321–8508
sumi-e classes

SAN DIEGO *SUMI-E* CLASS
2222 Ledge View Lane
Spring Valley, CA 92077

TAKAHASHI SHUNKIN
565 Fifth Ave.
Brooklyn, NY 11215
(212) 768–9345
calligraphy classes

TANAKA, JOMYO
27 Grove St.
New York, NY 10014
(212) 989–2078
calligraphy classes

YAMAMOTO, KOHO
64 McDougal St.
New York, NY 10012
(212) 673–5190
            533–4608
ceramics classes

YAMASHIRO ART CLASS
1203 Keniston Ave.
Los Angeles, CA 90019
(213) 934–7043
sumi-e classes

COOKING

ELIZABETH ANDO'S COOKING CLASS
Culinary Center
100 Greenwich Ave.
New York, NY 10036
(212) 255-4141

THE COOK'S PLACE
Worthington Square Shopping
  Center
Worthington, OH 43085
(614) 885-5729

FUKAMI, SACHIKO
7135 Lindell
St. Louis, MO 63108
(314) 727-2528

IMAI, TAKEO: JAPANESE COOKING
2427½ Wabash Ave.
Los Angeles, CA 90033
(213) 262-0223

THE SUSHI SCHOOL
317 W. Palmer Ave.
Glendale, CA 91204
(213) 621-3009

UWATE MATAO COOKING SCHOOL
111 N. San Pedro St.
Los Angeles, CA 90012
(213) 628-4688

DANCE, THEATER, AND MUSIC

AUSTIN GAGAKU GROUP
Center for Asian Studies
University of Texas
Austin, TX 78712
(512) 471-5811

AWAYA, YOKO
16512 S. Brighton Ave.
Gardena, CA 90247
(213) 329-5965
koto classes

AZUMA SUMAKO II
824 S. Chapel Ave. #4
Alhambra, CA 91801
(213) 289-5765
dance teacher

BANDŌ KATSUFUYE
3229 N. Delta St.
Rosemead, CA 91770
(213) 283-1800
dance classes

BANDŌ MITSUHIRO
23708 Livewood Lane
Harbor City, CA 90710
(213) 539-8636
Japanese dance

BANDŌ MITSUSA
547 N. Westmoreland Ave.
Los Angeles, CA 90004
(213) 661-7742
Japanese dance

FUJIMA CHISEYE
1514 W. Compton Blvd.
Gardena, CA 90247
(213) 321-9763
Japanese dance

FUKIMA KANSUMA
1327 Gramercy #1
Los Angeles, CA 90019
(213) 731-4378
      388-9061
Japanese dance

HANAYAGI JUROKUMI
13777 Gavina Ave.
Sylmar, CA 91342
(213) 362-3074
Japanese dance

HANAYAGI ROYUMINE
405 N. Rura Dr.
Monterey Park, CA 91754
(213) 283-1827
      548-8912
Japanese dance

HANAYAGI TOMUYAE
320 N. Commonwealth Ave.
Los Angeles, CA 90004
(213) 661-1879
Japanese dance

HARA KOICHI
1317 S. Westgate Ave.
West Los Angeles, CA 90025
(213) 477-3123
Nō singing classes

HASHIBE, HIROMI
1229 S. Fifth St.
Alhambra, CA 91801
(213) 283-4259
koto classes

HAYASHI, ARAWANA
28 Whittier St., #2
Cambridge, MA 02140
(617) 868-9820
gagaku music and dance classes

HOSHIZAKI TSUYAKO
2001 Rockford Rd.
Los Angeles, CA 90039
(213) 664-6100
Nō singing lessons

IKUTA-RYŪ, KOTO
7884 Gloria Lake Ave.
San Diego, CA 92119
(619) 465-7590
koto classes

ITO, SACHIYO
128 W. 13th St.
New York, NY 10011
(212) 490-0077
Japanese dance

KAMATA, REIKO
509 E. 77th St.
New York, NY 10021
(212) 794-2387
koto classes

KIKUKAWA HŌGETSU
12030 Aneta St.
Culver City, CA 90230
(213) 398-2132
Japanese dance

KINEYA KABUTACHI
3091 Lanfranco St.
Los Angeles, CA 90063
(213) 265-2303
nagauta (Kabuki-singing) classes

KINEYA YAJURO IX
1500 Sombrero Dr.
Monterey Park, CA 91754
(213) 685-9171
nagauta (Kabuki-singing) classes

MAIKAWA, YOSHI
2022 E. Second St.
Los Angeles, CA 90033
(213) 262-8817
kouta classes

MATSUI KAZU
P.O. Box 42876
Los Angeles, CA 90042
(213) 254-4630
shakukachi classes

MORIWAKI, KAZUKO
58 Harrison Dr.
Larchmont, NY 10538
(914) 834-0545
Nō instruction

NAKASHIMA CHIHOKU
1636 W. Redondo Beach Blvd.
Gardena, CA 90247
(213) 770-3637
koto classes

NAKASHIMA CHIYOKO
3091 Lanfranco St.
Los Angeles, CA 90063
(213) 265-2303
koto classes

NEW ENGLAND CONSERVATORY
290 Huntington Ave.
Boston, MA 02115
(617) 262-1120
Japanese music classes

NISHIKAWA EIJYU
337 S. OCCIDENTAL #18
Los Angeles, CA 90057
(213) 385-9679
Japanese dance classes

NISHIMURA YAHACHIRŌ
2706 Hobart Blvd.
Los Angeles, CA 90018
(213) 732-4246
Nō singing classes

OKADA, NANCY
American Buddhist Academy
331 Riverside Dr.
New York, NY 10025
(212) 678-9213
Japanese dance classes

SANJYO KANYA V
1500 Sombrero Dr.
Monterey Park, CA 91754
(213) 685-9171
Japanese dance classes

SHAKUHACHI
Bill Gleason
188 Chestnut Ave.
Jamaica Plain, MA 02130
(617) 524-2251
Performance and Instruction

SHIMIZU SEIZAN
1911 S. Westgate Ave.
West Los Angeles, CA 90025
(213) 826-8657
shakuhachi instruction

SOCIETY FOR ASIAN MUSIC
Asia House
112 E. 64th St.
New York, NY 10021
(212) 751-3210

SOUTHERN CALIFORNIA BIWAGAKU ASSOCIATION
1146 Mississippi Ave.
Los Angeles, CA 90025
(213) 477-1792
biwa instruction

YAMADA-RYŪ KOTO AND VOICE
Performance & Instruction
Cathleen B. Read
Boston, MA
(617) 391-0909

YAMAGUCHI HODO
2109 E. Third St.
Los Angeles, CA 90033
(213) 269-1441
shakuhachi instruction

YOSHIDA, FUSAKO
231 W. 25th St. (4G)
New York, NY 10028
(212) 989-2884
koto instruction

IKEBANA AND BONSAI

AKEBONO BONSAI KYŌKAI
608 N. 21st St.
Montebello, CA 90640
(213) 723-6954
bonsai classes

ALLINDER, FUMIKO
201 W. 70th St.
New York, NY 10023
(212) 873-6115
sōgetsu ikebana

AMERICAN BONSAI ASSOCIATION
P.O. Box 358
Keene, NH 03431

BONSAI
Max Mendel
2345 S. Arlington Ave.
Indianapolis, IN
(317) 356-2693
bonsai gardening classes

BONSAI STUDY GROUP
Massachusetts Horticultural
  Society
300 Massachusetts Ave.
Boston, MA 02115
(617) 536-9280

FUKUYAMA BUSEN
2146 W. 31st St.
Los Angeles, CA 90018
(213) 734-7804
bonsai classes

**THE GRAND BONSAI—SOUTH
SIDE**
Richard Olson
(314) 355-1067
St. Louis-area *bonsai* club

MRS. HAMANO
2921 N. Halsted
Chicago, IL 60657
(312) 348-8604
ikebana

HANAYA FLORAL DESIGN
57A Cuttermill Rd.
Great Neck, NY 11021
(516) 466-4330
sōgetsu ikebana

HATA, SETSUKO
Dakota St.
Palisades, NY 10964
(914) 359-2615
sōgetsu ikebana

IKEBANA INTERNATIONAL
4059 Melrose Ave.
Los Angeles, CA 90029
(213) 661-0620

P.O. Box 9663
Washington, DC 20016
(703) 536-9275

IKEBANA TEACHERS' GUILD
1908 Westgate Ave.
Los Angeles, CA 90025
(213) 478-1121

**IKENOBŌ IKEBANA SOCIETY
OF AMERICA**
1737 Post St. #16
San Francisco, CA 94115
(415) 567-1011

KASHŪ BONSAI KYŌKAI
2833 Harcourt Ave.
Los Angeles, CA 90016
(213) 732-4556
bonsai classes

KONDŌ BUSEN
244 S. San Pedro St. #304
Los Angeles, CA 90012
(213) 625-8565
bonsai classes

MISHOKAI CLUB
Mrs. Arakawa
1620 N. Lasalle
Chicago, IL 60614
(312) 337-9427
ikebana

NANKA IKEBANA KYOJUKAI
3314 W. 30th St.
Los Angeles, CA 90018
(213) 734-7789
ikebana

OHARA IKEBANA CENTER
South Tower
31st St. & Seventh Ave.
New York, NY 10001
(212) 564-0841

RAFU BONSAI CLUB
3345 Second Ave.
Los Angeles, CA 90018
(213) 733-4910
bonsai classes

SHŌFŪ-RYŪ LA CHAPTER
406 N. Woods Ave.
Los Angeles, CA 90022
(213) 261-2604
ikebana

**SŌGETSU SCHOOL OF FLOWER
ARRANGING**
Mrs. Sally Mikawa
766 Polo Dr., N.
Columbus, OH 43229
(614) 888-9634

**SŌGETSU SCHOOL OF FLOWER
ARRANGEMENT**
Roxbury, CT
(203) 354-7062
Rajean Metzler

SUZUKI, BEN T.
608 N. 21st St.
Montebello, CA 90640
(213) 723-6954
bonsai classes

MARTIAL ARTS

AIKIDŌ ACADEMY
5019 N. Encinita Ave.
Temple City, CA 91780
(213) 286-9851
    281-5214

AIKIKAI
142 W. 18th St.
New York, NY 10011
(212) 242-6246
aikidō

AMERICAN KARATE SCHOOL
745 Grand Ave.
San Marcos, CA 92069
(619) 744-4493

BOND ST. DOJŌ
49 Bond St.
New York, NY 10002
(212) 477-0899

BOSTON KENDO CLUB
c/o Tohoku Judo Club
30 Temple St.
Somerville, MA 02145
(617) 623-9075

BUDŌKAN OF SAN DIEGO
5019 Santa Monica Ave.
San Diego, CA 92107
(619) 222-6000/6918

**CALIFORNIA KARATE
ACADEMY**
16906 La Salle Ave.
Gardena, CA 90247
(213) 324-8042

COMPTON JUDŌ DOJO
1500 S. Western Ave.
Gardena, CA 90247
(213) 566-4585

GOJŪ-RYŪ KARATE-DŌ
322 Rancheros Dr.
San Marcos, CA 92069
(619) 744-2291

GOJU KARATE
212 W. 29th St.
New York, NY 10001
(212) 564-6648

HARTFORD JUDO CLUB
942 New Britain Ave.
West Hartford, CT
(203) 247-9437

**HATCHETT'S SCHOOL OF
KARATE**
1174 E. Main St.
Bridgeport, CT 06608
(203) 579-0339

**HWANG'S KARATE, JUDŌ &
AIKIDŌ**
1626 Barnum Ave.
Stratford, CT 06497
(203) 377-5986

IAI-DŌ
Raymond Otani
2576 Broadway
New York, NY 10025
(212) 662-2626
sword

ISA SHOTOKAN KARATE
P.O. Box W
Solana Beach, CA 92075
(619) 436-3611

JAPAN JUDŌ-KARATE
6320 Bay Parkway
Brooklyn, NY 11204
(212) 331-6406

JAPAN JUDŌ & KARATE, INC.
43 Forest St.
Stamford, CT
(203) 327-6665

JAPAN KARATE ASSOCIATION
295 Huntington Ave.
Boston, MA 02115
(617) 536-1244

1440 W. Olympic Blvd.
Los Angeles, CA 90015
(213) 381-6095

2121 Broadway
New York, NY 10023
(212) 874-9868

**JAPAN KARATE-DŌ
ORGANIZATION**
3333 Midway Dr.
San Diego, CA 92110
(619) 223-7405

**JAPAN KARATE-DŌ,
RYOBUKAI**
1510 S. Euclid
Anaheim, CA 92802
(714) 774-5730

**HERB JOHNSON'S OLYMPIC
STUDIOS**
3921 N. Keystone
Indianapolis, IN 46205
(317) 545-6071

**KARATE-DŌ CENTER OF
ENCINITAS**
530 Second St.
Encinitas, CA 92024
(619) 942-1261

KENDO CLUB, NY
46 W. 83rd St.
New York, NY 10024
(212) 874-6161

**KENDŌ FEDERATION OF THE
U.S.**
1715 W. 256th St.
Lomita, CA 90717
(213) 326-4463

KODOKAN JUDO
152 W. 26th St.
New York, NY 10001
(212) 989-8370

KYOKUSHIN-KAI KARATE
640 Hilard St.
Manchester, CT 06040
(203) 646-4963

KYŪDŌ CLUB
c/o Tendai Center of Boston
15 Watson St.
Cambridge, MA 02139
(617) 547-0150
archery

STEVE LATTA
9 Brown Ave.
Athens, OH 45701
judō

LOS ANGELES KYŪDŌ-KAI
1853 S. Arlington Ave.
Los Angeles, CA 90019
(213) 733-7043
archery

MAS OYAMA'S KARATE
350 Avenue of the Americas
New York, NY 10011
(212) 477-2888

NEW ENGLAND AIKIKAI
2000 Massachusetts Ave.
Cambridge, MA 02140
(617) 661-1959
aikidō

OISHI JUDŌ CLUB
415 W. Broadway
New York, NY 10012
(212) 966-6850

SAN DIEGO JUDŌ CLUB
819 University Ave.
San Diego, CA 92103
(619) 295-9798

SEIDO KARATE
1095B Central Ave.
Albany, NY 12205

1242 W. Winnemac Ave.
Chicago, IL 60640

2203 Ridgemont Dr.
Finksburg, MD 21048

25 Spinnaker, #12
Marina Peninsula, CA 90291

(main branch)
61 West 23rd St.
New York, NY 10010

6103 N.E. 203rd St.
Seattle, WA 98155

1451 Fifth Ave.
Troy, NY 12180

19A Durham St.
Williamsville, NY 14221

SEINAN JUDŌ DŌJO
1442½ W. 36th Place
Los Angeles, CA 90018
(213) 733-1087
          731-9071

SEISHOKU AIKIKAI
17 Station St.
Brookline, MA 02147
(619) 524-2251

SHITŌ-RYŪ JAPAN KARATE FEDERATION
1429 N. Bristol
Santa Ana, CA 92706
(714) 543-5550

SHODOKAN
89 Canal St.
Salem, MA 01970
(617) 744-1232
aikidō, judō, karate

SHOTOKAN KARATE OF AMERICA
4300 Melrose Ave.
Los Angeles, CA 90029
(213) 664-0039

SHOTOKAN KARATE & JUDO
4850 W. Washington
Indianapolis, IN
(317) 243-3009

SOUTHERN CALIFORNIA KENDO FEDERATION
22710 Elm Ave.
Torrance, CA 90505
(213) 325-2473

TOHOKU JUDO CLUB
30 Temple St.
Somerville, MA 02145
(619) 623-9075

UECHI KARATE ACADEMY
188 S. Whitney St.
Hartford, CT
(203) 236-0530

RELIGION

AMERICAN BUDDHIST ACADEMY
331 Riverside Dr.
New York, NY 10025
(212) 749-8879
          678-9213

BUDDHIST ASSOCIATION
75 Sparks St.
Cambridge, MA 02138
(617) 491-8857

BUDDHIST CHURCH OF SAN FRANCISCO
1881 Pine St.
San Francisco, CA 94115
(415) 776-3158
classes in *ikebana*, go, martial arts,
    language, calligraphy, *sumi-e*

BUDDHIST TEMPLE OF CHICAGO
1151 W. Leland
Chicago, IL 60640
(312) 334-4661
classes in *ikebana*, tea ceremony,
    calligraphy, *sumi-e*

CAMBRIDGE ZEN CENTER
263 N. Harvard St.
Allston, MA 02134
(617) 576-3229

CLEVELAND BUDDHIST TEMPLE
East 214th Ave. & Euclid Ave.
Cleveland, OH 44117
(216) 692-1509

DAIBOSATSU ZENDŌ
Beecher Lake, Star Route
Livington Manor, NY 12758
(914) 439-4566

DŌSHIN-JI
Box 197
Mt. Temple, NY 12457
(914) 688-2228

MIDWEST BUDDHIST TEMPLE
435 W. Menomonee
Chicago, IL 60614
(312) 943-7801
tours, summer Japanese festival
    (obon)

MOUNTAIN VIEW BUDDHIST TEMPLE
575 Stierlin Rd.
Mountain View, CA 94043
(415) 968-9144/0975

NEW HAVEN ZEN CENTER
193 Mansfield St.
New Haven, CT 06511
(203) 787-0912

PALO ALTO BUDDHIST CHURCH
2751 Louis Rd.
Palo Alto, CA 94306
(415) 325-8991

PROVIDENCE ZEN CENTER
RFD #5, Pound Rd.
Cumberland, RI 02908
(401) 769-6464

SAN JOSE BUDDHIST CHURCH
640 N. Fifth St.
San Jose, CA 95112
(408) 293-9292

TENDAI BUDDHIST STUDY CENTER
(Boston)
(617) 547-0150 or
      253-6998

ZEN BUDDHIST TEMPLE
2230 N. Halsted
Chicago, IL 60614
(312) 348-1218

ZEN CENTER
300 Page St.
San Francisco, CA 94102
(415) 863-3136

ZEN CENTER OF NY
440 West End Ave.
New York, NY 10024
(212) 724-4172

ZEN COMMUNITY OF NEW YORK
5720 Mosholu Ave.
Riverdale, NY 10471
(212) 543-5530

ZEN INSTITUTE OF AMERICA
113 E. 30th St.
New York, NY 10016
(212) 684-9487

ZEN MOUNTAIN CENTER
Tassajara Springs
Carmel Valley, CA 93924

ZEN STUDIES SOCIETY
223 E. 67th St.
New York, NY 10021
(212) 861-3333

TEA CEREMONY

NATSUME-KAI TEA CEREMONY
16107 32nd Ave.
Flushing, NY 11358
(212) 988-6161

OGASAWARA SENCHA SCHOOL
Henry Onodera
920 S. Maple Ave.
Los Angeles, CA 90015
(213) 680-1865/1866

OMOTE SENKE DOMON-KAI
Southern California Chapter
19036 Owen Way
Cerritos, CA 90701
(213) 860-3035

URASENKE TEA CEREMONY SCHOOL
160 S. Occidental Blvd.
Los Angeles, CA 90057
(213) 387-8444

153 E. 65th St.
New York, NY 10021
(212) 988-6161

4691 Leathers St.
San Diego, CA 92117
(619) 272-5426

LANGUAGE AND LIBRARIES

ACADEMIA LANGUAGE SCHOOL
11 Mt. Auburn St.
Cambridge, MA 02138
(617) 354-6110
language

ANTIOCH COLLEGE
Asian Studies
Yellow Springs, OH 45387
(513) 767-7333

ARNET LANGUAGE SCHOOL
798 Boylston St.
Boston, MA 02116
(617) 247-0687
language

ASIA RESOURCE CENTER
803 SSB Tower
University of Missouri-St. Louis
8001 Natural Bridge Rd.
St. Louis, MO 63121
(314) 453-5521

ASSUMPTION COLLEGE
500 Salisbury St.
Worcester, MA 01609
(617) 752-5615 ex. 364
language

ATSUMI ASSOCIATES
19 Birch Rd.
Stow, MA 01775
(617) 897-2628
language

BATES COLLEGE
Lewiston, ME 04240
(207) 784-9105
Japanese studies

BOSTON UNIVERSITY
Boston, MA 02215
(617) 353-2000

BROWN UNIVERSITY
East Asia Center
Box 1850
Providence, RI 02912
(401) 863-1000

CHICAGO EAST ASIAN RESOURCE & EDUCATION CENTER
University of Chicago
5848 S. University Ave.
Kelly Hall, Rm. 403
Chicago, IL 60637
(312) 753-2632

COLUMBIA UNIVERSITY
116th St. & Broadway
New York, NY 10027
(212) 280-4676

CORNELL UNIVERSITY
Ithaca, NY 14850
(607) 256-1000
language

DONNELL LIBRARY
Japanese Section
20 W. 53rd St.
New York, NY 10019
(212) 790-6406

EARLHAM COLLEGE
Richmond, IN 47374
(317) 962-6561

HARVARD UNIVERSITY EXTENSION
20 Garden St.
Cambridge, MA 02138
(617) 495-4024

HARVARD UNIVERSITY SUMMER SCHOOL
20 Garden St.
Cambridge, MA 02138
(617) 495-4024

HARVARD-YENCHING LIBRARY
Harvard University
2 Divinity Ave.
Cambridge, MA 02138
(617) 495-2756
reference and reading room

INDIANA JAPANESE LANGUAGE SCHOOL
Indianapolis
Contact: Noriko Uesuge
(317) 844-0594
also classes in tea ceremony, *ikebana*, cooking, calligraphy, origami, kite-making, *sushi*-making

INDIANA UNIVERSITY
Goodbody Hall
Bloomington, IN 47405
Contact: Dr. Eugene Eoyang
(812) 335-7537/3765

JAPANESE INSTITUTE OF SAWTELLE
2110 Corinth Ave.
West Los Angeles, CA 90025
(213) 479-2477
language

JAPANESE LANGUAGE SCHOOL OF GREATER CINCINNATI
7964 Kentucky Dr.
Suite 6
Forest, KY 41042
(606) 525-1616

JAPANESE LANGUAGE SCHOOL OF SAN DIEGO
2624 Market St.
San Diego, CA 92102
(619) 233-5858

LITTLE TOKYO CULTURAL CENTER
244 S. San Pedro #B-4
Los Angeles, CA 90012
(213) 879-8881
Japanese classes

MARINA JAPANESE LANGUAGE SCHOOL
12448 Braddock Dr.
Los Angeles, CA 90066
(213) 822-0444

MIDDLEBURY COLLEGE
Middlebury, VT 05753
(802) 388-3711, ex. 2520

MISSOURI SOUTHERN STATE COLLEGE
Newman & Duquesne Rds.
Joplin, MO 64801
(417) 624-8100
Asia-related books; Shintō shrine at Spiva Art Center

NEW SCHOOL
66 W. 12th St.
New York, NY 10011
(212) 741-5600
language

NEW YORK UNIVERSITY
Washington Square
New York, NY 10011
(212) 598-1212

NIPPON CLUB
145 W. 57th St.
New York, NY 10019
(212) 581-2223
language

NORTHEASTERN UNIVERSITY
360 Huntington Ave.
Boston, MA 02115
(617) 437-2400

ORANGE COUNTY JAPANESE LANGUAGE SCHOOL
909 S. Dale St.
Anaheim, CA 92804
(714) 827-9590

PRINCETON UNIVERSITY
Princeton, NJ 08540
(609) 452-3000

SETON HALL UNIVERSITY
South Orange, NJ 07079
(201) 761-9000

SMITH COLLEGE
Northampton, MA 01060
(413) 584-2700

ST. JOHN'S UNIVERSITY
Grand Central & Utopia Parkways
Jamaica, NY 11439
(212) 969-8000

UNIVERSITY OF MASSACHUSETTS
Asian Language & Literature Department
26 Thompson Hall
Amherst, MA 01003
(413) 545-0886

WASHINGTON UNIVERSITY
Box 111
St. Louis, MO 63130
(314) 889-5156

YALE UNIVERSITY
1504 A Yale Station
New Haven, CT 06524
(203) 436-1861

MEDIA

JAPAN-NEW YORK NEWSPAPER
141 E. 44th St.
New York, NY 10017
(212) 832-1215

NEW YORK NICHIBEI NEWSPAPER
27 Park Place
New York, NY 10007
(212) 964-3461

NICHIBEI TIMES
2211 Bush St.
San Francisco, CA 94119
(415) 921-6820
Japanese-American newspaper

OCS NEWS
27-08 42nd Rd.
Long Island City, NY 11101
(212) 392-2070
distributes *Japan Times Weekly* (in English)

MEDICINE

JAPAN SHIATSU CENTER OF U.S.A.
8641 Firestone Blvd.
Downey, CA 90241
(213) 771-4550

MAEDA TOI KENKO CENTER
1605 W. Redondo Beach Blvd. #203
Gardena, CA 90247
(213) 324-9901
oriental medicine

NATIONAL INSTITUTE OF ORIENTAL MEDICINE
8665 Wilshire Blvd. #303
Beverly Hills, CA 90211
(213) 659-7571

NIPPON SHIATSU SPA
3024 W. Ball Rd.
Anaheim, CA 92804
(714) 995-6936

OTSUKA SHIATSU CHIRYOIN
42 E. 64th St.
New York, NY 10021
(212) 355-1930

SANWA SPA (SHIATSU)
Hotel New Otani
110 S. Los Angeles St.
Los Angeles, CA 90012
(213) 629-1200

SHIATSU EDUCATION CENTER
52 W. 55th St.
New York, NY 10019
(212) 582-3424

SUZUKI SHIATSU CHIRYO CENTER
2118 W. Artesia Blvd.
Torrance, CA 90504
(213) 515-7169
        323-6815

TAWA SPA (SHIATSU)
362 E. First St.
Los Angeles, CA 90012
(213) 680-9141

TERUKINA CHIRYOIN
561 N. Saint Louis St.
Los Angeles, CA 90033
(213) 266-3111
oriental medicine

MUSEUMS

ACHENBACH FOUNDATION
Palace of the Legion of Honor
Lincoln Park
San Francisco, CA 94121
(415) 558-2885

ALLEN MEMORIAL ART MUSEUM
Oberlin College
Oberlin, OH 44074
(216) 775-8665
woodblock prints

ARNOLD ARBORETUM
The Arbor Way
Jamaica Plain, MA 02130
(617) 524-1718
bonsai collection

THE ART INSTITUTE OF CHICAGO
Michigan Ave. at Adams St.
Chicago, IL 60603
(312) 443-3600

ASIAN ART MUSEUM OF SAN FRANCISCO
Avery Brundage Collection
Golden Gate Park
San Francisco, CA 94118
(415) 558-2993

THE CHILDREN'S MUSEUM
Museum Wharf
300 Congress St.
Boston, MA 02210
(617) 426-6500
two-story Kyōto house, Japanese
joinery and tools, reading room,
circulating library on Japan

CINCINNATI ART MUSEUM
Eden Park
Cincinnati, OH 45202
(513) 721-5204
photographs of Japanese subjects

CLEVELAND MUSEUM OF ART
1150 East Blvd.
Cleveland, OH 44106
(216) 421-7340
outstanding collection

DALLAS MUSEUM OF FINE ARTS
Fair Park
Dallas, TX 75226
(214) 421-4188
small but representative collection

FOGG ART MUSEUM
Harvard University
32 Quincy St.
Cambridge, MA 02138
(617) 495-2387
fine collection

FREER GALLERY OF ART
12th & Jefferson Dr., SW
Washington, DC 20560
(202) 381-5344
outstanding collection

GEORGE WALTER VINCENT SMITH ART MUSEUM
The Quadrangle
222 State St.
Springfield, MA 01103
(413) 733-8265
strong in decorative arts and crafts

ISABELLA STEWART GARDNER MUSEUM
280 The Fenway
Boston, MA 02115
(617) 734-1359
small fine collection

HAKONE GARDENS
2100 Big Basin Way
Saratoga, CA 95070
(408) 867-3438
garden

HAMMOND MUSEUM
North Salem, NY 10560
(914) 669-5033/5135
Buddhist art and Oriental gardens

INDIANAPOLIS MUSEUM OF ART
1200 W. 38th St.
Indianapolis, IN 46208
(317) 923-1331
collection, plus classes in tea
ceremony, sumi-e, calligraphy

JAPANESE EMBASSY, WASHINGTON
2520 Massachusetts Ave.
Washington, DC 20008
(202) 234-2266
Japanese teahouse and garden

JAPANESE GARDEN
Arboretum
University of Washington
Seattle, WA 98195
(206) 543-8800

JAPANESE GARDEN
Brooklyn Botanical Gardens
1000 Washington Ave.
Brooklyn, NY 11225
(212) 622-4433

JAPANESE GARDEN
Hammond Museum
P.O. Box H
North Salem, NY 10560
(914) 669-5033

THE JAPANESE GARDEN AT THE DAWES ARBORETUM
7770 Jacksontown Rd., SE
Newark, OH 43055
(614) 323-2355

JAPANESE TEA GARDEN
Golden Gate Park
San Francisco, CA 94117
(415) 558-3706

JAPANESE TEAHOUSE AND GARDEN
Antioch College
Yellow Springs, OH 45387
(513) 767-7331

JOHN WOODMAN HIGGINS ARMORY MUSEUM
100 Barber Ave.
Worcester, MA 01606
(617) 853-6015
arms and armor

JOHNSON HUMRICKHOUSE MEMORIAL MUSEUM
300 Whitewoman St.
(Roscoe Village)
Cochocton, OH 43812
(614) 622-8710
decorative arts and crafts

KIMBELL ART MUSEUM
Will Rogers Rd., W.
Fort Worth, TX 76107
(817) 332-8451
wide range of Japanese art

LYMAN ALLYN MUSEUM
100 Mohegan Ave.
New London, CT 06320
(203) 443-2545

MISSOURI BOTANICAL GARDEN
2345 Tower Grove
St. Louis, MO 63110
(314) 772-7600
Seiwa-en, the largest Japanese
garden in North America

MITZIE VERNE COLLECTION OF ORIENTAL ART
3326 Lansmere
Shaker Heights, OH 44122
(216) 561-6069
contemporary Japanese graphics

MUSEUM OF ART & ARCHAEOLOGY
One Pickard Hall
University of Missouri-Columbia
Columbia, MO 65201
(314) 882-3591
Japanese prints, costumes,
ceramics

MUSEUM OF FINE ARTS, BOSTON
465 Huntington Ave.
Boston, MA 02115
(617) 267-9300

MUSEUM OF FINE ARTS
The Quadrangle
49 Chestnut St.
Springfield, MA 01103
(413) 732-8620
prints

NATIONAL ARBORETUM
24th & "R" Sts., NE
Washington, DC 20002
(202) 472-9100
bonsai

NEWARK MUSEUM
49 Washington St.
Newark, NJ 07101
(201) 733-6600

THE PEABODY MUSEUM
E. India Sq.
Salem, MA 01970
(617) 745-1876

PHILADELPHIA MUSEUM OF ART
26th St. & Benjamin Franklin Pkwy.
Philadelphia, PA 19101
(215) 763-8100

PRINCETON UNIVERSITY—THE ART MUSEUM
Princeton, NJ 08544
(609) 452-3787

RHODE ISLAND SCHOOL OF DESIGN MUSEUM
Two College St.
Providence, RI 02903
(401) 331-3511
Nō robes, kesa (Buddhist robes),
prints, sculpture, armor, lacquer

SEATTLE ART MUSEUM
Volunteer Park
Seattle, WA 98112
(206) 447-4708
(206) 447-4790

THE TEXTILE MUSEUM
2320 "S" St., NW
Washington, DC 20008
(202) 667-0441

TOLEDO MUSEUM OF ART
2445 Monroe St.
Toledo, OH 43620
(419) 255-8000
all periods: lacquer, tsuba, inro

WILLIAM ROCKHILL NELSON GALLERY OF ART
Atkins Museum of Fine Arts
4525 Oak St.
Kansas City, MO 64111
(816) 561-4000/4001/4002
one of the best East Asian
collections in the U.S.; classes in
calligraphy, sumi-e

WORCESTER ART MUSEUM
55 Salisbury St.
Worcester, MA 01608
(617) 799-4406
Edo prints and paintings

YESTERYEARS MUSEUM
Main & River Sts.
Sandwich, MA 02563
(617) 888-1711
Seven-hundred Japanese dolls

ZANESVILLE ART CENTER
1145 Maple Ave.
Zanesville, OH 43701
(614) 452-0741

PERFORMING ARTS

ASIA SOCIETY
Performing Arts Program
133 E. 58th St.
New York, NY 10022
(212) 371-4758
751-3280

CENTER FOR ASIAN STAGE AND THEATRE STUDIES
49 E. Passaic Ave.
Rutherford, NJ 07070
(201) 438-8348

MUSIC FROM JAPAN
7 E. 20th St.
New York, NY 10010
(212) 674-4587
programs of new Japanese music

NIPPON-KAN THEATRE
Chinatown Tours
628 S. Washington
Seattle, WA 98104
(206) 624-8800
restored historic theater

WESLEYAN UNIVERSITY
Middletown, CT
(203) 347-9411
Japanese court dance
performances

PHOTOGRAPHY CREDITS

KEY TO ILLUSTRATION CODES:
tl: top left; *tc:* top center; *tr:* top right; *bl:* bottom left;
bc: bottom center; *br:* bottom right; *r:* right; *l:* left

Courtesy Asahi, Inc.: *p. 115*

Courtesy The Asia Society/B. Kaplan: *p. .162 (bl, br)*

Courtesy The Asia Society Performing Arts Program: *p. 163*

Kate Bader: *p. 28, 47 (bl)*

Courtesy Comme des Garçon/Peter Lindbergh: *p. 40, 41*

Ehon Yamato Hiji: *p. 71 (r)*

Courtesy Hiroko Govaers: *p. 160, 161*

Thomas Haar: *p. 17 (bl), 18 (b), 25 (l), 29 (tr), 32, 33 (b), 36, 38 (l), 46 (br), 47 (br), 85 (tr, br), 100 (bc), 102, 105, 106, 107 (tl), 113 (br), 114, 123 (bc), 128, 130, 144 (l, tr, br), 145, 150, 151 (tl, bl, r), 178, 182 (tl), 184, 185, 188–9, 190, 194, 195 (tc, bc, r)*

Courtesy Marta Hallett: *p. 180, 186*

Courtesy Kazuko Hillyer International, Inc./Christian Steiner: *p. 125*

Holt, Rinehart and Winston: *p. 109*

Courtesy David Hughes: *p. 118, 123 (r)*

Courtesy Japan National Railways: *p. 174*

Courtesy Japan National Tourist Organization: *p. 25 (r), 27 (t), 42, 44, 45, 64–5, 92, 117, 140 (tc, tr, br), 147, 156, 157, 187 (tr)*

Courtesy Japan Publications Trading Co., Ltd. *p. 204, 205*

Dana Levy: *p. 16, 17 (tl, br), 19, 20, 21 (l), 22 (tl, tr, b), 23, 29 (tl, br), 30, 33 (t), 38 (r), 52, 58, 59 (tl, tc, br), 61, 66–7 (t), 82, 84, 86, 87 (tr, bc), 89, 93, 95 (tr, br), 96, 100 (t), 101, 107, 111 (tl, tr), 112, 113 (tr), 116, 131 (bc,br), 134, 135 (tr, tl), 137, 139, 142, 148, 149 (r), 152, 155, 164, 168, 169, 170, 171 (l), 175, 179 (tr, bc), 187 (bl), 197.*

Mark Lowe: *p. 26, 43, 110*

Courtesy James A. Michener, *The Hokusai Sketch-Books:* *p. 76, 77, 182, 183*

Tina Mucci: *p. 192*

Courtesy Music From Japan: *p. 120, 121, 124*

Courtesy Museum of Fine Arts, Boston: *p. 62, 63*

Courtesy Museum of Modern Art, New York: *p. 80, 81, 126, 193*

Collection of the Newark Museum: *p. 60*

Courtesy Isamu Noguchi: *p. 37 (l, r)*

Courtesy RCA: *p. 127*

Courtesy Reinhold-Brown Gallery: *p. 47 (t), 51 (t, b)*

Courtesy Sapporo, Inc.: *p. 115*

Sekai Bunka Photo Library: *p. 18 (t), 21 (r), 24, 27 (b), 46 (tc, tr), 54, 55, 56, 67 (r), 68, 71 (tl), 72, 75, 90, 94, 97, 98, 103 (bl, br), 107 (tr), 122, 138, 149 (tl), 154 (l, r), 158, 104*

Shiatsu Education Center of America: *p. 132 (bl, bc, br), 133*

Courtesy Oliver Statler: p. *166, 167, 171 (r), 172 (tl, tr), 173, 176, 177*

Courtesy Suzuki Carpentry Studio/Seiji Suzuki: *p. 34–5*

Courtesy Reizi Tamechika, *Hyakunin Isshu:* *p. 74*

Courtesy Tansuya, New York: *p. 50*

Yoshiharu Tsuge, Shogakukan Publishing: *p. 78, 79*

Courtesy Yohji Yamamoto: *p. 39*

Bruno Zehnder: *p. 48, 49 (br, bl)*

AUTHOR CREDITS

LIZA DALBY: Architecture; Clothing; Gardens; Gardening; Graphics; High-Tech; Packaging; Traditional and Folk Medicine; Massage; Games; Origami; Kite Flying; Modern Toys; The Bar; Geisha

PETER GRILLI: The Japanese Bath; Hot-Spring Baths; Domestic Baths and Public Baths

DAVID H. HUGHES: An Eastern Melting Pot; Drums, Flutes, and Strings; East–West Influence; Jazz

CHRISTINE GUTH KANDA: Folk Crafts; Textiles; Ceramics; Wooden Crafts; Dolls; Plastic Food; The Tea Ceremony; Rituals, Objects, Surroundings; Religion: Festivals, Rituals, Practices, Talismans

STEPHEN LONGSTREET: High Craft; Scrolls; Screens; Prints; Photography; Sculpture; Calligraphy; Yoshiwara

JON SPAYDE: High Craft; Scrolls; Screens; Prints; Photography; Sculpture; Calligraphy; Dutch-Studies; Poetry; Story; Diaries and *Zuihitsu*; Comics; Films; Sashimi and Sushi; Noodles and Bean Curd; The Japanese Meal; Ceremonial Food; Garnishes; Portable Meals; Sake; Whiskey and Beer; Coffee Shops; Nō; Kabuki; Bunraku; Modern Theater; Dance; Learning Japanese; Levels of Politeness; Characters

OLIVER STATLER: Cultural Travel; Ritual Travel; Fantasy Travel; Pilgrimage; Getting There; Lodging; Mountain and Sea

TERRY TRUCCO: Sumo; Baseball; Martial Arts

INDEX

Note: For ease of reading, macrons and foreign italicizations have been omitted in the index. They will be found in the text.